Interdisciplinary Inquiry in Teaching and Learning

Second Edition

Marian L. Martinello
The University of Texas at San Antonio

Gillian E. Cook
The University of Texas at San Antonio

Merrill,
an imprint of Prentice Hall
Upper Saddle River, New Jersey   *Columbus, Ohio*

Library of Congress Cataloging-in-Publication Data

Martinello, Marian L.
    Interdisciplinary inquiry in teaching and learning / Marian L.
Martinello, Gillian E. Cook. — 2nd. ed.
        p.   cm.
    Includes bibliographical references and index.
    ISBN 0-13-923954-5
    1. Interdisciplinary approach in education—United States.
2. Interdisciplinary approach to knowledge.   3. Education—United
States—Curricula.   I. Cook, Gillian Elizabeth.
II. Title.
    LB1570.M3675   2000
375'.000973—dc21   99-28065
                                                              CIP

Editor: Debra A. Stollenwerk
Editorial Assistant: Penny S. Burleson
Production Editor: Mary Harlan
Design Coordinator: Diane C. Lorenzo
Text Design and Project Coordination: Clarinda Publication Services
Cover Designer: Jason Moore
Cover photo: © FPG
Production Manager: Pamela D. Bennett
Director of Marketing: Kevin Flanagan
Marketing Manager: Meghan Shepherd
Marketing Coordinator: Krista Groshong

This book was set in Souvenir Light and Swiss by The Clarinda Company and was printed and bound by R. R. Donnelley & Sons Company. The cover was printed by Phoenix Color Corp.

© 2000 by Prentice-Hall, Inc.
Pearson Education
Upper Saddle River, New Jersey 07458

Earlier edition © 1994 by Macmillan Publishing Company.

Printed in the United States of America

10 9 8 7 6 5 4 3 2 1

ISBN: 0-13-923954-5

Prentice-Hall International (UK) Limited, *London*
Prentice-Hall of Australia Pty. Limited, *Sydney*
Prentice-Hall of Canada, Inc., *Toronto*
Prentice-Hall Hispanoamericana, S. A., *Mexico*
Prentice-Hall of India Private Limited, *New Delhi*
Prentice-Hall of Japan, Inc., *Tokyo*
Prentice-Hall (Singapore) Pte. Ltd., *Singapore*
Editora Prentice-Hall do Brasil, Ltda., *Rio de Janeiro*

We dedicate this book to our parents, who encouraged us to explore
worlds beyond their experience:
Rocco Martinello and Helena Terenzio Martinello
Harold T. Cook and H. Joyce Cook
and
to the teachers and children who will explore
worlds beyond those we can imagine.

Preface

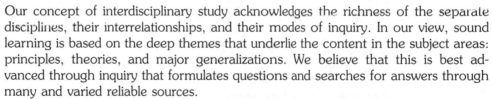

Our concept of interdisciplinary study acknowledges the richness of the separate disciplines, their interrelationships, and their modes of inquiry. In our view, sound learning is based on the deep themes that underlie the content in the subject areas: principles, theories, and major generalizations. We believe that this is best advanced through inquiry that formulates questions and searches for answers through many and varied reliable sources.

Interdisciplinary Inquiry in Teaching and Learning was written from the Deweyan premise that children will become lifelong, self-directed learners by engaging in inquiry processes with interdisciplinary content and that, from these explorations, upper elementary and middle school students can inductively formulate concepts and generalizations that help to explain the world and what it means to be human. We believe that teachers may choose from a continuum of roles to direct, guide, or mentor student inquiry across the fields of study of the curriculum, in response to student and teacher needs and the characteristics of their instructional situations and in order to achieve the highest standards for children's achievement.

ORGANIZATION OF THE TEXT

The book is organized in two parts. Part One presents theoretical bases for inquiry learning and describes some of the most notable historical experiments in integrated curriculum development. The intent is to explain the classic foundations for an inquiry-oriented interdisciplinary approach to teaching and learning. We believe that the approach to curriculum development that is detailed in this book rings true for teachers, administrators, and parents who apply our recommendations to their students' education. Through this work, we attempt to separate thematic studies and inquiry development from trendy and superficial uses of methods that bear the same titles. Interdisciplinary inquiry is all about clear thinking for instruction—about how to develop curriculum that supports children's explorations that know no subject-matter boundaries. Therefore, Chapter One covers the interdisciplinary qualities of inquiry, discussing its origins, modes and processes, content, contexts, products, and implications for teaching and learning. Chapter Two describes the experiments in integrated curriculum development at the Dewey School, 1902–1903; the Lincoln School, 1926; the Houston City Schools, 1924–1930; and the Bank Street Workshops for teachers, 1943–1948. Using these historical contexts, this chapter discusses questions emerging from those experiments that are germane to interdisciplinary curriculum design and development today.

Part Two is devoted to instructional practice. Chapter Three offers models, teacher roles, and starting points for theme studies. Chapter Four guides the reader in implementing a theme study: selecting a theme, converting topics to themes, brainstorming and identifying areas for inquiry, questioning, establishing criteria for evaluating students' growth in questioning, and meeting required standards. Inquiry relies on resources of the types described in the next two chapters. Chapter Five explains how to use print, people, places, and things for interdisciplinary theme studies. Chapter Six extends this discussion to include media and technology.

How to engage children in inquiry is the focus of Chapter Seven, which explores principles of inquiry, essential components of interdisciplinary inquiries in theme studies, unit studies, learning activities, and scheduling for thematic instruction. Finally, Chapter Eight examines the critical issues of accountability and assessment. It covers formative and summative assessments, assessment processes in theme studies, reporting about children's learning, using the portfolio as an alternative means for demonstrating progress and achievement in theme studies, using culminating activities in evaluation, and the role of the teacher in assessment.

SPECIAL QUALITIES

In addition to its philosophical base and historical examples, *Interdisciplinary Inquiry in Teaching and Learning* describes three teacher roles on a continuum to accommodate teaching styles, learner readiness for inquiry learning, and learning environments. These roles of director, guide, and mentor, which are new to this revision, provide optional ways for teachers to think about how they may most comfortably develop thematic studies that effectively involve children in constructing meaning from their experiences. The roles are introduced in Chapter Three and are explained as dimensions of interdisciplinary curriculum and inquiry learning in subsequent chapters. The special characteristics, benefits, and skills of inquiry learning are detailed and illustrated in Chapters Three through Eight. Our discussion of inquiry skills was specially written for this edition, giving primary attention to ways of questioning that children can be helped to refine as they become more precise in articulating what they want to explore. Because inquiry cannot proceed without good use of accessible resources, Chapters Five and Six contribute to the reader's understanding of the various resources for learning that can fuel, sustain, and inform children's inquiry. In these chapters, we demonstrate how many different types of resources that are found in everyday environments can be tapped both to spark and to deepen children's explorations.

The narrative makes ample use of examples taken from the work of practicing teachers we have worked with. Each italicized example is used to illustrate a particular idea or method that we discuss in the text. These illustrations offer readers concrete applications of teaching methods that integrate the curriculum areas and encourage children to discover big ideas.

USES OF THIS TEXT

We recommend that *Interdisciplinary Inquiry in Teaching and Learning* be used as a core text in graduate-level general curriculum courses for upper elementary and middle school students. The text is also appropriate for courses and staff development programs in inquiry learning and the development of theme studies.

Marian L. Martinello and Gillian E. Cook
San Antonio, Texas

Acknowledgments

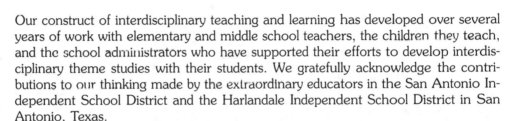

Our construct of interdisciplinary teaching and learning has developed over several years of work with elementary and middle school teachers, the children they teach, and the school administrators who have supported their efforts to develop interdisciplinary theme studies with their students. We gratefully acknowledge the contributions to our thinking made by the extraordinary educators in the San Antonio Independent School District and the Harlandale Independent School District in San Antonio, Texas.

Our teacher education students at The University of Texas at San Antonio have helped us to formulate important aspects of this book's treatment of interdisciplinary teaching and learning. We are similarly indebted to the elementary and middle school students who participated in theme studies conducted by the preservice and inservice teachers we have taught.

The Division of Education at The University of Texas at San Antonio is our academic home, and one of the most supportive places for professional inquiry we have experienced in our careers.

We greatly appreciate the help that our editors, Linda Scharp McElhiney and Debbie Stollenwerk, have given us throughout the development of this book, from its conception, through initial manuscript preparation and revisions, to the preparation of the significantly revised final document for the second edition.

Our reviewers also deserve recognition for helping us to refine our ideas and clarify their expression. They are: Maureen Gillette, College of St. Rose; Bob Hoffman, San Diego State University; Janet Juhlin, Southwest Baptist University; Paul L. Nelson, St. Martin's College; Connie H. Nobles, Southeastern Louisiana University; and Virginia Schwarzrock, University of Portland.

Many more people than we have space to acknowledge have influenced our thinking and encouraged us in this work. We gratefully acknowledge their many contributions to our thinking and our learning.

Contents

Chapter Five

Using Resources for Interdisciplinary Theme Studies: Print, People, Places, and Things   107

Part One

Introduction to Interdisciplinary Inquiry

Chapter One

The Interdisciplinary Qualities of Inquiry

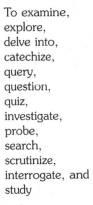

To examine,
explore,
delve into,
catechize,
query,
question,
quiz,
investigate,
probe,
search,
scrutinize,
interrogate, and
study

All these are synonymous with the act of inquiring. Even while referring to a process with common attributes, each term suggests different qualities of an activity that is defined as "the search for information, knowledge, and truth" *(Webster's Third International Dictionary, 1981),* p. 1167. What, then, are the qualities of inquiry? How do they vary with the discipline or field of study? The inquirer? The circumstances surrounding the search?

3

Inquiry is the source of new knowledge. Developing the ability to inquire is central to the education of those who devote their lives to explaining nature's mysteries, gaining access to them through the languages and paradigms of the sciences, mathematics, the humanities, and the arts. But inquiry is not solely the province of scholars. Inquiry is also what ordinary people do to learn and to add meaning to their lives. Some seem more adept at it than others. Why? It all depends on how we are educated.

At a time when the democratic ethic and processes are shaping the political structures and values of many of the nations on our planet, a major responsibility of the public schools is to educate thinking persons. Demographic projections predict that the twenty-first century will belong to people whose backgrounds are more diverse and less affluent than those of people in earlier times. The United States is an especially interesting case because of its multicultural population and democratic systems. Those systems may not survive without the education of all children through various ways of thinking and knowing, from their earliest days and throughout their schooling. The greatest contemporary challenge to American public education is to find ways to ensure that this is accomplished.

We tend to look to the separate disciplines of study for direction. Thus, movements in science education have worked for years to develop students' scientific thinking, and social studies education has fostered critical thinking and creative problem solving. Central to language arts instruction is the complex use of spoken and written language and interpretive skills in reading. Nurturing students' creative expression is the concern of instruction in the fine and performing arts. Yet American students are not known to be self-directed inquirers. What is missing from their education?

To understand inquiry, we need to know how it is done well and how we can recognize its processes in ourselves and others. We find evidence of inquiry in sports, in professional work, in occupations, and in everyday living—wherever problems and challenges require serious and sustained study. Most of the research evidence on inquiry draws from the same disciplines that define the academic curriculum. Therefore, we focus on those traditional fields of study, but ask you to think about extensions to other areas of human endeavor, especially those you know and live best.

In this book, we draw from the work of analysts of inquiry, such as Roe (1952) and Kuhn (1970) in the sciences and Hughes (1980) in the arts, and of some who explore thinking in several fields, such as Phenix (1964), Gardner (1983), and John-Steiner (1985). The reflections of scientists, mathematicians, computer scientists, writers and poets, and fine and performing artists have given us glimpses into the workings of their minds. Some appear in print, such as Watson's (1968) reconstruction of the search to discover the structure of DNA and Matisse's Notebooks of a Painter (in Flam, 1973). Some are found in video productions of documentaries and analyses of invention and discovery. Other accounts are from personal interviews with scholars at our own university and in our community.

In the quest for knowledge, every field is dedicated to clarifying the meanings of "real" and "true." Our interest is in the path toward those goals: How is the quest for truth carried on? How are the meanings of "real" and "true" uncovered? How is productive inquiry done in any field—what are its beginnings, its processes, its influences, and its products? And, then, how can we use this knowledge in the education of children?

ORIGINS OF INQUIRY

People who work in the *natural sciences* often say that their investigations start with puzzles. Watson and Crick were intrigued by the missing links in the alpha helix that fellow researcher Pauling had proposed toward explaining the structure of DNA. Feynman (1988) found anomalies in the temperature-tolerance data for the O-ring seals that ultimately explained the space shuttle *Challenger's* explosion shortly after liftoff in 1986. In a similar way, Birnbaum (personal communication, 1991) searches for discrepancies in the work of fellow geologists, looking for the gaps in their work, "the things they *don't* explain and the questions they *don't* raise" in their investigations. Scientists are intrigued by the unknown and unexplained. Their curiosity drives their inquiry more often than does their human desire for recognition and material reward. Even Watson, who claims he wanted the Nobel Prize, was helped through the unproductive periods of the search for the DNA double helix by the desire to understand the chemical origin of life.

The studies of *mathematicians,* like those of theoretical physicists, often begin with the test and proof of theories that may have been formulated intuitively. To search for a solution to the "traveling salesman problem," a question that involves finding the shortest tour around a group of cities, K. Robbins (personal communication, 1992) tried testing the theory of cooperating processes. The theory offers a different perspective on the problem, suggesting a solution strategy that connects independently working computers to share data generated from random searches for the shortest routes. The problem supplies the intrigue; the theory offers a new perspective. Hardy (1940) speaks eloquently about the mathematician's search for proofs. Wiles's seven-year quest to prove Fermat's Last Theorem is a good example (Lynch, 1998). Fermat noted that the Pythagorean Theorem, $x^2 + y^2 = z^2$, which explains the interrelationships of the hypotenuse and the sides of a right triangle, is true only for the squares of each side. The equation does not hold true for larger multiples, and, therefore, $x^n + y^n$ does not equal z^n when n is greater than 2. Wiles had been intrigued with this problem from childhood. Fermat had not offered a proof, although he said he had one. Wiles likens his search to a journey through a dark building (Lynch, 1998):

> You enter the first room of the mansion and it's completely dark. You stumble around bumping into the furniture, but gradually you learn where each piece of furniture is.

Finally, after six months or so, you find the light switch, you turn it on, and suddenly it's all illuminated. You can see exactly where you were. Then you move into the next room and spend another six months in the dark. So each of these breakthroughs, while sometimes they're momentary, sometimes over a period of a day or two, they are a culmination of—and couldn't exist without—the many months of stumbling around in the dark that precede them.

Writers inquire into scenarios, characters, and experiences that capture their interest. Welty (1983) listened for stories in the dialogues of relatives and friends. Short-story writer and poet N. Cuba (personal communication, 1992) searches her experiences with people for insights into the relationships that infuse her stories and poems. Cuba's story about a brother-sister relationship is drawn from her experience with an adored older brother, but the scenario is imagined. Its "trueness" derives from the integrity of the characters and the setting and from the author's deep understanding of each. The same interest is expressed by fiction writer B. Oliver's (personal communication, 1991) intimate study of his characters. Knowing their favorite scents, tastes, music, and textures, as well as their innermost thoughts, is important to his ability to depict them as authentic characters, even though that specific information may never appear in print. The setting, too, is often imagined in greater multisensory detail than what the writer shares on the printed page.

Inquiry in the *fine arts* derives from a desire to know more about oneself and the universal "self." Printmaker, photographer, and painter K. Rush (personal communication, 1992) defines his purpose as "to find something beyond what I already know. To get closer to myself so that tangible forms of my work reflect me—the part of me that is more like all of you." It often starts with play, the artist's exploration of ways that images can be used to express perceptions. Matisse (Flam, 1973) talked about forming different perceptions of line, form, color, and light and experimenting with ways to express the designs perceived. In his study of modernism, Hughes (1980) describes the Cubists as trying to depict *process* by recording all the possible perspectives of their subjects at the same time. Their problem was to capture on canvas ways of seeing that had not yet been expressed in the visual arts.

The *humanities* are similarly driven by questions about human experience. The study of the ancient people of the Lower Pecos River (Ancient Texans: Rock Art and Life Ways along the Lower Pecos, Witte Museum, San Antonio, Texas, 1987) started with the excavation of their rock shelters, their homes. When sites near the Alamo were excavated, I. W. Cox and his team of archaeologists at the Center for Archaeological Research, University of Texas at San Antonio (personal communication, 1991), found artifacts that caused them to wonder about the lifestyles of people who had lived in the area over the years. The work of historians such as W. Smith (personal communication, 1992) in his studies of China, G. Hinojosa (personal communication, 1992) on the Hispanic experiences in south Texas, and Van Kirk (1980) on women's role in the fur-trade society of western

Canada strive to make sense of the past and to explain change. They probe gaps in the historical record about the needs, wants, and life patterns of those who lived at different times in close or distant places and in similar or different cultures. These researchers devote years to their studies because they want to discover the unknown or, by challenging or enlarging existing interpretations, come to better understand human experience.

In all of these fields, the driving force is *passion* to explore and to understand. John-Steiner (1985) found evidence of passion in the thinking of men and women in every field of study. Inquiry for educators is framed by this question: How can children experience that insatiable drive to learn?

MODES AND PROCESSES OF INQUIRY

In *Frames of Mind* and a later article, Gardner (1983, 1997) presents the concept of *multiple intelligences:* linguistic, logical-mathematical, spatial, bodily-kinesthetic, musical, interpersonal and intrapersonal, and naturalist. Each is a different *form* of thinking that uses particular abilities in varying degrees for special purposes. Gardner's theory describes the diversity of ways in which people perceive and construct meanings. Phenix's (1964) classic study of *realms of meaning* classifies the areas of knowledge by form and content, the languages of thought, and the focus of their inquiries. Propensities for ways of learning affect how questions are studied and what is learned. John-Steiner's (1985) analyses of thinking in scholars present ways of thinking as visual, verbal, musical, choreographic, and scientific. She asserts that while many of these modes of thinking are used by thinkers in every field, thinking in some inquiries may be dominated more by one than another.

Several modalities are believed to be important in the acts of perceiving and expressing our thoughts to ourselves and others. These have been variously described as intelligences (Gardner, 1983, 1997), vehicles (McKim, 1980), and ways of knowing (John-Steiner, 1985). In our search to understand the similarities as well as the differences in inquiry across the fields of study, we have found evidence of several modes of thought that seem to fall into three major categories: symbolic, imagic, and affective. The *symbolic* modes include the use of symbol systems usually associated with the languages of words and numbers. Our spoken and "inner" speech represent symbolic means of expressing thoughts, as do the symbols used to construct a mathematical equation. Musical notation is another symbol system used to convey tonalities and their relationships. These *imagic* ways of thinking include visual, tonal, and kinesthetic-sensate ways of knowing. The images of the mind's eye—and ear and hand and, in fact, all sensory representations in imagination—offer different ways of forming ideas to solve problems, to analyze experiences, and to invent and to create. Dreams and drawings, paintings, photographs and moving images, graphs, maps, blueprints, models, and graphic designs are conveyances of visual thinking. The design of graphics to communicate complex information, causal relationships, and evidence for multivariate interactions requires fluency in visual language: the "pictures of numbers," "pictures of nouns," and pictures of verbs" (Tufte, 1983, 1990, 1997). Emotions and feelings, including intra- and interpersonal understanding and communication, are associated with *affective* thought. These—such as keen interest and curiosity, competitiveness and cooperation, and the act of forming hunches—serve to frame, drive, direct, and color an inquiry.

Thinking processes go by several names, too. Some call them operations (McKim, 1980); others liken them to habits of mind (Rutherford & Ahlgren, 1990). Whatever the label, the allusions to rational and intuitive thinking typically use terms such as critical analysis (Hawes, 1990), problem solving (Perkins, 1990), and creative thinking or synthesis (Wallace & Gruber, 1989). Such terms imply that thinking is all of a piece; that inquiry is inquiry is inquiry, no matter what the content. We test that idea in this chapter.

Figure 1.1
The Modes and Processes of Inquiry

Symbolic: The use of words, numbers, and other symbol systems to perceive, construct, and express meanings and to form and frame inquiry.

Imagic: The use of images, sounds and tonalities, and kinesthetic-sensory ways to perceive, construct, and express meanings and to form and frame inquiry.

Affective: The use of feelings and emotions to perceive, construct, and express meanings and to color, direct, and drive inquiry.

Some Habits of Mind

Finding and keeping focus
Asking good questions
Simplifying questions and problems
Being attentive
Seeing anomalies
Thinking fluently and flexibly
Forming hunches
Designing tests and experimenting
Searching for patterns
Using models and metaphors; thinking by analogy
Finding elegant solutions
Taking risks
Cooperating and collaborating
Competing
Persevering and having self-discipline

All these modes and processes, summarized in Figure 1.1, appear in our readings and discussions about thinking in the arts, the sciences and mathematics, and the humanities. They refer to both the form in which information is perceived and worked with and the ways in which it is expressed and communicated. While some fields of study may rely on certain modes or processes more than others and individual inquirers may be more talented in the use of some over others, all have something to offer every inquiry because each provides the inquirer with a different way to perceive the subject and a different form in which to shape and convey ideas. The more diverse the modes of thinking used by an inquirer, the greater the potential for discovery. The power of interdisciplinary inquiry lies in its ability to encourage diversity of thought and, therefore, to increase the explorer's chances of making creative connections and "going beyond the information given" (Bruner, 1973).

THE CONTENT OF INQUIRY

The Languages of Disciplines and Fields of Study

The arts, the sciences and mathematics, and the humanities are distinguished from one another by their specialized languages, their laws and theories, the accepted bodies of knowledge in their disciplines, and the methodologies used to conduct their inquiries. It is widely assumed that knowledge of a field is prerequisite to productive inquiry in that field. Certainly, fluency in musical languages is as important to musical composition as literacy in the symbols of the periodic table is to inquiry in chemistry. But can knowledge of those languages constrain and even constrict a search? Nothing can lock us into a way of thinking about something as effectively as the name we give it. A classic example is how the term *atom*, whose Greek root means "indivisible," deterred atomic physicists from entertaining thoughts of the atom as a divisible unit. And what of the models and beliefs that are dominant in a field of study at a particular time? As Kuhn (1970) and Margolis (1993) point out, firmly held beliefs can severely limit inquiry because they fool us into thinking that we know all that needs to be known to understand the topic of study. Assumptions that the earth was the center of the universe retarded understanding of the solar system and the structure of the universe. Some (Griffin, 1984; Barber, 1993) contend that the anti-anthropomorphic bias in science blinds perception and understanding of thinking in animals.

Kuhn's (1970) analysis of scientific revolutions explains how new concepts open a field of study to questions no one thought to ask when older models molded thinking. Newtonian physics influenced what and how mathematicians thought about physical relationships until Einstein's theory of relativity challenged the ruling paradigms. The concept of plate tectonics dramatically altered the prevailing views of the earth's geological history. Non-Euclidean geometry allowed new geometric concepts to emerge. Modernism in art broke with the long-standing tradition of Renaissance perspective. Each paved the way for new ways of seeing and thinking, sometimes in several fields of study. For example, the concept of relativity affected work in the humanities and the arts as well as in the sciences. Every model, every belief, by its existence enables and limits inquiry. The accepted knowledge of a field both informs and biases our perspectives, as we look at our subject through that lens.

The language of a field influences how questions are formulated. Linguistic languages have their unique characteristics to describe things, depict action, and subtly distinguish and discriminate. The descriptive capabilities of adjective-rich English may be challenged by those of the Eskimo languages, and both may be challenged by the superior abilities of Spanish to express nuances in action. Every symbol system carries similar advantages and limitations for inquiry. Mathematical symbols permit some relationships to be expressed more clearly than others. Reflecting on the completeness of bubbles in a wave breaking on shore, Fuller said that nature hated π because the value is never resolved; 3.1415 . . . goes on forever. By hating π himself, Fuller looked past it for wholeness and found the geodesic dome, now understood as the molecule formed from charred carbon and referred to affectionately and respectfully as the "Buckey ball" (Perlmutter, 1991). Musical notation enables composers to record orchestrations for large symphony orchestras and very complex tonalities, yet is unable to communicate precisely some rhythmic patterns in jazz.

The Literary Arts.   Writers usually have what Gardner (1983) calls linguistic intelligence, the ability to perform verbal thinking with ease. They delight in the sounds and the symbolisms of words and are particularly adept at perceiving words in different ways and at expressing and communicating ideas through language by using their "inner voice," according to John-Steiner (1985). Most speak of their *love* of words. Welty (1983) was compelled by the characteristics of words from childhood. She delighted in how they *felt* in her mouth as she formed them, the ways they combined to express images and sensations, and the ways they enabled her to find meanings in people, places, times, and experiences. N. Cuba (personal communication, 1992) enjoys the detail that words provide, allowing her to work with her sensations, feelings, and images, as she did when describing the many dimensions of a fish in one of her stories. It all started for her with questions: "Is it possible to catch a fish with your hands? What kind of fish would be in this location? What would be inside it that would be fascinating?" She saw the fish as a metaphor for life. Everything inside of the fish is representative of life: pleasant and unpleasant, beautiful and ugly. Cuba's study of the fish became a study of the meanings of life.

Most writers are aware of the sensations that help them imagine as they write. There is evidence of visual as well as verbal thinking in their self-reports and by inference. The reader's ability to form images while reading is testimony to the writer's ability to communicate sensory ideas. The same may be said for the affective mode. Writers use words to speak from and with emotion and to cause feeling in the reader. Poets, in particular, seem to think simultaneously in imagic, verbal, and affective modes. While words may be their primary vehicle for expression and communication, the way they visualize the placement of each word on the page and the physical appearance and style of the letters influence the thought expressed. Poets may be in the vanguard of those who use verbal language to develop and to express their meanings through imagic, symbolic, and affective modes. The inquiries—the searches literary artists conduct to write in authentic and moving ways—use all of the modes of thinking. Only the product is primarily, though not exclusively, dominated by the verbal.

Writers use detective-like reasoning when they develop personas from bits of character traits and when they form a story from puzzle pieces of human experience. Welty (1983) explains how she uses facets of people she has known to create new characters with their own special constellations of qualities that make them unique, yet reminiscent of others, and therefore believable. Writers also develop insights into their subjects and settings by pulling from deep within themselves new interactions among ideas. "All serious daring," as Welty says, "starts from within." They often express those intuitive understandings through metaphor.

The Fine and Performing Arts.　Visualization is often used to think through and express concepts in the visual and performing arts. Images emerge from intuitive thinking, but can also arise as the artist analyzes a problem. Visual artists' descriptions of their inquiries are alive with metaphor. "Drawing," K. Rush says (personal communication, 1992) "is perception—a way of knowing." Drawing is also a way to play with visual ideas by encoding them. Gardner (1983, p. 66) includes the "susceptibility to encoding in a symbol system" as a criterion for the seven intelligences that he identifies (the spatial, bodily-kinesthetic, and musical among them). Visual artists do not claim a symbol system comparable to musical notation or the graphic language used to choreograph the dance or movement strategies in sports, but the physical elements of visual art (line, color, space, shape, and texture) may be building blocks of "symbol" systems for visual thinking.

Artists have much in common with the theoretical physicist, suggests S. Reynolds (personal communication, 1991). They develop imaginative ideas about the world by asking questions on the nature of things and reality. D. Hodges (personal communication, 1991) uses Ives's 1908 orchestral piece "The Unanswered Question" as an illustration of the composer's use of music to ask and seek answers to philosophical questions about the meaning of life in the universe. He argues that tonal thinking offers new perceptions of the question—new ways of understanding its character.

The artists we have interviewed underscore the emotional aspects of their work. Rush (personal communication, 1992) speaks of rapport—understanding that is nonverbal—as important to his work. He refers to this thinking as intuitive, holistic, divergent, spatial, and nonverbal. His purpose in inquiry is to intuit meaning from all elements of his life experiences, without contaminating them by his biases or predilections. He refers to Ryder's metaphor, which likens inquiry to an inchworm, its back legs holding fast to a leaf, its front end leaning forward, feeling outward into space for new experiences and discoveries. Reynolds (personal communication, 1991) characterizes artistic creativity as requiring risk taking, driven by the artist's need to investigate new sources and new processes to enable discovery. Intuitive feelings guide the sense of correctness of perceived shapes and forms, and analytical thinking provides the critical evaluation of one's work. "Art is a snail trail—the track that you leave," Reynolds says. It is a quest for truth that has continuity, pattern, and diversity—a challenge to find as many worlds as we can know.

Mathematics.   Central to Gardner's concept of logical-mathematical intelligence is the work with "long chains of reasoning" (Gardner, 1983, p. 139). Phenix understands the essence of mathematics as "a language of complete abstraction" (Phenix, 1964). Einstein's (Mantel, 1974) reasoning with images (for instance, his perspectives from a tram moving at the speed of light) and his conceptions of energy and time used imagery to develop a sequence of abstractions that led to the theory of relativity. Visual thinking is critical to Robbins's (personal communication, 1992) computer network to investigate the traveling salesman problem: "Workhorse" computers are linked to a central "blackboard" computer to simultaneously deliver data from their computations to the "blackboard" and be able to randomly select from that "blackboard" increasingly specialized sets of data. Analogies of teams of workhorses and a centralized blackboard contributed to this solution strategy, and the graphing of quantitative information makes the process possible. J. Keating (personal communication, 1991) also graphs statistical relationships to see quantitative patterns more clearly. Visual thinking merges with symbolic thinking as symbol systems are used to express discovered relationships between quantitative ideas. Much of this seems deliberate and reasoned, and it is. But equally important is the hunch that may give rise to an inquiry or direct its course: Robbins *senses* that the theory of cooperative functions is rich with potential to yield a solution to the traveling salesman problem. Keating often "sees" solutions to problems and then reasons out the proof. According to Gardner (1983, 139), "Many mathematicians report that they sense a solution, or a direction, long before they have worked out each step in detail." Explaining the idea requires the exercise of logic and its symbolic expression.

"No matter how talented you are in your field, no matter how much you know, the work is always difficult when you're at the frontiers of your knowledge. Inquiry is not easy when you're testing the limits of your abilities. But that is what makes it satisfying" (Robbins, personal communication, 1992). The need to understand, to discover relationships, and to invent new perspectives drives mathematical inquiry. And then there is the *joy,* the sheer pleasure of searching.

The Natural and Social Sciences.   We have tended to think of the scientific method as a clean and meticulous process of formulating hypotheses, organizing experiments, collecting data, and then analyzing and interpreting the findings in order to test the hypothesis and phrase new ones. Most natural and social scientists depict their inquiries as far less clear-cut and tidy. Watson's (1968) description of the search for the double helix is perhaps the best known testimony to the ins and outs, false starts, and detours of scientific detective work. Every scientist we have interviewed, and the many who contributed to John-Steiner's (1985) analysis, referred in some way to imagic thinking in their work. Most use metaphors and analogies. Many draw. Some, like Watson and Crick, construct models to clarify their thinking through kinesthetic-sensate experience. Sometimes the construction is highly analytical. At other times, it may be associated with flashes of insight. von Kekule's discovery of the molecular structure of benzene (which initiated the discipline of organic chemistry) came from a dream of spiraling images that merged in the snake-like shape of a ring (McKim, 1980). Artist K. Rush (personal communication, 1992) reminds us that dreaming is a form of thinking different from others. Eastern cultures use meditation to enable thinking that breaks the bounds imposed by our restricted sense of self. These are intuitive processes.

But science also involves critical, skeptical analysis of findings. And analysis requires symbolic thinking. Science measures with precision. It explicates hypotheses and builds theories. Scientific thinking challenges the known, searching out what is not understood and what is missing. It seeks to replicate and evaluate. The analytical processes may proceed in imagic modes, but they also need symbolic forms to advance the flow, expression, and communication of thought.

Playing with ideas is as characteristic of scientific inquiry as inquiry in any other field. Watson called it "tinkering." Bronowski (1973) called it "asking impertinent questions." D. Senseman (personal communication, 1991) refers to the pleasure of exploring the fascinating unknown. The affective dimensions of inquiry come through in many scientists' reports of their work. *Playfulness, delight,* and *pleasure* are words scientists use to try to explain the role of those clearly felt, but enigmatic, sensations that fuel their inquiries. These affective modes of thinking are also integral to the intra- and interpersonal abilities, associated with Gardner's (1983) personal intelligences, that contribute to collaboration, competition, perseverance, and joyfulness in inquiry.

The Humanities. Despite a tendency to think of their fields as primarily analytical, historians, anthropologists, archaeologists, and others who study human experience draw on both analytic and affective modes of thinking. W. Smith (personal communication, 1992) reminds us that history is a cultural activity. The language of history is the language of culture. Studies of human experience seek and search through and for the human voice. They can be inherently interdisciplinary, perhaps more than in any other field of study. Therefore, their inquiry can, and often does, use all the ways of knowing associated with the sciences and the arts. Humanities scholars reconstruct the past by interpreting and imagining the patterns suggested by clues in the artifacts of human presence. Understanding the lifestyles of a people, like those of the Lower Pecos, who dwindled away without trace by the middle of the first century, is an ongoing detective-like hunt (Ancient Texans: Rock Art and Life Ways along the Lower Pecos, Witte Museum, San Antonio, Texas, 1987). Still unanswered questions about why those ancient Texans painted diverse designs on the small round rocks found in their natural shelters along the Rio Grande haunt researchers. Perhaps more than any other, the subject matter of human experience demands of the inquirer a confluence of modes and processes of thinking.

THE CONTEXTS OF INQUIRY

Equally influential is the context of inquiry: its person, its place, and its time. Each and every inquiry has a unique context. The era in which it takes place and the idiosyncratic characteristics of the searchers must influence the ways questions are formulated and explored. Culture, gender, experience, personality, circumstances, good luck or bad—all these contextual factors seem important.

Individual inquirers bring their personalities, propensities, and backgrounds to bear on what and how they explore. Watson contributed a generalist's perspective that complemented Crick's specialist orientation. Watson's talents with synthesis, as well as his youth and American background, brought a special constellation of qualities to the search for the molecular structure of the gene with Crick's analytical powers, maturity, and British training. The inquirer's cultural rearing, including native language, influences ways of perceiving a problem and formulating a question. Growing up male or female in a particular culture will add other layers of influence on any study, some drawn from rearing practices, others from societal biases. Wilson (Knull, 1988) writes plays about universal human issues, but portrays them from the African-American cultural perspective because he wants to advance understanding of that heritage in a society that often seems uncaring about, as well as ignorant of, the black experience. McClintock's work on jumping genes went unnoticed and unappreciated in her field for decades, largely because of her gender in a male-dominated field. A different example of cultural bias is that for years research on heart disease has used only male subjects, yet those studies have been the source of treatments for women with coronary illnesses.

The environment in which the inquiry is conducted will also limit or advance its search. Laura Gilpin's photographs, like Ansel Adams's, were unique for their time. Today, with technological changes in photographic processes and the proliferation of images in the society at large, their inquiries would probably be quite different in character. Robbins's study of the traveling salesman problem would not be feasible without high-speed computers. And just as new tools change the kinds of questions asked, so do contemporary ideas influence how we interpret the past. "'The past is a foreign country, they did things differently there'" (Hartley quoted in Lowenthal, 1985, p. xvi) expresses in serious terms what Macauley (1979) presents humorously in *Motel of the Mysteries*. Macauley's fictitious archaeologists found it all too easy to find sacred meanings in the mundane objects of everyday life. Interpreters of the past must take care not to allow their contemporary knowledge or preconceived ideas to influence their perceptions.

Einstein found his work in the Swiss patent office helpful in developing his powers of observation and visual thinking. Hawking's (Freedman, Hickman, & Morris, 1991) thought experiments on the meaning of time and black holes extend and question some aspects of Einstein's theories. Advancing computer technology gives him special tools for his visual reasoning. Developing technologies during World War II greatly influenced engineering, just as the computer is empowering contemporary researchers who need to probe and interpret large quantities of data. The influence of context is clear in Wiles's response to a question about his proof of Fermat's Last Theorem: "Is your proof the same as Fermat's?" (Lynch, 1998):

> There's no chance of that. Fermat couldn't possibly have had this proof. It's 150 pages long. It's a 20th-century proof. It couldn't have been done in the 19th century, let alone the 17th century. The techniques used in this proof just weren't around in Fermat's time.

Increases in the quantity and quality of the resources needed to explore any question can empower and enlarge the inquiry. Lack of resources certainly hinders the search.

Social, political, and personal contexts can determine what questions can be asked, who may explore them, and when an inquiry can be done or be recognized. The gender, ethnicity, age, and background of the inquirer and the era in which the inquirer lives and works can affect the kinds of questions asked, the opportunities to explore those questions, and the degree of acceptance, within the field or among the general public, of an inquirer's empirical findings, interpretations, and theoretical constructs.

Every inquiry has the potential to change what and how we understand, but every inquiry is limited by what and how we know. Every inquiry is unique and can break the bounds of tradition, but each is limited by the courage and the imagination of the inquirer.

THE PRODUCTS OF INQUIRY

Every question, if explored with care and thoroughness, guides us toward knowledge, newly acquired by the individual or newly discovered in the field of study. Inquiry also raises additional questions that suggest further directions for study. The findings of one search generate ideas for others and sometimes suggest connections that give rise to new theories. Inquiry in any field may produce expanded symbol systems—ways of expressing concepts and interrelationships more clearly and succinctly. The process of inquiring helps us not only to develop content knowledge, but also to expand our skills in using the modes, processes, and skills of the search. People who do not consider themselves scholars in specialized fields of study use inquiry to learn about anything that interests them, to solve problems that affect their lives, to direct their personal experiences, to find their own truths, and to hone their habits of mind. The ordinary person's inquiry may explore an area of interest, an intriguing question, a mystery, the meanings of an idea, and even the secrets held by the things we see and use every day. Whatever the problem, subject, or issue, any careful and enthusiastic inquiry will encourage us to practice some of the same modes and processes of thinking regularly used by those who search for new knowledge in their chosen disciplines, professions and occupations, sports, hobbies, and, indeed, the many facets of living.

Habits of Mind

Margolis (1993, 8) says that just as physical traits are associated with patterns of movement, habits of mind "yield patterns of thought, intuitions, images, intentions." Embedded in the testimonies of the sources we consulted are references to abilities that seem to course through inquiry, supporting the use of the thinking modes and processes we detail in this chapter. Some habits of mind can, of course, be inflexible and, therefore, severely limit authentic inquiry. But those we discuss here are ways of thinking that we all need in order to become better learners.

Interestingly, some of the same habits appear important for inquiry in every field. They include the abilities to focus, to question, to simplify, to attend to details, to see anomalies, to think fluently and flexibly, to form hunches, to experiment, to search for patterns, to use models and metaphors, and to find elegant solutions and the affective dispositions of taking risks, cooperating/collaborating, competing, and persevering or being capable of self-discipline. Certainly, there are others. We start with these, inviting you to contribute to the set as we continue this inquiry into interdisciplinary inquiry learning.

Finding and Keeping Focus. "Keep your focus," the coach directs the Olympic athlete before the competition. Good advice. But staying focused is more difficult than it seems. Finding a focus hinges on the way questions are posed. Maintaining the focus depends on which questions are selected. An inquiry can be only as probing as its questions.

Asking Good Questions. "That's a good question!" We praise questions because we don't have an easy answer, the question offers a new angle on the topic or problem, or the question spotlights a brand new idea. Every discipline of study, profession, and occupation is nurtured by those good questions that can, through their exploration by specialists in the field, expand its body of knowledge.

The idea of questioning as problem definition is commonly associated with the scientific method. Natural and social scientists define their experiments through hypotheses, which are really proposed answers to their questions. Although a question may be phrased in different ways, it focuses and delimits the inquiry. The geologist who explores relationships among several variables in the physical world is asking operational questions. An anthropologist studying cultural characteristics of social groups may ask descriptive questions. Both scholars formulate their questions in ways that determine where they will look for answers. The questions of theoretical mathematicians are inherent in their search for proofs; those who apply mathematics, such as statisticians, translate questions from other fields into mathematical language. While writers may not highlight the questions that drive their writing, their poems, stories, and essays are clearly attempts to communicate answers to questions about human experiences, behaviors, and qualities. In effect, they are writing figurative answers to a universal set of questions about the human condition. The works of fine artists, often considered *problems,* are the manifestations of experiments with elements such as light, color, texture, shape, tone, and rhythm. All experiments are framed by questions. The character of the query can determine the success of the experiment. But not all questions are equally clear in guiding investigation. Not all questions can be answered in substantive ways. How well the question is formulated determines the extent to which its answers contribute insights to a study.

Simplifying Questions and Problems.   Research is advanced by questions that are simply and clearly phrased. No matter how complex the subject under investigation, most researchers claim to search for the simplest and most direct language to express their query. Scholars in every field maintain a continuing quest for the most succinct, most clarifying "language" to express and communicate what they want to find out. The clearer the question, the greater its ability to isolate significant variables, suggest critical relationships, provide clues to sources of substantive data, and, in effect, point to the problem's solution. The ability to remove from a problem its complicating, extraneous features is a hallmark of the successful inquirer.

Being Attentive.   Eastern philosophy advances attentiveness as the ultimate habit of mind—the means for becoming one with the universe. In Western thought, too, attentiveness is valued. The natural scientist speaks of this as observation and collection of precise data. Some say that it is more important to have impeccably accurate data than a clear interpretation because interpretations may vary, but the data must always be true. Inquirers in the humanities talk about clearly recording measurements of the observable. The mathematician and the theoretical scientist may place less emphasis on observing their environment than on theorizing about it, but they, too, refer to attending to specific components that complete an idea. Their thought experiments examine details in the same way that inventors report seeing all parts of their inventions in their mind's eye. Literary artists refer to knowing every detail of their character's persona, whether or not they ever write them down. Visual artists are equally concerned with details— a drop of color, a shadow, or a spot of light—that contribute to the image, although most casual viewers are oblivious to them. Musicians cannot help but attend to the tone and texture of individual notes.

"The devil is in the details," we're told because attention to detail can uncover problems with general ideas. Meaning and *evidence* are also in the details. Tufte (1997) gives one of the most compelling illustrations of this in his discussion of how the decision to launch the *Challenger* spacecraft was made without careful inspection of all the details. It was really very simple. The issue was whether the O-rings on the *Challenger's* booster rockets would function properly in the very cold temperatures at Cape Canaveral on the launch date, when seven astronauts were scheduled to be propelled into space, teacher Christa McCauliff among them. As Tufte's statistical and visual mind reconstructs the investigative events in that decision making, he shows how a complete set of data was not compiled or clearly presented to show all the information the engineers had about O-ring response to a range of temperatures. By constructing his own complete graphic of detailed data, Tufte shows how a decision *not* to launch would have been most likely, no matter what the political concerns and institutional norms of the day.

Attentiveness requires open-mindedness and appreciation of how a whole is a collection of individual pieces that can be comprehended only by perceptual precision.

Seeing Anomalies.   Like magic, the unexpected, the discrepant event, the contradiction to what we believe to be true demands explanation. Anomalies are paths to discovery (John-Steiner, 1985) because they raise questions.

Martinello (1987) was intrigued by an erasure in the dowry wish list kept by a young rural German-Texan bride, Emma Mayer Beckmann, in the early years of the twentieth century. The erasure itself was not unusual. The bride had chosen to lower the price of the stove on her list, apparently in order to retain a parlor suite and sofa on her list and still remain within her budget. Curiously, though, the bride knew that she would be moving into a log house, with no parlor at all and no room for parlor furniture. Emma also knew that cooking would be one of her important daily tasks. Yet, according to prices of stoves in the Sears & Roebuck Company catalogs of the day, Emma sacrificed a large range for a very modest wood-burning stove in order to keep the parlor suite and sofa in the dowry her parents were providing. This anomaly gave rise to a search for Emma's hopes and dreams and their origins.

When experience and prevailing theories are misfits, when there is an apparent discrepancy or contradiction, inquiry is advanced by the inquirer who takes another look at the problem. Bronowski (1973, p. 153) reminds us, "Ask an impertinent question and you are on to the pertinent answer." Anomalies make you wonder about what is, and, therefore, they spawn questions that can probe what others may take for granted.

Thinking Fluently and Flexibly.   Based on the work of Guilford (1956), Torrance (1962, 1970) described characteristics of creative thinking associated with the generation of many and varied ideas. He termed these ways of thinking *fluent* and *flexible,* respectively. When asked about their inquiry, natural scientists often cite the ability to look at their problem or their data in new ways. This flexibility in perspective can suggest different interpretations and, most important, new questions for exploration.

The ability to think in maverick ways fuels controversy in every field; it may also overturn cherished ideas, challenging established knowledge. Historians may search for clues to support interpretations of people's lives or events that are different from earlier ones. Journalists look for the new angle on a story. Writers distinguish themselves by finding different ways to speak to universal human experience. Metaphors can give new dimensions to old ideas. Artists combine different media to create unique visual and auditory images. The ability to generate lots of ideas with ease and to use different perspectives to examine any idea is central to creative production; it is also critical to interdisciplinary thinking.

Forming Hunches.   Analysis and intuition play complementary roles in anticipatory thinking. Some predictions and hypotheses are reasoned out; others, such as conjectures, speculations, and projections, are intuited. Those who work in the "hard" sciences are as likely to talk about the importance of their hunches as those who inquire in the arts and humanities. From the hunches, formal hypotheses may emerge. Natural scientists are concerned with relating variables in hypothetical statements that focus their inquiry. Mathematicians and theoretical scientists work to prove the theorems, principles, and laws that are the hypotheses of their imaginative reasoning. Even when the hypotheses are not couched in formal language, inquirers engage in "if-then" thinking. Historians may search for reasons to justify an interpretation or to project a consequence from historical precedents in the sense that "the past is pro logue." Writers also use projection to make their characters behave in response to certain circumstances and to the behaviors of others. This hypothetical thinking may result in the forms sculptors chisel out of an undifferentiated mass of material, in the images painters create, in the tonal themes that composers weave into variations, or in the cadenzas and improvisations of performers. Though less formal and sometimes more spontaneous than the hypotheses of research scientists, these creations are nonetheless *experiments* that test hypothetical ideas often born of hunches.

Designing Tests and Experimenting.   Experimentation is generally associated with the sciences. It's what natural scientists are expected to *do*. But experimenting is more inclusive than only doing lab experiments. Social scientists use the experimental method to control and test variables cited in their hypotheses; their methods of data collection might be surveys and behavioral observation. Mathematicians test mathematical theorems, principles, and laws by logically developing proofs and trying out their applications. Humanities scholars also experiment by searching for evidence that supports or refutes their ideas. The process of finding the evidence is an experiment in its own right. Anthropologists experiment by gathering descriptive data on their subjects, sometimes to find patterns that may suggest hypotheses and sometimes to test an idea. Writers and performers play out their hunches to see if their audiences can tell whether the actions of characters ring true and the plot is gripping. Attempts to solve problems in the fine arts are evaluated in the studio and rehearsal hall as they are created and recreated; the edited versions are then tested during exhibition and performance.

Searching for Patterns.   No matter how good we are at finding new ways of looking at a problem or topic, no matter how prolific our questions, there can be no synthesis without the organization of ideas. The search for patterns is integral to all learning and, therefore, to the generation of new knowledge. Natural scientists are detective-like when they categorize the data they collect. This integration of "little" notions into "big" ideas is also a part of the social scientist's investigative method. Literary artists develop their characters from the interaction of human traits and form their stories by articulating the associations among happenings in human experience. The search for patterns takes different routes for a painter or sculptor, composer or playwright, performer or actor. But none can solve his or her special problems without being able to achieve an integrated wholeness.

Graphic organizers are particularly useful in pattern searching. Tufte's work (1983, 1990, 1997) speaks about the language of graphics. His analyses of the most creative graphic displays of information explain how relationships among quantifiable variables will show up in some graphics, but not others. A good graphic can also reveal relationships among qualitative variables. So, it seems, part of this ability to find patterns is connected to making hypotheses, attending to potentially interrelated details, and visualizing ways to display them.

Using Models and Metaphors; Thinking by Analogy.   Models are means we use to shape and communicate our ideas about potential answers to our questions. The scientific method is a model of inquiry that scientists embrace and use as their touchstone. That model has been adopted by many social scientists, who, in turn, have adapted it to their special problems, language, and types of data. The physical representation of molecular structure is another kind of model that explains abstract ideas. Mathematical rules and principles are also long-standing models of criteria for quantitative inquiries. Even so, as mathematical fields expand to include the applicative methods of computer science and statistics, models for their use are formed and reformed. Humanities scholars use ethnographic models to research their subjects, experimenting with varied approaches to better comprehend the complexity of their subjects. In the fine arts, models for inquiry and expression are formed and reformed by inventive scholars. Inquiry is invention.

Weber and Perkins (1992) find analogy to be central in stories of invention. "Like a snake caught in a rat hole" is the graphic way in which Edward Rosinski expressed how the long petroleum molecules were caught and held for cutting by zeolite catalysts. They also mention that Bell's view of the telephone in terms of the way the ear works is a homely, but useful analogy. The analogy's value is in the imagery it prompts.

Metaphors are a special type of model. They can ascribe concrete and sensual qualities to abstract ideas: for instance, the physical model of chemical bonds in the double helix of DNA. Models can help the strange become familiar by calling up known images that prompt multidimensional associations: The mechanical DNA model is reminiscent of a spiral staircase or the twist in the honeysuckle stem.

There is often an interplay of rational thinking and feeling through metaphors. Poets and writers use them regularly, as Milligan (1998) did in his poem "The Poet Tree," in which he likens a gnarled old tree to his own aging. The work of fine artists includes visual, textural, and tonal metaphors. Metaphors give ideas a larger form. They help to uncover ways to group-related concepts. Scholars in the sciences and humanities use them to advance their search for meaningful patterns. Metaphors and models are vehicles for communicating complex ideas with clarity and succinctness. Knowing how to create and to use models and metaphors is a tool of every inquirer.

Finding Elegant Solutions.   Computers might not have developed to their contemporary power without the application of the binary system. A simple "one-zero, on-off" relationship permits some of the most complex technology and computation in human experience. The binary system's role in the development of the computer is an example of an elegant solution. Physicists claim that energy will not be completely understood until its aesthetic is found. Whatever the problem or question, its inquiry seeks solutions that are transcendent in their richness and simplicity. The search in any field is not for any answers, but for answers that are clear and unambiguous and convincingly true—answers that are beautiful. Elegant solutions explain complexities in all fields. Knowing where and how to look for them is a function of any inquiry.

Taking Risks.   The pursuit of elegant solutions to problems sometimes demands breaking with old, established traditions. Inquirers in all fields speak to the ability to do that in calculated ways. Sometimes this means pursuing interests and methods of investigation that are not valued in the field of study. Scientists in any discipline may have to risk loss of acceptance in the field in order to question an established idea or to follow their individual bent. Mathematicians may face professional ostracism if their work challenges accepted beliefs or pursues directions that are not yet accepted. The same is true of the humanities, the social sciences, and the literary and fine arts. Yet change is not possible without the courage to study an inherently interesting topic before its legitimacy is recognized or to subject the patterns one sees to criticism. Knowing when and how to take risks can determine success in any endeavor.

Cooperating and Collaborating.   Despite the tendency for most disciplines to value individual over group efforts, the ability to cooperate and collaborate with others who are working with related problems can advance an inquiry. This is increasingly true in the natural and social sciences, where team efforts can contribute to interdisciplinary studies. Opportunities to bring different points of view to bear on the same problem can lead to richer solutions. Although mathematicians are usually more solitary experimenters, they, too, claim to benefit from collaborative work with others who are intrigued by the same problem. Literary artists tend to work alone, as do many composers and visual artists. But writers have editors with whom they share a project and with whom they fine-tune the expression of their ideas. And those who work with sounds or visual images often prefer to be members of colonies of similar-minded and artistically talented people who can serve as respondents and reactors to one another's work. Knowing how to be a productive partner or group member often enhances the search for solutions (Johnson & Johnson, 1990).

Competing.   The desire to discover directs inquiry. The drive to excel fuels it. Scientists may strive to be first in cracking a code or finding a pattern that earns a Nobel Prize. They want their findings to appear in the literature before other scholars "steal their thunder." Grantsmanship is a highly competitive enterprise. Mathematicians also work to be first with the proof for a theorem—or with a new theorem. Creative artists may be less concerned with racing others to publish, exhibit, or perform their work, but they, too, push against the limits of their fields' knowledge and their personal creative talents by competing with their peers or with themselves. Without competition, there would be few revisions and new drafts. The competitive spirit often provides the discipline needed to continue an inquiry even when it is not going smoothly. Knowing how and when to compete most effectively is a habit of mind that is useful in many of life's phases, stages, and circumstances.

Persevering and Having Self-Discipline.   Every inquiry has its stalemates, its barriers, and its frustrations. No matter how interesting the study may be, there is always a point at which it becomes difficult. At that point, the inquirer may be pushing against the frontiers of personal knowledge or even the knowledge of the field. This applies to sports and occupations as well as to academic pursuits. For instance, barrel racing is a rodeo event in which horse and rider zigzag through a course defined by strategically placed barrels. The competitors' scores are registered in units of time it takes to complete the course. Overturned barrels deter progress and mar the performance. But overturned barrels are the price of testing the limits of horse and rider. As one barrel-racing champion told us, "If I don't turn over barrels once in awhile, I'm not running close enough. I have to keep trying" (C. Dodwell, personal communication, 1998).

People persevere in those efforts that have special significance for them. The motivation to continue derives, in part, from the degree of intrigue the search holds. How well individuals can exercise self-discipline also determines how long each is willing to "hang in" when the going gets rough. Learning to exercise self-discipline and to assess the origins of and influences on one's motivations has much to do with productive inquiry.

IMPLICATIONS FOR TEACHING AND LEARNING

What about children's inquiry? What do the ideas discussed in this chapter mean for students—all students, but especially those in elementary and middle schools? Our ideas are not new. Socrates would have endorsed them. In American education, Dewey (1933) was among the first to equate education with problem-solving skills, offering these steps from scientific problem solving:

▾ Becoming aware of a difficulty
▾ Analyzing the problem
▾ Generating possible solutions
▾ Testing the solutions
▾ Accepting or rejecting the tested solutions

Bloom's (1956) classic, *Taxonomy of Educational Objectives: Cognitive Domain* names categories of thinking:

▾ Knowledge (recalling information)
▾ Comprehension (understanding concepts and interrelationships of information)
▾ Application (using information in many contexts)
▾ Analysis (finding the component parts of larger ideas)
▾ Synthesis (creating new big ideas from component parts)
▾ Evaluation (applying criteria for making judgments)

Later, Taba's research (1962) defined stages in children's inductive thinking that could be guided by teacher questioning:

1. Formation of concepts, guided by questions to encourage observation, comparison/contrast, and categorization
2. Interpretation of data, guided by questions to help children examine their findings and see causal interrelationships
3. Application of principles, guided by questions prompting hypotheses and generalizations drawn from data interpretations

Educational philosophers, theorists, and empirical researchers have built on these concepts over many years, helping to clarify them for the practice of teaching and learning. The most common influences of these ideas are found in programs to develop thinking skills, science as process, writing across the curriculum, the project method, integrated curriculum, and theme studies. Each has special merit, but none focuses on inquiry across all curriculum areas in the ways we propose.

The modes and processes of thinking discussed in this chapter are drawn from Dewey's philosophy of education for democracy, from Taba's research on ways that critical and creative thinking can be developed in children, from Bloom's categorizations of thinking processes that are central to all learning, and from the authors on ways of knowing and thinking who have contributed to subsequent literature on these issues. Though long respected as the hallmarks of the educated person, these ways of thinking are more critical for meaningful living in our technological world than ever before.

In our study of how scholars conduct inquiry in their respective fields of study, we have found important implications for the ways to design curriculum and to develop learning. Each field's ways of thinking and exploring invite children's development of the modes and processes of inquiry that we have described here. Learning in the elementary and middle school years must prepare children for secondary and postsecondary studies by offering them solid foundations in the major ideas, generalizations, principles, and theories in the natural and social sciences, the literary and fine arts, and mathematics. They must also learn to use, with increasing capability, the particular imagic, symbolic, and affective modes of thinking that enhance inquiry in each field of study. To become well educated, children should be offered experiences with many types of content in different contexts that develop productive habits of mind. We believe, as Dewey did, that learning results from doing, that habits of thinking are formed by actually thinking, and that the real world is the best laboratory for meaningful learning. It follows then that the most natural curriculum for novice inquirers is modeled after the inquiry of experts in their respective fields. But the primary responsibility of elementary and middle school teachers is not concerned with specialization in any one field. Their charge is to develop in their students foundational knowledge from all fields and, in the process, to offer children the generic tools for self-directed life-long learning. We believe that this is best accomplished through interdisciplinary thematic curriculum and instruction that is question-driven and investigative.

Our View of Inquiry for Children

The concept of interdisciplinary inquiry for elementary and middle school curricula is really very straightforward.

Within almost any topic selected from the literary arts, the sciences and mathematics, the humanities, and the fine arts, there are natural connections to the other fields. Those connections are easily found in big ideas, that is, the concepts, generalizations, theories, laws, and principles that become umbrella themes for substantive content from each discipline. By exploring these big ideas through inquiry, children will

- ▾ learn the content of several disciplines germane to the topic of study,
- ▾ discover the interdisciplinary meanings of the big ideas,
- ▾ develop fluency with the language of each discipline,
- ▾ learn the methodologies of each discipline for developing new knowledge,
- ▾ develop facility with the modes of thinking and the habits of mind associated with open-ended inquiry, and
- ▾ become proficient in self-directed learning.

The process of open inquiry involves the following:

Questioning: Formulating questions that are clearly focused on what children want to find out and organizing them into sets of logically related issues

Searching for Resources: Finding many and various resources that are most germane to the questions selected for study

Consulting Resources: Probing different types of resources for the clues they hold to help children better understand their questions and find answers to them

Organizing Findings: Collecting the clues uncovered in resources and organizing them in different ways to tease out the patterns they form

Interpreting Findings: Knowing how to *read* the patterns of meaning found in the organized data.

Asking New Questions: Formulating new, more probing questions from the findings uncovered in response to earlier questions

In Part Two of this book, we offer ways to build thematic curricula for grades 4–8 that derive from this model of inquiry for the education of all children in substantive content across the curriculum and in ways to inquire for lifelong, self-directed learning.

REFERENCES

Arnheim, R. (1969). *Visual thinking.* Berkeley: University of California Press.

Barber, T. (1993). *The human nature of birds.* New York: St. Martin's Press.

Bloom, B. S. (Ed.). (1956). *Taxonomy of educational objectives: The classification of educational goals: Book 1. Cognitive domain.* New York: Longman.

Bronowski, J. (1973). *The ascent of man.* Boston: Little, Brown.

Bruner, J. (1973). *Beyond the information given: Studies in the psychology of knowing.* New York: Norton.

Dewey, J. (1933). *How we think.* Lexington, MA: D. C. Heath.

Feynman, R. P. (1988). *"What do you care what other people think?"* New York: Bantam Books.

Flam, J. D. (1973). *Matisse on art.* London: Phaidon Press.

Freedman, G., Hickman, D., & Morris, E. (Producers and Directors). (1991). *A brief history of time* [Film]. Hollywood: Anglia Television/Gordon Freedman Productions and Paramount Pictures.

Gardner, H. (1983). *Frames of mind: Theory of multiple intelligences.* New York: Basic Books.

Gardner, H. (1997). The first seven . . . And the eighth. *Educational Leadership, 55* (1), 8–13.

Griffin, D. (1984). *Animal thinking.* Cambridge, MA: Harvard University Press.

Guilford, J. P. (1956). The structure of intellect. *Psychological Bulletin, 53,* 267–295.

Hardy, G. H. (1940). *A mathematician's apology.* Cambridge: Cambridge University Press.

Hawes, K. (1990). Understanding critical thinking. In V. A. Howard (Ed.), *Varieties of thinking* (pp. 47–61). New York: Routledge.

Hughes, R. (1980). *The shock of the new.* New York: Knopf.

John-Steiner, V. (1985). *Notebooks of the mind: Explorations of thinking.* Albuquerque: University of New Mexico Press.

Johnson, D. W., & Johnson, R. T. (1990). *Cooperation and competition: Theory and research.* Edina, MN: Interactions.

Knull, K. R. (Producer & Director). (1988). *A world of ideas with Bill Moyers: August Wilson* [Video]. Alexandria, VA: PBS Video.

Kuhn, T. S. (1970). *The structure of scientific revolutions* (2nd ed.). Chicago: University of Chicago Press.

Lowenthal, D. (1985). *The past is a foreign country.* Cambridge: Cambridge University Press.

Lynch, J. (Producer & Director). (1998). *The proof* [Video]. NOVA: Adventures in Sciences. Boston: WGBH-TV.

Macauley, D. (1979). *Motel of the mysteries.* Boston: Houghton Mifflin.

Mantel, H. (Producer & Director). (1974). *Einstein: The education of a genius* [Film]. Princeton, NJ: Films for the Humanities and Sciences.

Margolis, H. (1993). *Paradigms and barriers: How habits of mind govern scientific beliefs.* Chicago: University of Chicago Press.

Martinello, M. (1987). *The search for Emma's story: A model for humanities detective work.* Ft. Worth: Texas Christian University Press.

McKim, R. H. (1980). *Experiences in visual thinking* (2nd ed.). Monterey, CA: Brooks/Cole.

Milligan, B. (1998). Growing a poet tree. In M. Martinello, G. Cook, & L. Woodson. (Eds.), *Modes of inquiry: Voices of scholars across the fields of study* (pp. 19–23). Carrollton, TX: Alliance Press.

Perkins, D., & Weber R. (1992). Effable invention. In R. Weber & D. Perkins (Eds.), *Inventive minds: Creativity in technology* (pp. 317–336). Oxford: Oxford University Press.

Perlmutter, A. H. (Producer). (1991). *The creative spirit* [Television series, 4 parts]. Public Broadcasting System and IBM. New York: Ambrose Video.

Phenix, P. H. (1964). *Realms of meaning.* New York: McGraw-Hill.

Roe, A. (1952). *The making of a scientist.* Westport, CT: Greenwood Press.

Rutherford, F., & Ahlgren, A. (1990). *Science for all Americans.* New York: Oxford University Press.

Taba, H. (1962). *Curriculum development: Theory and practice.* New York: Harcourt, Brace, Jovanovich.

Torrance, E. P. (1962). *Guiding creative talent.* Englewood Cliffs, NJ: Prentice-Hall.

Torrance, E. P. (1970). *Creative learning and teaching.* New York: Dodd Mead.

Tufte, E. (1983). *The visual display of quantitative information.* Cheshire, CT: Graphics Press.

Tufte, E. (1990). *Envisioning information.* Cheshire, CT: Graphics Press.

Tufte, E. (1997). *Visual explanations.* Cheshire, CT: Graphics Press.

Van Kirk, S. (1980). *Many tender ties.* Norman: University of Oklahoma Press.

Wallace, D., & Gruber, H. (1989). *Creative people at work.* New York: Oxford University Press.

Watson, J. D. (1968). *The double helix.* New York: Mentor Books.

Weber, R. & Perkins, D. (eds.) (1992). *Inventive minds: Creativity in Technology.* Oxford: Oxford University Press.

Webster's third international dictionary (1981). Springfield, MA: Merriam-Webster.

Welty, E. (1983). *One writer's beginnings.* New York: Warner Books.

Additional Reading

Boslough, J. (1985). *Stephen Hawking's universe.* New York: Avon Books.

Cheney, M. (1981). *Tesla: Man out of time.* New York: Laurel Books.

Gardner, H. (1993). *Creating minds: An anatomy of creativity seen through the lives of Freud, Einstein, Picasso, Stravinsky, Eliot, Graham, and Gandhi.* New York: Basic Books.

Hoskin, M. (1971). *The mind of the scientist.* New York: Taplinger.

Howard, V. A. (Ed.). (1990). *Varieties of thinking.* New York: Routledge.

Kidder, T. (1981). *The soul of a new machine.* New York: Avon.

Preble, D., & Preble, S. (1985). *Artforms.* New York: Harper & Row.

Ryle, G. (1949). *The concept of mind.* London: Hutchinson.

Shafer, H. J. (1986). *Ancient Texans.* San Antonio, TX: Witte Museum of the San Antonio Museum Association and Texas Monthly Press.

Shamos, M. H. (Ed.). (1959). *Great experiments in physics.* New York: Dover.

Chapter Two

Historical Experiments in Integrated Curriculum

In this chapter, we look at four examples of experiments in integrated curriculum that span fifty years, from the Dewey School, which opened its doors in 1898, to the Bank Street Workshops, which were in operation until 1948.

The stories of these experiments were told by people deeply involved in them: Katherine Camp Mayhew and Anna Camp Edwards at the Dewey School, James S. Tippett and his colleagues at the Lincoln School, E. Oberholtzer in the Houston City Schools, and Lucy Sprague Mitchell at the Bank Street College of Education. Oberholtzer describes a research study designed to examine the effects of a massive curriculum effort in integrated curriculum in Houston between 1924 and 1930. The other three describe smaller experiments in curricula that they did not term "integrated," but that incorporated many of the principles and practices that are part of curriculum integration and interdisciplinary inquiry.

In this chapter, we use imaginary scenarios, based on information given by these authors, to build a picture of life in these schools. Our focus in this book is on upper elementary and middle school grades. However, for each site, we have selected a first grade and a fifth grade class to exemplify the activities of the school.

The purpose of this chapter is not to relate the entire history of integrated curriculum design, development, and implementation. That would be far beyond the scope of this text. Rather, we have selected four experiments in curriculum that have been described and analyzed by those involved, and in which the participants have struggled with issues and questions that are still critical and relevant in any attempt to develop integrated curriculum and opportunities for interdisciplinary inquiry. These issues and questions reemerge at intervals throughout this book. Looking at ways that the questions have been addressed in the past may help you to approach them with more insight and wisdom as you develop your own integrated curriculum.

THE DEWEY SCHOOL, 1902–1903: THE SCHOOL AS A COOPERATIVE SOCIETY

The Laboratory School of the University of Chicago, later known as the Dewey School, first opened in January 1896 with sixteen pupils and two persons in charge. By 1898, after three moves, it was located in an old residence on Ellis Avenue and had a student population of eighty-two. By 1902, the numbers had risen to 140 children, 23 teachers, and 10 graduate assistants.

The main goals of the Dewey School were, first, the development of the school as a cooperative community that would meet the social needs of students and, second, the intellectual development of the child through activity.

Two major assumptions about children were basic to the philosophy of the Dewey School. The first emphasized the differences between children and adults: A child is not a "little adult," and a child's main work is learning. The second assumption was that "the conditions which make for mental and moral progress are the same for the child as for the adult. Therefore the school must meet the unique needs and interests of the child, while providing a situation where the problem-solving processes used by both children and adults can be brought to bear upon those interests and needs" (Mayhew & Edwards, 1936, pp. 250–251).

This learning occurred within a community setting. In *The School and Society* (1900), Dewey speaks of a school as "an embryonic community life" that will "reflect the life of the larger society." This "embryonic community" will, in turn, produce citizens that can improve the "larger society" by making it "worthy, lively, and harmonious" (Cremin, 1964, pp. 117–118).

In the school, therefore, a major focus was the *social* purpose of education, which can be seen clearly as we look at the interactive work of the six-year-olds in dramatic play and of the ten-year-olds in the construction of the Colonial room (see below). Children learned to work together to achieve common goals.

Activities were perceived to arise from the child's own interests and from the need to solve problems that aroused the child's curiosity and that led to creative solutions. In turn, activity itself led to inquiry and to the development of skills (Tanner & Tanner, 1980).

Subject matter was seen as a resource for social and intellectual problem solving. In accord with principles of child development, the subject matter selected was related to children's experiences and interests and moved from primarily concrete and physical experiences for the younger children to more abstract and intellectual pursuits for the older groups.

Group 3 (about 17 six-year-olds) was located in a big, sunny room that also served as the Biological Laboratory. During the 3 hours of their school day, they spent 1½ to 2 hours in this room; the rest of their day was spent with the seven-year-olds for play and games or with the younger children for play and music (Mayhew & Edwards, 1936).

The room contained blackboards and a sand table and had plenty of room for games and activities. A vivarium and an aquarium provided homes for the living things brought in by the children. In this scenario, the teacher shows us around.

Here's the children's first project, the farm. They built the farmhouse and barn from large blocks. This chicken coop is made roughly to scale. The whole class discussed what would be on the farm. We decided to grow corn and wheat and to have sheep and a dairy. Notice that the pastures have stone walls; the children decided that the animals needed something stronger than these stick fences.

This project involved them in a lot of measuring and number work. They even learned to use a square, triangle, and ruler to help them in the construction. They understood the inch and half-inch, but had some difficulty in using quarter-inches.

Let's go outside. They grew winter wheat on this little 5- by 7-foot plot, which they measured by themselves. They figured out how to plant the wheat, and when they had harvested the grain, they invented a two-piece flail to separate the seeds from the hulls. It worked really well!

Their dramatic play has centered around the farm. We worked out a complicated scenario to get the wheat to the mill and then to the stores, and after they had played it out, the children recorded the process by making diagrams to show what had happened.

The next area of study was the animals on the farm. The children learned about cows and dairy products. At the same time, our cooking lessons focused on the use of milk, butter, and cheese in recipes. We even tried to tan leather in our science lessons, but that didn't work very well.

Next, we studied sheep and wool production. From there, the children wanted to know about other fabrics, so we had an extensive unit on cotton.

Look at the sand table. They are working out how to get water from the mountains to the desert. They've learned a lot about water levels. They even invented a water tower.

Reading and writing are an important part of all their work. The skills grow out of the activities. At the end of the unit on cotton, we put together a play to show how the cotton came from the plantation to the factory and then to the wholesale stores. We also composed a written record of the process that was read at assembly.

I really enjoy this way of learning. The children are so interested in every-thing, and they constantly absorb new knowledge of materials and processes. Of course, it demands a lot from the teacher, but it is exciting to see the chil-dren using their inventive ability to develop these activities. It helps them to understand social relations and organizations and to be part of them. (Based on Mayhew & Edwards, 1936, pp. 80–88.)

The ten-year-olds (Group 7) were in two groups, under the direction of the head of the textile department and the director of history. They met in one of the dining rooms and at one end of the kitchen laboratory. In this scenario, the head of the history department shows us around the Colonial room, which the children built under the supervision of the shop director, Elizabeth Jones.

The children really had to work together closely on this project. The boys chose to work mainly on the furniture, and the girls on the bedding and rugs, but they both worked together on the construction of this fireplace. They had quite a difficult time with this. The first time they built it, the lime was not properly slaked, and the mortar crumbled. They learned that the lime needed to be left in water all night in order to slake adequately. You should have seen their ex-citement when they first lit a fire and found that the flue drew well! They were very pleased with themselves.

Look at the furnishings of the room. One boy made this little spinning wheel at home. We find that there has been a marked increase in the time chil-dren spend on their chosen activities in out-of-school hours. For example, this bedstead was constructed here, but the feather bed and bedding were made by the girls at home.

The children are learning a great deal about early communities and how peo-ple depended on each other, since in projects like these the children themselves have to act as an interdependent community. This study focuses on the growth of unity among the different colonies and the resulting movement toward inde-pendence from England. As we go on with the study, we will also examine the social and political development that followed independence. I think that the children understand how the pioneer families had to depend on themselves at first and how specialization of labor occurred. As we progress with the study, we will follow the expansion of trade among the colonies and with Europe. We want to involve the children in concrete experiences at all times. One of the teachers suggested that we have each child become an imaginary sea captain who de-scribes his travels and what goods he carries. This could lead into a study of the Navigation Laws, which are difficult to understand if they are too abstract.

The children have also learned the importance of research. At the begin-ning of the year, we found that many of the children could not read with ease or proficiency, so for three months we gave much time to collateral reading related to the historical and geographical background to the study. We also gave writing lessons and drill exercises on words and constructions that were troublesome to the children. They did not enjoy this much, but they understood the need to be able to get information from books, and now they are finding the research much easier.

All through the study, the children are acting as independent learners within a community. Our aim is not so much to cover ground as to give the children some knowledge of how social processes were used by the colonists to secure social results, how obstacles were overcome, and the means contrived to attain these results. We want the children to identify intellectually with the problems, just as the younger children identify with situations through dramatic play.

The main study for this group is historical, but it also moves into geography, science, and mathematics as the children construct maps, experiment with materials, and use number concepts to help with scale and proportion. They are also conducting other studies in science, and they really enjoy experimenting with numbers and mastering number processes. They also engage in activities related to the main project in art and music and cooking, and in their French classes, they talk about what they are doing in the activities.

The main value of this approach? I think it is that the children learn to work together and to handle all kinds of social activity, and at the same time, they become independent problem solvers. I must say I really enjoy watching the social and intellectual development of the children in this group. (Based on Mayhew & Edwards, 1936, pp. 166–171.)

The Integrated Curriculum in the Dewey School

Integration of the curriculum emerged both from beliefs about learning as derived from children's interests and occurring through inquiry and from beliefs about the purposes of schools as microcosms of society. Children's interests are not subject-specific; they cross the traditional disciplines. The acquisition of skills emerges from activities and inquiry that are related to a broad central theme and explored in the community of the classroom.

Curriculum integration was expected to occur naturally as subject-area specialists designed activities to explore the problem each group was investigating. However, teachers were not afraid to encourage the children to explore other topics not directly related to the central problem. For example, the group of six-year-olds, in addition to the counting and measuring they used as they learned about the farm, used dominoes and blocks to help develop concepts of tens and units, and they read and wrote books unrelated to the farm study. Similarly, some of the ten-year-olds' science studies were focused on Colonial history, but they also studied plants and animals unrelated to the study, and their number work allowed them to explore abstract mathematical principles and processes, such as the relationship between multiplication and division.

It must be noted also that the central problems studied in each age group tended to have a strong social studies orientation, which makes sense considering the social purposes of the school. Studies in subjects such as science, mathematics, cooking, art, music, and even French were related to the central social, historical, or geographical central theme.

THE LINCOLN SCHOOL, 1926: THE CHILD-CENTERED SCHOOL

In 1916, Abraham Flexner published his essay "A Modern School" in the *American Review of Reviews,* calling for a school designed "'to give children the knowledge they need, and to develop in them the power to handle themselves in our own world'" (quoted in Cremin, 1964, p. 280). This school would be based on scientific standards and would provide a "laboratory from which would issue scientific studies of educational problems."

This "model school" came into existence as the Lincoln School of Teachers College. Situated in Manhattan, the school built a curriculum based on units of work that took into account children's development and that used the city of New York itself as a laboratory for exploration and activities.

In 1921–1922, the school moved into a new building in which the children studied units designed to deal in depth with some important aspect of contemporary civilization.

Each classroom was perceived as a real workshop, and children's learning was seen as real work. The goal of the school was "the development of an all-round, harmonious personality." The criteria for units of work developed by the staff of the elementary division (Tippett, Coffin, and the staff of the elementary division of the Lincoln School of Teachers College, Columbia University, 1927) gave a clear indication of the school's philosophy:

1. The unit of work must be selected from real-life situations and must be considered worthwhile by children because they feel that they have helped select it and because they find in it many opportunities to satisfy their needs.

2. The unit of work must afford many opportunities for real purposes and real projects, and it will be something that children can carry into the regular curriculum.

3. The unit of work must stimulate many kinds of activities and so provide for individual differences.

4. The unit of work must make individual growth possible.

5. The succession of units of work must provide for continuous group growth from one level to the next.

6. Each unit of work must furnish leads into other related units of work and must stimulate in children the desire for a continued widening of their interests and understandings.

7. Each unit of work must help meet the demands of society and must help clarify social meanings.
8. Each unit of work must be accompanied by progress in the use of such tool subjects as contribute to that unit.
9. Each unit of work must lead to the development of desirable habits.

Teachers themselves were expected to have a sound background: a thorough knowledge base, an understanding of children and their development, and a lively personality (Tippett et al., 1927). The teacher was expected to use a specific technique that included the following elements (Tippett et al., 1927):

1. To give time for orientation
2. To set the stage for the initiation and development of educative situations or units of work
3. To work as a member as well as a guide of the class
4. To select the educative factors in any unit of work
5. To do something with the facts and meanings that have been stressed

Let us look at "real work" in progress in a first grade classroom.

The first grade turned their classroom into a "play village." Houses were constructed out of cartons and cardboard and lovingly painted. Blocks enclosed yards and formed elegant walls and gates. Toy people and animals populated the village; the houses were filled with handmade furniture, drapes, and rugs. Engines, cars, and wagons provided transportation. A theater, a hotel, and stores made the village more than a collection of homes.

In this village, the children worked and played. They left it to take real trips throughout New York City: to markets, farms, and factories; to museums and a fire station; and to docks and ferries. From the trips, they brought back new knowledge and experience that they used in their dramatic play, language work, science, cooking, and math. They composed their own class stories and learned to read them. They made up plays and composed songs. They used money constantly in their dramatic play: to pay rent, to buy and sell, to go to the theater or the circus, to ride on buses or trains. They used measurement in construction and cooking. Science was an integral part of the exploration: The children conducted an experiment with the power of steam. Artwork centered around the trips and the project itself, from painting pictures to designing booklets to printing fabric for curtains for the houses.

The fifth grade unit on water transportation grew out of a third grade boat unit, and out of the children's own interest in boats and their uses. In the fifth grade, students were able to explore the subject in more depth and detail than was possible at the third grade level.

During the first three weeks of the year, the class studied the topic in a general way and developed an extensive list of questions to be explored:

Do we really know when boats began?
Why did people need larger boats?
Why did the Roman galleys have several banks of oars?
Why did sailboats change to steam?

In order to prepare for individual study, the whole class worked together on two topics, "Primitive Boats and How They Began" and "Early Sails and How They Began." Students then selected different topics and worked on them individually or in very small groups. Each student set a date for the completion of the report. The report was read to the whole class, criticized, and either accepted as complete or returned for revision. Completed reports were contributed to a class "boat book."

From the beginning, the unit took a historical approach to the topic, and this led to two major class projects: a book of linoleum-block prints of ships and a painted burlap frieze depicting the history of water transportation from the earliest history to the modern day. These projects were organized and developed through extensive committee work by the students.

Field trips related to the study included a ferryboat ride from Manhattan to Staten Island to see harbor boats, and visits to a square-rigger that had been turned into a museum and to the Brooklyn Navy Yard.

Work on the unit incorporated extensive reading and writing, research, vocabulary work, accurate measuring and elementary geometry, scientific study of navigation and flotation, geographic study of maps, artwork, music, dancing, and industrial arts, all related to the topic.

The year's work culminated in a special school assembly where the students gave a variety of reports, songs, and dances. (Based on Tippett et al., 1927, pp. 74–88, 184.)

The Integrated Curriculum in the Lincoln School

The curriculum in the Lincoln School was deliberately organized around broad, cross-curricular units of work designed to provide children as nearly as possible with "real-life situations" (Tippett et al., 1927). These units of work might incorporate virtually all the traditional subjects or be closely focused on one subject area, such as social studies, science, or music. In their reports for the year, teachers were required to indicate the subject areas that had been incorporated in the units of study (Tippett et al., 1927).

More than one unit of study was frequently in progress at one time. Sometimes a smaller unit was related to the major unit. For example, in the second grade class, a mapmaking unit might be going on concurrently with a study of how foods reach the city from the farm. At other times, unrelated units might be going on simultaneously. In a fifth grade class, a study of marimbas and marimba making instigated in the creative music class might be concurrent with a larger unit on Colonial history.

Skills subjects, such as math and reading, were frequently linked to a unit, but, if necessary, were taught separately. For example, if a unit did not include any opportunities for arithmetic, separate lessons would be taught, or if a specific skill or knowledge was needed, special lessons would be given. Sometimes, as in a second grade classroom, daily reading or other skill lessons were built into the schedule (Tanner & Tanner, 1980).

Flexibility in meeting the goals of the school was a hallmark of the Lincoln School—and these goals were clearly child-centered. Children were involved in the selection of units, and the units were designed to be broad enough to allow for individual interests. The teacher was guided by two considerations: "The unit must be kept near to present needs, and it must be thought worthwhile by the child" (Tippett et al., 1927, p. 31).

THE HOUSTON CITY SCHOOLS, 1924–1930: INTEGRATING CURRICULUM IN A LARGE CITY SCHOOL DISTRICT

Curriculum change in a large urban school district is a ponderous business. At the time of the study conducted by Oberholtzer (1937), 1929–1930, the Houston school district had a population of 325,000, a student body of 60,000, and 1,800 teachers. The Houston City Schools spent eight years in research and study and produced more than 300 bulletins (over 10,000 pages) before beginning to implement the integrated curriculum (Oberholtzer, 1937).

This "scientific" development of the curriculum followed the guidelines described by Bonser (1926) in Part 1 of the *Twenty-Sixth Yearbook of the National Society for the Study of Education,* which were as follows:

1. The development or choice of acceptable criteria or standards for selecting materials
2. The organization and presentation of selected materials for children under conditions as exactly comparable as possible to those of other children using different materials
3. The testing of results to find the outcomes of teaching the selected materials and the comparison of these with the outcomes from the materials used by the control groups

When implementation did occur, it was carefully controlled and "scientifically" monitored. The curriculum was introduced gradually, and an experimental study was conducted with selected fourth and fifth grade teachers to examine the effects of the integrated curriculum.

A first grade teacher speaks.

I teach first grade in the Houston City Schools. I have taught here for twelve years. We have had many changes in our district in the past few years. First, they changed the organization of the schools. We used to have grades 1–7 in the elementary schools. Now we have K–5 in the elementary school, and grades 6, 7, and 8 are placed in junior high schools. Kindergarten is optional.

At the same time, the district decided to try a new type of curriculum called "the integrated curriculum." It was really hard work to get it in place! Committees were working on it for years. We kept hearing about it, but we weren't sure what it meant. I was selected two years ago to try out a unit on family life. It is now an eighteen-week unit, but I just tried part of it for six weeks. The children enjoyed thinking about things they know and understand.

Last year we started this new program by introducing what they called a "fusion course" in social studies; we taught a general social studies course instead of separate classes in history and geography. It worked really well with my little ones. We were encouraged to work on topics drawn from the children's interests instead of learning dates and places. We learned about homes, the responsibilities of family members, and our own neighborhood.

This year we are using the district Handbook for Teachers *to help us plan integrated units on family life and community life. The controlling theme is interdependence. That theme is used in all the grades, but in different ways. In a faculty meeting, one of the district supervisors talked to us about the philosophy of the new curriculum. Basically, it is a problem-solving approach. Education must teach pupils to grapple with the economic, social, and political problems of life. The new curriculum uses an activity approach. Pupils learn to think intelligently about problems at their own level and to use material from any subject area to help solve the problem.*

The Handbook *has lots of ideas for us to use. My principal says we can try out the ideas, but he is a bit worried about reading and math. He says we should make sure the pupils learn all the skills they used to. That will be hard, but I think I can do it. I am looking for children's books I can use in place of the history and geography texts. He wants us to send the children to special teachers for art and music. I work well with Miss Black, the art teacher, and Miss Newman, the music teacher, so I hope we can plan some activities together. I am excited about the new curriculum, and I am looking forward to trying it in my classroom. (Based on Oberholtzer, 1937, chaps. 2, 3, 8; app. 4.)*

Fourth and fifth grade teachers participated voluntarily in a research study to examine the effects of the new curriculum. Three groups of teachers were identified, two experimental groups and one control group. The first experimental group, type A, was selected to use the integrated curriculum without restrictions as to time distribution, choice of materials, or specified expected outcomes. The second experimental group, type B, used the integrated curriculum, but with specific objectives and desired outcomes and with specified time distribution. The control group, type C, was divided into two halves. One half used the old curriculum taught in traditional ways, but incorporated the fusion course in social studies; the other used the new units in the integrated curriculum, but taught them in traditional ways, using the old time distribution for different subject areas.

In this imaginary scenario, a fifth grade teacher describes her experiences.

I was very excited when I was selected to be in a study of the new integrated curriculum. My principal recommended me, and I filled out a questionnaire. I was to be a type A teacher. That meant that I had lots of freedom to use the new curriculum. I had to cover all the fifth grade topics, but I could do it at my own rate. I had the pupils all day, and I was not allowed to divide the day into subjects; the pupils did not even go to art or music! I used the district Handbook for Teachers *to help me plan the units, but I used other materials as well.*

The theme I found most interesting was the one on "Life on the American Frontier." It was related to the controlling theme of adaptation. Some of the problems we explored in this unit were these:

How are houses built to adapt to the environment?

How did settlers change their eating habits?

What clothes did people wear, and why?

What kind of education did the children have?

What kind of inventions and tools helped the people adapt? (Later, this question was explored again in the unit on cotton.)

How was the land divided up for the settlers? How did they know where to settle?

The pupils studied how different settlers in Texas adapted to life here: Indians, Mexicans, Anglos, Germans, and others. Some of the pupils brought family keepsakes to make an exhibit of different cultures. The pupils were also very interested in the historical characters, and some of them wrote biographies of important leaders in Texas history. These questions involved the pupils in history, geography, science, math, music, art, and even cooking, and they did a great deal of reading and writing all through the unit. I think their reading and writing improved. One child said, "I have read more books than I have ever read before because I wanted to find out new things for myself."

The parents were very supportive. One parent wrote, "My son has done better this term than he ever did. I think one reason is that the increased freedom in the room keeps him from getting so nervous. He feels more at ease."

We also covered units on the cotton industry (related to the theme of interdependence) and two other historical units, "From the Old World to the New" and "The Making of Americans." All the units were related to life in Texas and in Houston.

For the study, we had to keep records and answer questionnaires. I really liked this approach. As I said in the questionnaire at the end of the year, "Each school day has been a day of real living for both the teacher and the children." (Based on Oberholtzer, 1937, chaps. 2, 3, 8; apps. 4, 25.)

The Integrated Curriculum in the Houston City Schools

The integrated curriculum was based on the work of Dewey and Kilpatrick. The school was seen as "an effective social agency" in which two prime considerations were "the nature of the child" and "the social function of the school." The curriculum was designed to promote the development of the child both as an individual and as "a member of the social group who participates in promoting social progress" (Oberholtzer, 1937, p. 9). Dewey's twin themes of the "embryonic community" and the school as an agent for social progress are apparent here.

This curriculum, unlike those of the Dewey School and the Lincoln School, which were expected to emerge from the interests of the children, was carefully developed around "big themes." *Interdependence* was addressed at all grade levels except grade 4, *control over nature* in grades 2 through 7, *adaptation* in grades 3 through 7, and *cooperation* in grades 6 and 7. There seems, therefore, to be a pattern of development from more concrete themes to those that are more abstract.

The topics addressed within each theme were all clearly in the area of social studies and followed three organizational patterns that may reflect the old course of study and the state-adopted texts. There was a chronological study of history, from "Primitive Life" in grade 2 to "The Industrial Revolution" in grade 7, and a mixture of the "expanding environments" organization and topical study in geography. It is not clear just how the other subject areas were incorporated into the curriculum, but the teachers were encouraged to use the *Handbook for Teachers* for ideas and to teach skills as the need arose.

The Houston curriculum manifests some of the limitations and frustrations of large-scale curriculum development in the public schools. The committees struggled with the existing situation: a curriculum already defined by a subject-oriented course of study and by state-adopted texts, a mixture of well-trained and less adequately trained teachers, a perennial shortage of resources in a growing city, and the lack of means for educating the general public. In spite of all this, the curriculum incorporated the flexibility necessary for a child-centered approach, with provisions for varied activities in large and small groups.

As in most integrated curriculum work, the teacher had a high degree of flexibility and responsibility in organizing the classroom, selecting resources, deciding when to emphasize concepts and when to focus on skills, and planning activities that "serve best as a means to an end."

The results of the experimental study demonstrated measurable success in skills achievement; more time for "enriched education," problem-solving activities, and creative work; higher levels of achievement; and more learning among the experimental groups than in the control groups. In addition, comments from principals, teachers, children, and parents indicated gains in the development of "pupil initiative and self-reliance, . . . pupil attitudes and appreciations, . . . motivation of study habits and skills, . . . organization and procedure, . . . [and] teacher improvement" (Oberholtzer, 1937, app. 25).

It seems that in Houston the integrated curriculum was carefully planned, conceptually based, and thoughtfully implemented.

THE BANK STREET WORKSHOPS, 1943–1948: TEACHER EDUCATION FOR CURRICULUM DEVELOPMENT

The Bank Street Workshops were designed to take the principles and practices of curriculum from the Bank Street College of Education into the public schools. The Bank Street College of Education developed out of the Bureau of Educational Experiments, founded in 1916 by Lucy Sprague Mitchell to try to bring together the movement toward building experimental schools with the movement toward developing a science of education (Cremin, 1964).

The purpose of the first workshop, in 1943, was "to work with [New York] teachers in *their* school, with *their* children, in *their* physical and social neighborhood, and in that concrete situation to work with them realistically to build a curriculum suited to children in modern-day United States" (Mitchell, 1950, p. 81). For the first three years, three of the Bank Street staff worked intensively with about half the teachers and three of the administrators in a large urban elementary school of some 1,700 students. The curriculum was revised twice during the Workshop experience, with increasing involvement and ownership among the teachers. In 1946, the program was expanded to two additional schools, and three teachers from the original school were assigned to work full-time with the Bank Street team in the new Workshops.

In the following imaginary scenarios, two teachers describe the program.

I am a first grade teacher, and I have been in the Workshop for 1½ years. I was one of the first twenty-six teachers in the Workshop program at our school. When the Bank Street leaders told us about it, I was excited, but also worried. It all seemed so strange! I liked the idea of using and widening children's interests, but I didn't know how. All I wanted at the beginning were concrete suggestions that I could use in my classroom. Now, at the end of a year and a half, I understand how naive I was! The Bank Street staff were wonderful. They helped us to develop our own ideas, but they showed us how to do it. For example, Miss P., the Bank Street leader who worked with the kindergarten and first and second grades, helped me to develop a neighborhood study for my first grade children. She suggested trips around the school and in the neighborhood that would help children to explore topics like "Workers in the School and the Neighborhood," "Transportation," and "Food." The children loved the trips, and so did I. They were so interested in everything they saw. We explored the school and the local neighborhood, visited the Hudson River and the Harlem River and the pushcart market on Eighth Avenue, and looked at all kinds of transportation. When they built a new curb along our street, the children were fascinated and asked the men all kinds of questions.

I now understand that this approach means thinking about the curriculum in a completely new way. I was amazed to see how many of the old subject areas were included in the home-school-neighborhood unit: health education, reading, language, literature, art, science, penmanship, and number. I have seen the children growing as thinkers, as artists, as scientists, and as social beings. And I thought that this was just a social studies unit!

I think one of the most important things about this approach is that children begin to see relationships, and as Miss P. pointed out, seeing relationships is thinking. The children are beginning to identify with an ever-broadening group of people, and I think this will help them in later grades to identify with people they can't know personally.

I've changed in the ways I think about learning. At the beginning, I thought that the trips, the related play, and the art activities were just to get children motivated for real learning. Now I understand that these activities are real learning experiences in themselves.

Now I want to know more for myself. I want to learn more about my own city of New York. I have learned to ask questions! This approach is very hard work, but it gives me a lot of satisfaction because I am learning and I see the children's development, too.

I am looking forward to the next stage in the Workshop. We are already thinking about the curriculum for the whole school. I used to think that curriculum was the curriculum guide we had to follow. Now I see that it is based on our philosophy and beliefs, on our understanding of children and their development, and on the physical and social setting in which the children live. Our first grade curriculum will still focus on home and school in relationship to our neighborhood, but this time around, I think we will understand more clearly how the parts fit together and what we are trying to do. I am so glad to be involved. (Based on Mitchell, 1950, pp. 93–95, 129–141, 198–213, 472–476.)

At the same time, a fifth grade teacher describes the program from her point of view.

I sometimes think that the Workshop approach is easier for the younger grades than it is for us. We have so much content to cover! In grades 5 and 6, we have to address the general theme "Living Together in the United States and in the World." That means we have to cover the history of the United States from the explorers to the present, the geography of the United States, the rest of the Western Hemisphere and Europe, and now a new addition called "Living and Working Together in the World."

The fifth and sixth grade teachers are working on this challenge in the Workshop. Last year we put all the U.S. history into grade 5 and the relations with the rest of the world into grade 6. It really didn't work. We had too much content, and the sixth grade curriculum was too abstract and mature for the students.

In our planning discussions, the committee did agree on some approaches. It was agreed that the way people lived and worked together was always to be linked to the physical environment: landforms, waterways, climate, native vegetation and animals, and natural resources. The opening topic in each grade would be focused on the present, and a study of present life and work in New York City was to continue all year. We decided to look at history in terms of significant movements and events rather than dates, wars, and political history. And we wanted to include an increasing focus on social values and relationships among people.

These discussions led to practical questions of what to put in each grade and how to integrate history with geography. We decided to base our curriculum on what we know about ten- and eleven-year-old children—their intellectual curiosity, their desire for adventure, and their growing sense of values. We looked at two big themes: the relationships of people to their environments and to one another. Within these two big themes, we wanted the children to use direct experiences that would help them to see the world as a laboratory, a place to find out things that interest them. Science is a big part of our curriculum. And of course we want children to think! We finally put together a curriculum we can work with.

It hasn't been easy though, even with the new curriculum outline. At the beginning, I didn't see the point of beginning with the present. It seemed more sensible to put it at the end, after we had studied the past. Miss B., one of the Bank Street workers, helped me to find a theme, "How We Became What We Are." I must admit that this has helped the children—and me!

We began work on a mural. At first, it didn't work too well. All the children had different ideas, and anyway they don't draw too well. Miss B. suggested that we use their ideas anyway and then try to find a theme. We took a trip to the Museum of the City of New York so that the children could compare transportation of long ago with that of today. We never really did find a narrow theme, but the mural showed the flow of history. We also put on a play with scenes about ideas like "Trade" and "Traveling." It worked pretty well, and one girl even said that it made history come alive.

Miss B. thinks that we could use the play and the mural to help children develop more questions to explore about the people in our history. Where did people come from? What were they like? Where do their descendants live? I think this is a good idea. The children are beginning to be able to do their own research in the library now.

I have learned a lot from the Workshop. At first, I did not see how you could put history and geography together. Now I see that history and geography and science are all parts of the same discovery method.

The Bank Street workers have been very helpful. They come in sometimes and work with my class. Then I can understand what they mean. They listen to us in the discussion sessions and help us to clarify our ideas. This new curriculum comes from the Workshop, not from Bank Street. We meet every week to talk about what we are doing. Sometimes we have guest speakers, like the high school science teacher. Last year we made maps. I learned a lot about map projections and why my unit wasn't working. They even took us on a field trip around the neighborhood so that we could learn how to help children look more carefully and raise good questions.

Perhaps the most important thing I have learned is to look at children's development and their environment and then to work out the social ideas that we will bring out in discussion and activities whenever we have an opportunity. These big social ideas have made my teaching make more sense. I have always liked history; now I'm beginning to understand why I like it and how to help the children like it, too. (Based on Mitchell, 1950, pp. 97–98, 142–183, 246–272.)

The Integrated Curriculum in the Bank Street Workshops

The story of the Bank Street Workshops is an account of how teachers changed over time. The implied assumption is that improvement of teaching leads to improved learning. This example is particularly interesting because of this focus on teachers' professional development.

In the early days of the Workshops, the participating teachers did not understand the integration of the curriculum. They liked the idea of units as experiences in which content from various areas of the curriculum might be used, but they perceived the units as something to be added onto the regular course of study.

Social studies was deliberately selected as a starting point in the curriculum, since this subject area lent itself most readily to student involvement and social interaction. History, geography, and civics were obviously part of the new social studies, and science was also added. Major themes were identified for different grade levels: "Living and Working in the Home, School, and the Neighborhood" for kindergarten and first and second grades; "Living and Working in New York City and in Different Kinds of Communities" for grades 3 and 4; and "Living and Working Together in the United States of America and the World" in grades 5 and 6, an organization that exemplifies the "expanding environments" pattern still common in the elementary social studies curriculum.

As the Workshop meetings continued, teachers explored with Bank Street staff ways in which activities in dramatic play, art, language, music, and other subjects grew out of the core experiences. However, in the Workshop program, there was never any effort to build a completely integrated curriculum. Indeed, in the second phase of the Workshops, the emphasis was on building a sound vertical social studies curriculum rather than broadening the curriculum across other subject areas. Integration continued to be informal rather than structured.

At the beginning of the Workshops, the teachers were interested in *how* to implement the new ideas, not in the underlying philosophy or assumptions about children and learning. In the second phase, there was an important shift in the teachers' approach to curriculum building. After three years in the Workshop, they began to see how knowledge of children's development, of the environment, and of a basic philosophy of education were essential bases for curriculum development.

The story of the Bank Street Workshops is a fascinating story of intensive staff development and curriculum building. Some of the findings from the Workshop experience are significant in any curriculum development in which teachers are involved.

The teachers went through the following stages of professional growth:

1. an early lack of self-confidence that led them to seek specific directions and prescriptions,
2. a desire to acquire more background knowledge and content,
3. growth in understanding the concept of curriculum building, and finally
4. the ability to relate their job to the world outside the school (Mitchell, 1950).

It is interesting to note that these findings closely parallel the "stages of concern" identified by Gene Hall and his colleagues as they studied teacher development some thirty years later (Hall & Loucks, 1978).

As the teachers developed more self-confidence in their own ideas and their ability to work creatively with children, their professional attitudes changed. They became enthusiastic, inventive, and willing to experiment. They worked hard, but they obtained deep satisfaction from their creative endeavors (Mitchell, 1950). While they became increasingly impatient with the strictures and limitations of public school teaching, they were also better equipped to deal with these problems and to develop true learning environments for their students.

QUESTIONS THAT EMERGED FROM THESE EXPERIMENTS IN CURRICULUM

In each of these settings, from the Dewey School to the Bank Street Workshops, common questions emerge that are of great significance to anyone engaging in the development of integrated curriculum. The questions have no easy answers, but they must be explored for every new endeavor. How was each issue handled by these experimental schools?

How Is a Philosophy Developed and Implemented?

The Dewey School was designed as a laboratory to test Dewey's ideas about methods, curriculum, and organization. These ideas emerged from twenty years of study of philosophy, teaching, writing, and social service. The basis for his philosophy has been traced to sources such as Kant, Hegel, Rousseau, James, and Addams (Brickman, 1962; Cremin, 1964; Tanner & Tanner, 1980).

This philosophy was clearly articulated in Dewey's own writings and was put into practice by a small group of dedicated teachers under Dewey's own leadership.

The Lincoln School, too, was founded largely on the work of one man, Abraham Flexnor, who, in turn, was strongly influenced by Dewey. In the early years of the twentieth century, new experimental schools were developing rapidly in many places across the United States. Flexnor, who had undertaken a survey of the Gary (Indiana) schools in 1917 (Cremin, 1964), took a strong stance against the remnants of the traditional curriculum that he saw even in some of the so-called progressive schools. He argued that "if a subject serves a purpose, it is eligible to the curriculum; otherwise not" (Flexnor, 1923, p. 99) and insisted that the "scientific spirit" was to infuse the model school and to make it a place in which to test educational beliefs (Cremin, 1964).

The Lincoln School was created as an educational laboratory in which to try out Flexner's ideas. The teachers were committed to the principles on which it was founded, and the story of the Lincoln School, *Curriculum Making in an Elementary School,* written by the staff of the school in 1927, shows clearly their commitment and involvement (Tippett et al., 1927).

In Houston, the philosophy that supported the integrated curriculum was based strongly on the work of Dewey and Kilpatrick. The ideas for implementation of the new curriculum seem to have come from the administration in the district, but there was a commitment to teacher involvement in its development. The committees that met for eight years before the curriculum was implemented included teachers as well as administrators. Implementation was not imposed, but teachers were encouraged to use the new curriculum to the extent that they felt able. Indeed, the experimental study identified three groups of teachers: one group who implemented the new ideas fully, one group who implemented the new curriculum within the old framework, and a control group who continued to teach in the traditional way.

The Bank Street Workshops also involved teachers. Indeed, the purpose of the Workshop was to enable teachers to develop the new curriculum at their own speed and in their own way. The first Workshop initially involved only about half the teachers in the school. It was three years before the principal decided to make the Workshop curriculum the official social studies curriculum for the school. The philosophy supporting this curriculum was clearly Deweyan. It was, however, introduced by the Bank Street staff in a way that supported their beliefs that the school was a place where experiments and scientific problem solving were carried out at all levels, including the level of curriculum development.

It is apparent from these examples that the development of integrated curriculum should be based on certain principles and practices:

- ▼ a sound vision of the larger purposes of schooling;
- ▼ a long-term commitment to change, understanding that real change takes time;
- ▼ the involvement of teachers as experimenters in an experimental setting where children, too, are experimenters;
- ▼ a willingness to allow teachers to make choices about the amount and types of involvement they wish to have; and perhaps above all,
- ▼ the importance of putting principles into practice at all levels of the school community: in administration, teaching, and learning.

In this book, we support the same principles. Our own philosophy is presented in Chapter One and serves as the foundation for the entire book.

It is important to recognize that in each case the philosophy was not fully understood or fully developed at the beginning of the experiment. In the Dewey School, the teachers were working with an incomplete theory, which was developed gradually through practice and reflection over time (Mayhew & Edwards, 1936; Tanner, 1997). Development of the philosophy at the Lincoln School is described as "a cooperative enterprise" in which "each [member of the staff] has contributed, each has planned and criticized" (Tippett et al., 1927, p. 1). In Houston, the integrated curriculum "enlisted the staff of executives, supervisors and teachers . . . in a scientific study of curriculum problems related to the improvement of learning in the classroom" (Oberholtzer, 1937, pp. 2–3). In New York, the Bank Street staff described themselves and the teachers they worked with as "a cooperative, experimental group of school people and research workers" (Mitchell, 1950, p. xxv).

In each case, the philosophy and beliefs, though based on a common vision and a common understanding of how children learn, were developed slowly over time by those involved. As you read this book, we invite you to define your own vision and beliefs for your own situation and to continue to develop and reflect on your own philosophy.

Who Determines the Content of the Curriculum?

In any curriculum that is built around children's interests, there is a tension between meeting the needs of the children (as perceived by adults) and satisfying the desires of children (as perceived by the children themselves). This tension is an underlying factor implicit in the accounts of the Dewey School, the Lincoln School, the Houston City Schools, and the Bank Street Workshops.

At the Dewey School, the children had limited choices. Dewey stated that the Dewey School would offer "'a much larger degree of opportunity for initiative, discovery, and independent communication of individual freedom than was characteristic of the traditional school'" (quoted in Mayhew & Edwards, 1936, pp. 6–7). However, it was clearly the task of the teacher to determine both the broad curriculum, albeit related to the children's interests and developmental stages, and the daily business of the classroom. The teacher provided the major ideas and framework for the curriculum; within that framework, each child was encouraged "to contribute, either out of his past experience or his imagination, ways and means of meeting the problem of needs that might arise under new circumstances" (Mayhew & Edwards, 1936, p. 81). The role of the teacher was that of a guide, where the activity of the child was self-initiated, and the teacher's responsibility was to provide necessary materials, instruction in technical skills, and direction or suggestions when needed (Mayhew & Edwards, 1936).

At the Lincoln School, the tension is more evident. Flexnor, writing in 1917, suggested a curriculum "built out of actual activities in four main fields which I shall designate as science, industry, aesthetics, civics." Children "would be interested in problems and the theoretical basis on which their solution depends" (Flexnor, 1923, p. 103). This sounds like a fairly teacher-centered approach. However, the guidelines for the selection of units described by Tippett and his colleagues in 1927 reflect a more child-centered approach. The unit was to be selected from "real-life situations" that the child should consider worthwhile "because he feels he has helped select it." The unit was required to give "opportunities for real purposing and real projects," to "provide for individual differences," and to "stimulate in the child the desire for a continual widening to his interests and understandings" (Tippett et al., 1927, pp. 31–37). The children's questions and interests were an integral part of each unit, but the teacher had the responsibility for developing the units, planning learning activities, and maintaining high standards of growth and development for every child (Tippett et al., 1927).

At the Lincoln School, the teacher was seen as a co-learner with the children and, at the same time, as a guide with the responsibility for ensuring that the children developed the appropriate work habits of questioning and research, independence and self-confidence, and the social skills of orderliness and cooperation (Tippett et al., 1927).

The Houston curriculum was designed by committees of teachers. The individual classroom teacher was given considerable flexibility in its implementation so that students could "be recognized as individuals and permitted to progress in accordance with their learning ability" (Oberholtzer, 1937, p. 10). As teachers became more confident in implementing the integrated curriculum, "pupils were assisted in setting up their own objectives and in helping to organize activities" (Oberholtzer, 1937, p. 17).

In Houston, teachers were assigned to specific roles. Some of those teachers who demonstrated "considerable ingenuity and resourcefulness" were assigned to the Type A group, where they were not bound to the regular school schedule of classes, and were asked to "plan the program in terms of problem-solving, creative expression, and drill for individuals or groups as the need is seen." Type B teachers implemented the integrated curriculum within certain restrictions and structure related to time distribution and specific aims, objectives, and outcomes. Type C teachers used the new integrated curriculum only in place of the old history and geography units (Oberholtzer, 1937, pp. 22–23).

The Bank Street Workshops were clearly designed to enable teachers to develop curriculum to meet the needs of their own students within their own unique situations. Learning about child psychology became an integral part of the teachers' training, and by the second stage of the Workshops, three years into the project, teachers wanted to experiment within the framework of the curriculum to "interpret the prescribed curriculum content in ways that were best for children's growth." They learned to give the children freedom to explore their own interests within the broad units and discovered that this resulted in "new interests, new zest for observing and finding out, new habits of tackling a problem by thinking out relationships, [and] new ways of expressing their thinking and feelings" (Mitchell, 1950, p. 337). In the Bank Street program, teachers were perceived as "changing their status from docile followers to constructive creative initiators and thinkers" who worked together with children "exploring the world of things and people" (Mitchell, 1950, p. 29).

From these examples, some principles emerge as we consider the question of who determines the content of the integrated curriculum:

- ▼ Teachers have the responsibility for designing the broad framework of the curriculum.
- ▼ The curriculum is built around known developmental stages and interests of students.
- ▼ When the integrated curriculum is first introduced, teachers take responsibility for selecting specific topics and learning activities.
- ▼ As teachers become more confident and comfortable with the new curriculum, they are more willing and able to give children more responsibility in selecting learning activities.
- ▼ As children work in a free, problem-solving atmosphere, they are able to make better curriculum choices for themselves.
- ▼ Teachers can take the role of director, guide, or mentor, depending on the situation and the needs of the learners.

As you think about developing your own integrated curriculum throughout this book, you need to think about the current situation—the levels of understanding, commitment, and experience concerning the integrated curriculum among the teachers. The developmental level of the children and the amount of prior experience they have had in making curriculum choices are even more important considerations.

To What Degree Does an Integrated Curriculum Incorporate All Subject Areas?

This question has been addressed for each of our examples earlier in this chapter. A brief review may help to give additional focus.

In the Dewey School, social studies was the major area of study, which is in accord with Dewey's ideas of the school as an embryonic community. Other subject areas were included as they occurred naturally in the major "activities," but skills areas were also addressed as separate subjects.

The Lincoln School curriculum was deliberately organized around "units of work," which were based on a variety of subject areas: social studies, science, music, arts and crafts, or a combination of two or more of these. Each unit was expected to incorporate a variety of subjects, but skills were also taught separately, either as a regular part of the school day or as the need arose.

The Houston curriculum was consciously designed as an integrated curriculum. However, it had a strong social studies bias; indeed, the names of the units seem to have been drawn directly from the old history and geography syllabi.

The Bank Street Workshops were centered clearly and deliberately on social studies, with science integrated as closely as possible. Here the integrated nature of the curriculum emerged slowly and naturally over time. The degree of integration seems to have varied from fairly limited attempts in a sixth grade unit on "Earth Forces in China" to a broad interdisciplinary unit on "Our Neighborhood" in the first grade.

How much integration does an integrated curriculum involve? It depends primarily on the type of topic or theme. Generally speaking, the more abstract the theme, the greater the ease of integration. Specific topics tend to limit the amount of integration. For example, "Transportation" can apply directly to nearly all the major subject areas, while "The Civil War" is more likely to be focused in history with some geography. For any theme study, however, the exploration of significant "big ideas" is central. (See Chapter Three for a broader discussion on the selection of themes.)

There is no magic formula. It is more important that the curriculum be relevant and significant to the learner and that activities and ideas naturally involve interdisciplinary and cross-disciplinary thinking and questioning than that every subject area be forced into the "integrated curriculum."

How May Skills in Reading and Math Be Taught?

This question is, of course, related to the previous one, but because it is a perennial question that you will face as you engage in integrating the curriculum, it deserves special attention.

In all the examples, it is clear that while reading and mathematics are part of the units and activities, the theme studies did not provide complete coverage of the skills needed in these areas. There was, therefore, provision for specific skills instruction.

In the Dewey School, for example, the children engaged in "number work" that explored mathematical principles through games and inquiry unrelated to the major areas of interest. In the Lincoln School, arithmetic and reading were taught separately if the unit of work did not make adequate provision for skills instruction, or specific skills were taught as needed.

The Houston curriculum did not really address this problem. The study of fourth and fifth grade teachers incorporated three different approaches, from totally integrated to totally subject-oriented. In the totally integrated group, skills were taught "when a teacher saw a need, and to whatever extent the teacher decided," while in the control group, skills were "taught in regular subject periods as set up in the daily schedule" (Oberholtzer, 1937, p. 25). It is interesting to note that a comparison of the results of the experimental and control groups showed similar achievement in reading, spelling, and arithmetic. As Oberholtzer pointed out, "The pupils . . . using the integrated units did not suffer in their achievement in the subjects commonly known as the 'three R's'" (Oberholtzer, 1937, p. 131).

The Bank Street staff worked hard to help the teachers see how the activities in one subject area led to activities in reading and mathematics, and the teachers began to understand how children learn "to read and write by being 'taught backwards'—that is, by getting interested in something they could really do" (Mitchell, 1950, pp. 345–346). It appears, however, that formal skills instruction, particularly in math, was continued along with the activity curriculum.

The extent of additional skills instruction needed depends on the selected theme and the children's needs. The main question here is not so much how to incorporate reading and math *into* the curriculum as it is to see how activities emerging naturally from children's inquiry and problem solving help them in the development of verbal and numerical literacy.

At the same time, external standards can help teachers recognize appropriate levels of knowledge and skills. National standards developed by professional educational associations, standardized testing, state and district curriculum guides, and adopted texts all communicate expectations about students' levels of achievement at different age or grade levels. These standards can provide a framework within which teachers and children can make decisions about curriculum, teaching, and learning.

How Is Success Evaluated in the Integrated Curriculum?

Apart from the study conducted by Oberholtzer in Houston, our examples show little evidence of formal evaluation, and we think that this relates directly to the goals and purposes of the schools and programs. If you look at their stated purposes, then the story of each example is itself the evaluation.

The Dewey School was set up as a social experiment. The descriptions of the groups in action reflect that social experiment, where children did work together on projects that both mirrored the larger world and helped them develop skills to live productively in that larger world.

The story of the child-centered Lincoln School is a series of accounts of child-centered units of work in which the children explored their neighborhood and through those experiences learned to make sense of the larger human community.

The Bank Street workers modeled, demonstrated, and, true to the philosophy they were teaching, enabled teachers to build curriculum based on beliefs about learning, understanding of children, and knowledge of the environment. Their book chronicles that process, and, again, the story is the evaluation.

Meanwhile, in Houston, Oberholtzer posed questions and collected data from experiments designed to answer those questions. The success of the experiment is measured by the degree to which the responses satisfied the questions.

It is tempting to think of evaluation only in terms of cold, hard data, scientifically collected and collated, and, indeed, this type of evaluation has its place. But the integrated curriculum is dynamic, interactive, situational, and creative. There is no single model; thus, there cannot be a single model for evaluating success.

This does not let us off the hook, however. If we choose broad and far-reaching goals, we must find broad and far-reaching means of evaluation. In Chapter Seven, we explore some of these approaches. Mayhew and Edwards, Tippett, Oberholtzer, and Mitchell tell us stories that themselves reflect the beliefs of the storytellers. Because these authors were deeply involved in the projects they describe, their evaluations *are* subjective, and they ring true through the richness of the stories.

How Is the Larger Community Related to Schooling and the Curriculum?

This final question goes far beyond the details of teaching and learning, yet is probably the most important of all. It comes full circle to the vision and the philosophy of each of the experimenters in our four examples; each in his or her own way saw the school as a microcosm of society and as a learning community in its own right.

For Dewey, the answer to this question was clear. He wrote that "education could prepare the young for the future social life only when the school was itself a cooperative society on a small scale" (Mayhew & Edwards, 1936, p. 5). At the same time, the school has a responsibility to the larger society. In 1901, Dewey wrote of the social purpose of curriculum "in maintaining the intellectual continuity of civilization" (Dewey, 1901, pp. 193–194; Cremin, 1964).

The Lincoln School put into practice Flexnor's vision of a model school—a school with two major purposes: the intellectual and aesthetic development of the child—that would, in turn, serve a society in which "abstract thinking has probably never before played so important a part" (Flexnor, 1923, pp. 100–101).

In Houston, Oberholtzer pointed out that "the wealth of the nation is bound up in the welfare of its youth" and that "the child with an inquisitive mind and a creative desire . . . is now generally recognized as the center of interest around which all forward-looking changes in American public education should be made" (Oberholtzer, 1937, p. 4).

In all these examples, we see a common purpose: the development of the individual, leading to the development of society.

This purpose is reflected at another level in the Bank Street Workshops. Mitchell (1950) describes graphically the professional development of the teachers as curriculum thinkers and as continuing learners and then indicates that as the teachers became more creative in their own jobs, they also related their jobs increasingly to the world outside the school, both in the profession and in the larger community.

In all four examples, there were close links between the school and the parents. In the Dewey School, parents provided the financial support to keep the school alive and at the same time supported the school's philosophy, even when they were uncomfortable about some of the new ideas (Tanner, 1997). At the Lincoln School, where it was believed that "a school cannot safely go faster in its educational procedure than parents will allow," parents were actively involved in the Parent-Teacher Association, the Parents' Study Group, and classroom conferences (Tippett et al., 1927).

In Houston, there is no evidence of parental or community involvement in the development and implementation of the integrated curriculum, but parents were asked to submit written, anonymous appraisals of their children's learning and any change in their children's attitude and interest while they were involved in the integrated curriculum. These reports form an important part of the evaluation of the project (Oberholtzer, 1937, pp. 349–350).

At Bank Street, there was a clear recognition of the importance of cooperation between parents and teachers, between home and school, in the process of education. At the same time, there was a growing understanding of the mutual responsibility of school and community, where each must contribute to the welfare of the other (Mitchell, 1950).

Schools inevitably reflect the current values of society and, in fact, are intended to conserve dominant values. This may help to explain why the apparently successful ventures in integrated curriculum described in this chapter did not survive and why this approach appears to require reinvention. Schools tend to be reactive to societal demands rather than proactive in preparing children to shape society as adults. However, in places where primary attention is given to examining how children learn and what they will need for the world of the future, child-centered, inquiry-based movements in curriculum continue. Cases in point are found in the current concerns for developmentally appropriate practice, whole-language instruction, writing across the curriculum, emphasis on science process, approaches to developing mathematical literacy, inquiry learning, discovery learning, cooperative grouping, and the development of schools as learning communities. But these are partial attempts. Curriculum for integrative learning applies these concepts in all subject areas. Although the four experiments described in this chapter did not continue intact, there are schools where successful interdisciplinary programs have been in progress for years. Among these are the Town and Country Schools and lab schools at places such as the Bank Street College of Education in New York City and Nova Scotia's Dalhousie University. Such experiments in secondary education as Foxfire and the Dalton School are additional examples.

Our four examples give us a view of the integrated curriculum in action. How may we understand their stories, adapt their ideas, and answer their questions in our own world, with our own students, in our own time? These questions frame the inquiry of this book.

REFERENCES

Bonser, F. G. (1926). Curriculum making in laboratory schools of experimental schools. *Twenty-sixth yearbook of the National Society for the Study of Education* (Pt. 1). Bloomington, IL: Public School Publishing.

Brickman, W. W. (1962). Introduction. In J. Dewey & E. Dewey (Eds.), *Schools of tomorrow* (pp. ix–xxviii). New York: Dutton.

Cremin, L. A. (1964). *The transformation of the school.* New York: Vintage. (Original work published 1961)

Dewey, J. (1900). *The school and society.* Chicago: University of Chicago Press.

Dewey, J. (1901). The place of manual training in the elementary course of study. *Manual Training Magazine, 2,* 193–194.

Flexnor, A. (1916). A modern school. *American Review of Reviews, 53,* 465–474.

Flexnor, A. (1923). *A modern college and a modern school.* Garden City, NY: Doubleday.

Hall, G., & Loucks, S. F. (1978). Teacher concerns as a basis for facilitating and personalizing staff development. *Teachers College Record, 80,* 36–53.

Mayhew, K. C., & Edwards, A. C. (1936). *The Dewey School.* New York: Appleton-Century.

Mitchell, L. S. (1950). *Our children and our schools.* New York: Simon & Schuster.

Oberholtzer, E. (1937). *An integrated curriculum in practice.* New York: Teachers College Press.

Tanner, D., & Tanner, L. N. (1980). *Curriculum development: Theory into practice* (2nd ed.). New York: Macmillan.

Tanner, L. N. (1997). *Dewey's Laboratory School: Lessons for today.* New York: Teachers College Press.

Tippett, J. S., Coffin, R. J., & the staff of the elementary division of the Lincoln School of Teachers College, Columbia University. (1927). *Curriculum making in an elementary school.* Lexington, MA: Ginn.

Additional Reading

Dewey, J. (1956). *The child and the curriculum* and *The school and society.* Chicago: University of Chicago Press. (Original work published in 1900, 1902)

Dewey, J., & Dewey, E. (1962). *Schools of tomorrow.* New York: Dutton. (Original work published 1915)

Kilpatrick, W. H. (1918). The project method. *Teachers College Record, 19,* 319–335.

Kilpatrick, W. H. (1931). A reconstructed theory of the educative process. *Teachers College Record, 32,* 530–558.

Part Two

Development of Interdisciplinary Theme Studies

Chapter Three

Models, Teacher Roles, and Starting Points for Theme Studies

MODELS IN THE LITERATURE ON THEME STUDIES

Theme studies are at the heart of the curriculum, not ancillary to it. Gamberg (1988, p. 10) describes theme study as at "the core of what children do in school." The model explained and illustrated in *Learning and Loving It: Theme Studies in the Classroom* requires that a theme meet several criteria: it must be of interest to the children, sufficiently broad to contain subtopics, not limiting in a geographic or historical way, supported by many and varied resources, appropriate to cross-disciplinary study, and capable of involving children with their community. Gamberg et al. ask teachers to select the theme and identify resources. Specific directions for studying the theme later emerge from the children's questions about it.

Short et al. (1996) follow the authoring cycle as a framework for inquiry: building from the known, finding questions, exploring various perspectives on the topic, examining differences, sharing learnings, planning new explorations, and taking action on what is learned. They view the teacher's role as "planning to plan" to provide a framework for developing curriculum directly from the children's questions. Teachers select the broad concept around which the curriculum will be developed and locate resources, often in the form of collections of children's literature about the selected concept. These text sets are used to launch an inquiry journey, which the children navigate.

Using a model of open inquiry drawn from the natural sciences, Whitin and Whitin (1997) offer children extensive involvement in curriculum development. In Whitin and Whitin's model, children use the methods of scientists, starting with sustained and precise observation of natural phenomena. With the teacher's guidance, the children formulate questions, determine the strategies most suitable for exploring them, and conduct their studies with resources obtained by both the teacher and the children. In this model, the teacher helps the children better develop their questions, find and use resources for exploring the questions, reflect on what they have found, and define new directions for their continuing research. This scientific approach to exploration is also found in Doris's (1991) work with children in *Doing What Scientists Do*. Inquiry-oriented theme studies that use established scientific methods of research offer children opportunities to practice authentic inquiry as co-inquiring members of research teams under the guidance of a senior researcher, their teacher.

TEACHER ROLES

In working through the process of designing theme studies with several groups of classroom teachers, we have found that different teachers use different approaches to developing equally successful theme studies. There appears to be a continuum that presents the teacher's role: director, guide, or mentor. Teacher-directors structure and present, teacher-guides model and prompt, and teacher-mentors participate and edit.

Teachers who are new to theme studies or whose primary teaching style is like that of a director or conductor often prefer to monitor the development of the curriculum by thinking through the process in considerable detail before beginning a theme study with their students. Others on the continuum between director and guide may like to begin with their own ideas, then ask their students for input, and synthesize the two sets of data as they plan theme studies. Throughout their planning, these teachers will structure the theme study so that it is well integrated with the regular curriculum guidelines. These will be influenced by national and professional organizations, adopted texts, district curriculum guides, and district and state standards.

Teachers who are very comfortable serving as instructional guides will often introduce a thematic idea to their students and solicit student-generated ideas for its exploration in the earliest planning stages. Using the students' ideas as the primary focus of the study, these teachers plan the interdisciplinary thematic curriculum with reference to district and state standards. Their curriculum plans become "maps" to guide the students' exploration of their own interests within the boundaries of teacher-framed options.

The mentor role is taken by teachers who are experienced with interdisciplinary thematic teaching and who feel comfortable working with their students in open-ended ways, while staying true to established curriculum standards. In this role, the teacher becomes a member of the research team, collaborating with students in identifying themes for study, reacting to their ideas for exploration, suggesting ways to proceed, and even participating in some of the searches.

Throughout this text, we explore these three different teacher roles and their implications for teaching and learning through theme studies. Each is challenging in its own way: teacher-directors assume major responsibility for planning and conducting a theme study; teacher-guides must find the appropriate balance between doing for students and facilitating student-generated inquiry; teacher-mentors bring to their interactions with children well-honed skills of diagnosing student needs, advising on all phases of the inquiry process, and providing support, that is, keeping the scaffold for each student's inquiry reinforced and stable. No matter from which place on the continuum you start or which combinations of roles you choose to use, you will experience highs and lows in inquiry-oriented theme studies. At times, your students will be fired with enthusiasm when they find a rich resource that advances their study or when they uncover a new piece of information or develop an insight from their inspection of collected data. But they will also experience the frustration that occurs when they hit dead ends in their search, the boredom that sometimes attends having to sort through details, and the distress of discovering that their understanding of important concepts is partial or incorrect. Those who devote their lives to inquiry in their chosen fields attest that the "bad" times are as characteristic of sustained and substantive inquiry as are the "good" times (John-Steiner, 1985). Students who learn to cope with and to work through the problem situations of inquiry develop the self-discipline that enables lifelong, self-directed learning. They may also catch the "disease" that Nobel Laureate Richard Feynman (Dallas, 1993) said he had: the compelling need to ask questions and to find answers.

Following are descriptions of how teacher-directors, teacher-guides, and teacher-mentors develop theme studies. These three roles, and the approaches to curriculum development that they represent, are illustrated in the various chapters of this text that discuss methods of teaching for inquiry learning through interdisciplinary theme studies.

Teacher as Director

When you serve as director for inquiry-oriented interdisciplinary curriculum development, you make most of the decisions, leading your students to work within a predetermined structure. First, you select study topics. For instance, if the standard curriculum includes the topic of photosynthesis in plants, you examine the content of that topic for concept definitions and/or generalizations that serve as umbrella ideas for the children's study. An example of a concept definition is *Photosynthesis is the process by which green plants use light to synthesize carbohydrates from carbon dioxide, water, and inorganic salts using the chlorophyll and other pigments present in leaves.* A related big idea might be *Green plants adapt to conditions of low light by maximizing their abilities to capture and use available light.* As teacher-director, you find ways to engage children with questions that, when explored, will help them to discover this concept definition and/or generalization. The challenges you face as teacher-director include:

1. motivating the children to study photosynthesis;
2. formulating questions that they might enjoy studying and that, when explored, will help the children understand the concept and big idea; and
3. locating various types of resources that are accessible to the children, that is, resources they can use and understand as they explore their questions.

An anomaly—something unexpected or discrepant with what you know or understand—can be a strong motivator for inquiry.

One fifth grade teacher found an anomaly that led to the study of photosynthesis when walking along a creek where bald cypress grow. Despite a dense canopy of leaves, many and varied green plants were living quite well in the understory. How could they live there? How would they get enough light to photosynthesize their food? These real questions became the central questions for the interdisciplinary study. The teacher raised questions about understory plants from different disciplinary perspectives:

Biology:	*What adaptations do understory plants have that allow them to capture light?*
Physics:	*What degree and type of light filters through the canopy to the understory?*
Chemistry:	*How does photosynthesis differ for canopy and understory plants?*
History:	*Which and how many of these understory plants have been noted to grow in this creek's environment since the first travelers recorded their presence?*
Math:	*How have understory plant populations changed over time?*
Fine Arts:	*What are the shapes, sizes, and colors of leaves and their adaptations in the understory plants?*

Finding resources to research these questions is the next task. In the role of teacher-director, you find and collect books, magazine articles, historical records of flora at the creek, resource people (e.g., botanical experts, parks and wildlife rangers, and local residents) who have information to share about the plants along the creek, photographs of the plant leaves that are adapted to conditions of low light, and videos of understory plant life in other parts of the world—in addition to using the local creek site itself. As teacher-director, with big idea in mind, main questions and subordinate questions formulated, and resources in hand, you decide which of the standards for student learning will be met when students study the questions and resources. You draft an instructional plan to present the anomaly to the students, during a visit to the creek site or through videos or still pictures of the site that are brought to the classroom, and involve the students in formulating questions that are similar to those planned. You plan specific individual and/or group tasks for examining particular resources to help the children explore assigned questions. These are not learning activities in the traditional sense. They are invitations to consult the supplied resources with particular questions in mind. You structure this data collection with worksheets or other organizing formats and lead the discussion to share findings. The objective is to have all students find the answers to the several research questions and to understand the overarching concept definition or generalization.

As these explorations continue, you determine which skills the students need to develop, such as the skills of interviewing people, reading and interpreting images, gathering information from videos, and taking notes. Then you provide skill development lessons for the entire class or small groups as needed.

You choose the evaluation methods. For instance, if portfolios are used to collect student work, you determine which work is included and what rubrics are applied. You may offer students some options for reporting their learnings, but typically these options are limited to those you deem most germane to the theme study and most meaningful for the assessment of student achievement of specified objectives.

Teacher as Guide

As a teacher-guide, you allow the students choices within the limits that you set. You select a thematic idea and then solicit student-generated ideas for its exploration in the earliest stages of planning. Using the students' ideas as the primary focus of inquiry, you develop the curriculum with reference to district and state standards. At each stage of the theme study process, you develop a variety of options for your students.

For example, if the major focus for a theme study is *Change,* as teacher-guide you ask the students to brainstorm on the concept. A web or other thematic organization helps you to see the major areas of interest emerging from the students' associations. You then develop a curriculum around these major topics and structure it to meet district standards. You determine a sequence so that students will select those areas that you want them to explore. You also determine the big idea that you want students to develop (e.g., *Change in one area causes change in other related areas*). And you guide the children's inquiry so that they will discover that big idea.

Major questions to be investigated are developed when students brainstorm on what they would like to know about the given topic. Often a KWL exercise will help the students to identify what they know (K) and what they want to know (W). You then build these questions into the structure of the curriculum so that they are addressed within the thematic unit. At the end of the unit, you can use the KWL chart to assess student learning (L).

Finding resources for the study is a critical part of thematic inquiry. As teacher-guide, you identify and collect resources for the students to select from. You may obtain books from the school library and the public library, identify and schedule appropriate guest speakers, organize field trips, bring in artifacts, and suggest the types of resources that students might bring in.

As the theme develops, within a specific area, students work with you to select from a variety of possible learning activities. For example, if one aspect of the theme study is *Urban Development,* one group of students might compare a series of maps that over time shows the growth of their own city, while another group might interview neighborhood storekeepers whose businesses have been affected by highway development.

In assessing students' learning, you work with the students to develop a common rubric to be used throughout the unit, or you provide a number of different evaluation options for individual students or groups to select. You determine in advance the major types of assignments and procedures for assessment so that the students have clear expectations and a structure within which to work. For example, one teacher-guide allots percentages of the grade to evaluation of students' content knowledge at the end of the unit and to their demonstration of the skills they are expected to learn and use throughout the unit. Another teacher-guide gives grades for assignments at different points of the unit's development, such as notes on research, learning activities that help the children to synthesize and apply their knowledge, and completion of a final product.

Portfolio assessment allows for flexibility within a given structure. The teacher-guide specifies the types of materials to be included in the portfolio and then allows the students to select their own examples of work for each category. For example, you may require that each student submit notes on research, a bibliography, a piece of written work, an illustration, and a reflection on his or her learning in the unit. The students then select the specific examples of each category to put into their own portfolios.

Teacher as Mentor

As teacher-mentor, you become an advisor and co-inquirer. In classrooms where the mentor approach to inquiry-oriented theme studies prevails, students select the topic and theme of study (which may be initiated by a common experience provided by the teacher, but without a predetermined focus or theme); determine the questions for exploration; identify, find, and consult resources; decide how they will organize and report their findings; and determine criteria to apply for the evaluation of their work. You guide and maintain quality control of the process, but the students are the drivers. This role is particularly demanding. To be a teacher-mentor, you must be a master of inquiry and also be able to develop the requisite skills in others: You must understand the component skills, be able to determine how and when to use them, and be skilled in guiding the novice in applying them to topics of study that you know little about. As teacher-mentor, you become a co-inquirer with children, participating in the inquiry as a partner, but also as an experienced inquirer.

Teacher-mentors usually start with a common experience. One teacher-mentor worked with fourth grade children at a wilderness trail. She set them to "wandering and wondering" (Whitin & Whitin, 1997) along a creekside, asking the children to make observations and to articulate what they wondered about. Another started with a guitar and asked the children to make observations about the artifact. As they become more precise and focused, student observations yield questions that, in addition to seeking facts ("What's the name of this plant?" or "Who made this guitar?"), compare and contrast ("What's the difference between the trees that live along the bank of the creek and those that live farther away from the water?" or "How are the sounds of the guitar different when you pluck or strum it?"), suggest hypotheses ("Do trees that live along the bank of the creek need more water than those that live farther away?" or "Can I make low-pitched sounds by holding the strings low down on the neck of the guitar?"), and generally reflect higher-order thinking. In the role of teacher-mentor, you become a vigilant overseer of this process, directing the children's attention to details they may have missed, asking for clarification of the children's wonderings, and assisting them to refine and more clearly articulate the variables that their questions seek to examine.

As questions are collected, you help the students find those that cluster around the same subtopic or subissue (in the above cases, trees living along the creekside and sounds produced by a guitar). All of these question sets are evaluated, just as an adult researcher would examine them, as possible foci for inquiry. The applied criteria include as primary ones the degree of student interest ("Do I really want to know about this?") and the availability and accessibility of resources ("Can I find lots of resources to answer my questions?" and "Will I be able to use and interpret those resources, given my knowledge and skills?")

There are no learning activities per se in teacher-mentors' classrooms. Students engage in true inquiry, finding and consulting the various resources in a detective-like hunt for clues to understanding and answering their questions and especially using them as sources that suggest new questions to continue, to deepen, and to expand the search.

The big idea (concept definition, generalization, principle, law) is not determined at the start of theme studies that are guided by you, in the role of teacher-mentor, although you monitor prospective selections of topic and subtopics to ensure that the study will not be trivial. You allow the big idea to emerge from the inquiries. You discover it along with the children. The difference between your role and the children's is that you must be attentive to the need to discover an idea of universal significance that transcends the particular topic under study. Furthermore, you will evaluate the progress of any inquiry for its multidisciplinary facets and its interdisciplinary connections. Most topics are naturally interdisciplinary, but you monitor each student's inquiry to make sure that questions from several disciplinary perspectives are entertained as the study progresses. Equally important, you keep watch for the types of skills each child needs to use and to learn how to use for productive inquiry. Teaching for skill development frequently is offered in a "just-in-time" manner, sometimes with individuals and sometimes with small groups of students with similar needs. In the role of teacher-mentor, you offer the purest form of individualized instruction: one-to-one or one-to-few, usually on demand by the student.

Methods of organizing data and reporting findings are selected and created by students, sometimes individually and sometimes collectively, on your advice. These might include many forms from conventional written and oral reports to multimedia presentations and creative productions and exhibits. Students also are responsible for determining the criteria they will apply to their work, whatever its form, in consultation with you. You keep watch over the validity and reliability of suggested measures and their pertinence to prescribed standards for student learning.

STARTING POINTS

How do you begin a theme study? There are many sources of starting points for interdisciplinary inquiry, and each applies equally well to curriculum development by teachers enacting any one of the roles, or a combination of roles, on the continuum we described earlier in this chapter. Categories of starting points include the following:

- ▾ children's common interests
- ▾ children's and adolescent literature and trade books
- ▾ textbook topics
- ▾ current events
- ▾ objects and artifacts
- ▾ local sites
- ▾ special interests
- ▾ cultural heritage
- ▾ abstract concepts

We discuss each in this section, with reference to the teacher role continuum, to help you choose those starting points that are best matched to your students' interests and inquiry skills and best supported by the accessible resources for inquiry in your instructional environment. We also suggest how a teacher enacting the role of director, guide, or mentor would work from those starting points so that you may choose those that best match your teaching preferences and the learning needs of your students.

Children's Common Interests

Children may demonstrate interest in a topic by talking about it, choosing books related to the subject, bringing in related toys or pictures, or drawing and writing about the topic. The list is limitless, but some of the most familiar topics include dinosaurs, animals, foods, and sports. One favorite is *Native Americans,* a topic that has the advantage of being well supported by resources in most parts of the country. Too often, however, a unit on native peoples becomes a superficial retelling of selected stories and stereotypes, with attractive, but meaningless accompanying art activities.

If you look for themes rather than topics, however, a study of Native American cultures can become an exploration of significant ideas, such as *Satisfying Basic Needs* (food, shelter, work, community, education, etc.), *Adaptation* (to the terrain, the physical environment, the climate, and the ecology of a region), and *Communities* (families, tribes, etc.). For example, a teacher working with students in a study based on the 1987 exhibit *Ancient Texans: Rock Art and Life Ways along the Lower Pecos,* at the Witte Museum in San Antonio, Texas, helped the children to explore the generalization that *Human beings all have the same basic needs; the culture and environment in which they live affect the way they meet those needs.*

As teacher-director, you might present an advance organizer for the unit, like the one in Table 3.1, to ensure that students explore ways that different groups of

Table 3.1
Methods people use to satisfy basic needs

	Examples	Food	Shelter	Security	Clothing
Northeastern Peoples					
Northwestern Peoples					
Alaskan Peoples					
Southwestern Peoples					
Local Peoples					

Native Americans, living on different parts of the continent, satisfied their basic needs. While this is clearly a social studies theme, you can expand the concept of *Basic Needs* to include generalizations such as *Animals satisfy basic needs through adaptation and migration.* Comparative tables, such as Table 3.2, serve as advance organizers for investigating different groups of animals.

In the role of teacher-guide, you may develop the same theme of *Satisfying basic needs* by brainstorming with the children to determine what they know and what they want to know about satisfying these needs. Particularly useful for this are the first two cells of the KWL chart, those that ask "What do I *Know*?" and "What do I *Want* to know?" (And at the end of the unit, the question in the third cell— "What have I *Learned*?"—helps to frame summary discussions.) When each child keeps a chart, all children can have some input into class discussions of the study. You work with the children to organize a web into areas of study such as homes, food, and clothing of one or two local tribes of Native Americans, or alternatively you might structure the web so that a student could select two or more Native American Indian tribes from different parts of the country and then find out how each tribe satisfied its basic needs. You help the students identify a limited number of areas of study to focus on so that the theme study has a manageable structure and does not require too many resources from outside the classroom. Throughout, you keep the children focused on defining the interrelationships among the concepts that comprise those big ideas you want them to discover, such as *Humans invent ways to use natural resources of their environment to meet basic needs.*

As teacher-mentor, with the same starting point, you encourage students to talk about their prior knowledge of Native Americans and to raise significant questions about how these people satisfied basic needs, and then you help them to locate primary and secondary resources to explore those questions. Note that in a teacher-mentor's classroom, children's explorations will move beyond the study of Native Americans to broader topics, such as nutrition, home construction, or clothing design, that contribute to the class's discovery of a major concept, like *Basic Needs,* and generalization, such as *Human beings all have the same basic needs; the*

Table 3.2
Methods non-human animals use to satisfy basic needs

	Examples	Food	Shelter	Security	Adaptations
Carnivores					
Herbivores					
Omnivores					

culture and environment in which they live affect the ways they meet those needs. This big idea may be the same as one a teacher-director or teacher-guide plans for his or her students. The difference is that the teacher-mentor encourages students to arrive at big ideas that were not necessarily anticipated by the teacher. Please don't confuse this with laissez-faire teaching. As teacher-mentor, you are constantly looking for many big ideas that emerge from students' explorations. Participating as co-inquirer, you heighten students' awareness of them.

Children's and Adolescent Literature and Trade Books

Whole-language instruction emphasizes the use of sound children's literature to help children learn to read and write. The purposes for using children's literature as a central focus in curriculum and instruction have been clearly defined. One major goal is to build children's enthusiasm for reading and to strengthen their reading skills (Chatton, 1989; Moss, 1984; Somers & Worthington, 1979). Literature is also seen as a way to provide a new aesthetic dimension to the more content-focused learning found in textbooks; at the same time, content knowledge enriches the child's understanding and enjoyment of literature (Johnson & Louis, 1987; Sebesta, 1989). A literature-based curriculum develops higher-order thinking: analysis, synthesis, and evaluation, processes that are used across the fields of study (Chatton, 1989; Johnson & Louis, 1987; Moss, 1984; Sebesta, 1989). Furthermore, the themes found in good literature are those that are significant, universal, and worthy of continued exploration. The wide realm of children's literature is a rich resource for interdisciplinary topics and themes.

Lists of children's literature, organized by topic, are found at Internet sites of booksellers and professional associations (such as ⟨www.ncte.org⟩ of the National Council of Teachers of English) and in anthologies and analyses of children's literature. Frequently studied at the upper elementary level is Jean Craighead George's Newberry Medal–winning *Julie of the Wolves* (1972). However, the story can lend itself to fragmented study of Eskimos, wolves, the arctic environment, and so on. Studies derived from the book are more meaningful if they are linked to a theme that leads to children's discovery of significant generalizations.

Such concepts could include *Survival, Adaptation,* and *The Relationship between Nature and Civilization.* Resulting generalizations might be *Survival depends on the ability to adapt to the environment* and *Nature and civilization can support each other or can be in conflict.* These broad generalizations could lead to inquiries into animal adaptations such as camouflage, plant adaptations to various climates, and human adaptations to new areas of settlement and into literature on survival through adaptation.

As teacher-director, you introduce a major theme, such as *Survival,* by reading the opening pages of *Julie of the Wolves* and asking the children to think about ways in which Julie learned to survive being lost in the wilderness. Using the children's ideas, you develop a list of ideas and structure the unit around them, making sure that every experience supports the children's learning of the big idea you have selected. You require all children to complete each of the activities you planned to cause them to arrive at the understandings you have set as objectives of the study.

In the role of teacher-guide, you read the opening chapters of *Julie of the Wolves* with the children and then help them develop a web of their interests and questions related to the story. By keeping the themes of *Survival* and *Adaptation* and the related generalizations or "big ideas" clearly in mind, you help the children select those areas of the web they have created that are particularly related to the theme you have chosen.

As teacher-mentor, you begin in the same way, by reading the opening chapters of *Julie of the Wolves* with the children and by helping them to identify their major questions and areas of interest by means of a KWL chart, a web, brainstorming, or other means. At this point, though, your method changes dramatically. You work closely with the children to help them develop researchable questions and to think about potential resources. Co-inquiring with the children, you and they look carefully at the collection of questions and areas of interest, group them as appropriate, and look carefully for key ideas and underlying interests. Questions are reworked to make them more researchable. One approach is to apply the journalistic questions *who, what, where, when, how,* and *why* and to estimate the extent to which these questions can be explored, given accessible resources. Another way is to use a variety of perspectives to see whether the resulting questions are capable of opening up a rich field for exploration (see Chapter Four for details of this approach).

Textbook Topics

Interdisciplinary study can be limited by textbooks, which are usually written to serve vast audiences and to cover large amounts of material. However, textbooks can provide a starting point, resources for children and teachers and reference guides. They can help to meet special goals, needs, and interests of particular groups of students. A topic treated summarily in a textbook can be developed into a larger study. The teacher's guide often identifies concepts that relate to a particular topic covered in the text, but that can also be developed or incorporated into a larger theme. Topics may come from textbooks in any of the curriculum areas, but usually are derived from social studies and science content.

For example, a fifth grade text discusses the American Revolution. Concepts presented in the teacher's guide include *Liberty, Democracy,* and *Rights of Citizenship.* Any one of these lends itself to a theme study, but it would tend to have a strong humanities orientation. A broader theme of *Revolution* itself suggests studies in physics, astronomy, and biology; art and literature; pottery and mechanics; and, of course, politics. Each of these can be examined within the study, and the exploration of each contributes to students' better understanding of all the others and of the larger idea of *Revolution.*

If you assume the role of teacher-director, you begin with the textbook account of the American Revolution and ask the children to think about the theme of *Revolution* and what it meant to the participants: the leaders, the colonists, the English government, and so on. You strive to have the children arrive at a concept statement for revolution that meets the criteria for that definition that you have in mind. To get there, you can record and organize the children's ideas into a chart or time line to guide the theme study. Or you may use a time line or graphic from the textbook to help the children stay focused on the theme.

As teacher-guide, you present the theme of *Revolution* as described in the social studies textbook and then invite the children to think of other examples of the concept. Keeping your definition of revolution in mind, you encourage the students to pose questions about their associations with the term. These suggest different subtopics of *Revolution* that become options for different groups of students to study in depth.

Enacting the teacher-mentor role, you ask the students to use the textbook account of the American Revolution as a starting point for thinking about what *Revolution* means. Children first develop questions about the American Revolution and then broaden those questions to move to other areas of exploration. For example, a question about Paul Revere might lead to questions about craftsmen of his time and about the economic effects of political revolution. Another question might explore the meaning of the word *revolution*. You might suggest that the students look to the term's Latin roots to enhance their inquiries to include things that "turn again." Other social, political, and personal revolutions; changing beliefs in disciplines of study; and major shifts in philosophies suggest additional areas for research. Most important to the integrity of your teacher-mentor role is that all questions raised for inquiry are raised by the children *with* you (not *by* you or *for* you). Your task is to help the children refine and expand their questions and to help them design and carry out their inquiry, using many types of reliable sources (see Chapter Five for a discussion of resource types and how to use them for children's inquiry).

Current Events

Current events lend themselves to classroom study because of their immediacy and their relevance to everyday life. It is easy, though, to teach about an event rather than exploring underlying themes that make it immediate and relevant to children. Just as teachers can work from children's expressed interests, they can develop children's interests in topics, events, and issues.

For many significant current events, materials are made available from government agencies, museums, private corporations, or educational publishers. However, topical events in the immediate community can also spark an interdisciplinary theme study. For example, a neighborhood may be considering the development of a nature trail along a creek bed that runs through suburban and downtown neighborhoods. Children can explore the implications of such a plan for home and business owners, for local wildlife, for the economics of the city, for the health of the citizens, and for the beauty of the area as they examine the broad generalization that *Widespread changes have far-reaching and unexpected results.*

Taking the role of teacher-director, you might begin by collecting newspaper articles, editorials, letters to the editor, and other print materials on the topic and arranging for local experts to speak to the class. Statistics about the project and other similar projects are presented or developed by the students. You determine the major questions and topics to be explored in depth and collect and organize the needed resources for this study. In addition, you carefully structure the unit plan to be followed in this theme study to ensure that all major areas are covered in depth, with carefully designed goals and objectives, learning activities, and means of evaluation.

As teacher-guide, you present one or two articles offering opposite points of view and brainstorm with the children on what effects the proposed plan might have for different members of the community. You contact key community personnel and then work with groups of children to help them plan and develop appropriate interview schedules, questionnaires, letters, and telephone conversations with these authorities. You provide a structure within which children stay sharply focused on the major theme and generalizations.

In the role of teacher-mentor, you present the issue to the students and ask them to develop a way of finding out what effects the proposed change might have. The children identify the major participants and design appropriate strategies for communicating with them. They also research similar situations in other areas by way of the Internet. You help them determine the best way to access and report information, all the while encouraging them to assume responsibility for developing their own skills as investigative reporters or scientific observers and experimenters.

Objects and Artifacts

Objects and artifacts are starting points for inquiry because they are directly observable. In our discussion, objects typically refer to naturally occurring tangible things not made or modified by humans, for example, parts and wholes of rocks, plants, and animals. Artifacts are constructed or modified by human beings, whether in contemporary times or in the past. They include all types of manufactured and crafted items, purchased as new or found in an attic, flea market, or museum. A short list of artifacts follows:

- ▼ papers: letters, advertisements, brochures, menus, personal notes, timetables, posters, catalogs, event tickets, postcards and greeting cards, labels, book plates, calendars, ledgers, and, of course, diaries
- ▼ still images: photographs and snapshots, drawings, paintings, sculptures, maps
- ▼ tools and utensils
- ▼ containers and packaging
- ▼ toys

▼ clothing, linens, and household textiles
▼ furniture
▼ machinery
▼ decorative items and trinkets
▼ anything fashioned and used by people

Objects and artifacts may be commonplace items, so asking questions about them helps us realize how much we take for granted. Think about the questions you could ask to find out about a cup, a shirt, or a pencil. Older artifacts are especially engaging because they speak to us of times past and people who often are no longer living. Questioning a bottle someone uncovered in a basement or attic, a great-grandmother's wedding gown, or a rusty nail is like exploring a mystery.

The skills of object/artifact reading need to be learned. They begin with careful observation, which wrongly has been associated with lower-order thinking. Whitin and Whitin (1997) note that observing with precision is a sophisticated skill. It involves seeing details, comparing/contrasting observations, forming categories of observations, uncovering anomalous findings, forming analogies to relate unknowns to personal experience, and making inferences and hypothetical statements about what is observed. Observations of these types naturally flow into questions that articulate the comparisons and contrasts, categories, anomalies, analogies, and inferences and hypotheses. Children need guidance in searching out details to become literate in object/artifact reading.

Depending on the role selected for implementing inquiry-oriented theme studies, teachers will use objects/artifacts differently as starting points, although the skills students need to interpret them are the same.

As teacher-director, you select objects/artifacts that are pertinent to the theme you have in mind, present the stimulus to the students, and involve them in its reading. You schedule skill-development lessons in object/artifact reading as prerequisite to student engagement with the object/artifact that is germane to the theme study. You model the process of interacting with an object/artifact, giving students practice activities, prior to introducing an object/artifact intended to actually initiate the students' theme study. You will do this as a whole-class activity. For instance, in a theme study concerned with the big idea *Changes in tools are enabled by developments in technology,* you bring to class examples of a digging stick, a hoe, and an automated plow. These are observed by the students, whom you instruct to raise comparative questions about the items.

For a theme study on *Changes in tools are enabled by developments in technology,* in the role of teacher-guide you present a digging stick or a hoe or an automated plow and engage the students in "reading" it and thinking about other examples of tools that accomplish the same purpose. You then ask the children to identify examples of the same category of artifacts that they and you find to further their comparisons through artifact reading. Following this, you guide the children to formulate questions about the objects and artifacts—helping them to frame questions that are germane to the theme. You are unlikely to schedule preparation lessons or to present a model of how to interact with an object/artifact before your students actually do so. Instead, you suggest ways that students may examine objects/artifacts. You ask questions to focus their attention on theme-salient qualities of the stimulus and to develop object/artifact reading skills. You ask students to look for details, make comparisons/contrasts, form categories, find anomalies and analogies, formulate inferences and hypotheses, and generally become engaged with the stimulus. You do all this, in small-group and individual interactions, to launch the theme study.

As teacher-mentor, you suggest objects/artifacts to study, encouraging students to *supply* the items for observation themselves. You talk with students about tools that they know have changed over time and ask them to find examples to bring to class. Together with individuals and small groups, you evaluate the objects/artifacts the children supply to uncover their research potential. You take turns with the students in searching for details, making comparisons and contrasts, forming categories, finding anomalies and analogies, formulating inferences and hypotheses, and wondering aloud about what mysteries each object/artifact holds. Questions derived from these conversations launch the theme study toward interests the inquirers have. The larger ideas to be discovered emerge from those interests rather than from the teacher's preconceived plans.

Local Sites

Nearly all schools provide some funds for field trips to local sites, such as

- ▼ homes and historic houses;
- ▼ museums and zoos;
- ▼ nature parks and trails;
- ▼ factories and professional offices;
- ▼ places of retail business, such as supermarkets and service stores;
- ▼ social agencies;
- ▼ political entities, such as city hall and the county courthouse, and the like:
- ▼ neighborhoods;
- ▼ local streets, yards, lawns, and dumps;
- ▼ cemeteries;
- ▼ depots and bus stops; and
- ▼ all other ordinary and unique places in our environment.

While it is necessary to provide transportation to some sites, others, like natural areas and local businesses, may be within walking distance from the school. Buildings are artifacts that you can physically enter and experience in three dimensions. They also contain starting points and resources for inquiry. Museums, zoos, nature parks, factories, professional offices, places of business, and social and political agencies contain objects, artifacts, documents, visuals, and resource people.

Field trips can easily become merely time away from the classroom. But if a local site is used as the starting point of interest for a theme study, it can help students ask increasingly specific questions about what they see there, questions that may lead to understanding concepts, generalizations, principles, theories, and/or laws.

Children who visit a local site at the start of a theme study with you as teacher-director will "take the tour" given by you or a tour guide at the site. For example, a theme study that explores *Lifestyles of people who settled in local communities were determined by ethnocultural and socioeconomic factors* could start with a visit to a farmhouse at a historical site. You select the house and the questions to be explored during the tour: questions about furnishings, their cost, and sources; about methods of preparing food, doing laundry, and maintaining the household; and about building materials of the house and its ancillary structures, such as the smokehouse and barn. The children are asked to make question-specific notes about what they see during the tour. Later, during debriefing sessions in the classroom, you lead them to identify the most salient observations pertaining to those questions. Your intention is to engage your students in exploring the specific questions you phrased to support the big idea that you selected.

As teacher-guide, you structure visits to local sites so that small groups of students may simultaneously engage with different resources at the site. In this role, you follow the same program of studies that you designed as teacher-director, but rather than having the entire class take the same tour, you'll have some children exploring furnishings, others exploring the kitchen and food preparation, another small group examining laundry items and talking with house interpreters about laundry days at the farm, and still others studying the contents of the smokehouse and barn. You ask the children to raise their own questions about the areas they explore. Their questions, not yours, determine further explorations and the direction the theme study will take.

The historic house offers more open-ended explorations for you as teacher-mentor and your students. Rather than going to the house with specific assigned areas of study in mind, you and the children *visit* the house rather than tour it: individuals move through its rooms and furnishings in the spirit of open-ended inquiry. The children explore the place both individually and cooperatively and consult one another about their questions.

Special Interests

Teachers know that their enthusiasm for a topic or subject of study can be infectious. Teacher-directors frequently look to their personal interests and knowledge as starting points for theme studies.

Railroads is a topic of special meaning for a fifth grade teacher who remembered playing with model railroads in her childhood. Her enthusiasm for miniature trains and the real thing had been fanned by her father, who had been riding the rails and collecting and making model railroads since his youth. The teacher told her students "stories" about her experiences with this topic, showing them arti-facts and suggesting that they watch the freight trains that rolled through their neighborhood. She designed a theme study around the history of railroads in the United States, defining the theme's study of railroads as a decisive force in ex-panding the American frontier and economically linking old and new areas of the country to illustrate these big ideas:

> Means of transportation change the way people live.
>
> People's needs and technology have influenced means of transportation.

This teacher-director developed her students' interests in a study she had planned for them.

Teacher-guides may also use their personal interests as starting points for theme studies, but they are more likely to search for children's special and temporal interests.

When armyworms infested the trees in a community, the curiosity of a group of second grade children was piqued. The boys brought to school as many of these moth larvae as they could carry—not to study them as organisms, but to see how the girls in the class would react to the wormlike creatures. Their teacher-guide saw a potential for theme study in those armyworms because the children were interested in them. She guided the children to ask questions about what they saw in the armyworms: Where do they live? What do they eat? Why do they build tentlike webs? Why are they called armyworms, especially if they're not worms? How many armyworms live in one tent? And if they're not worms, what are they? What do they become? How long do they live? Why do people kill them? The teacher arranged for children to conduct interviews, hold discussions, and read reference materials to find answers to their questions and to ask even more probing questions. Her goal was for them to understand the concept of metamorphosis and to infer several big ideas:

> Dramatic transformations occur in natural life cycles.
>
> Things are not always what they seem.

Using a more open-ended approach, teacher-mentors usually work from chil-dren's interests exclusively. These might be temporal interests like the armyworms noted above, but the teacher-mentor's approach differs from the teacher-guide's in two significant ways: (1) teacher-mentors ask questions along with the children, serving as co-inquirer, and (2) teacher-mentors do not attempt to influence or change children's focus on the topic. Instead, teacher-mentors help students refine their questions, wherever they may be focused, and also introduce their own questions to expand and deepen the study.

While teacher-mentors will encourage all students in a class to explore related issues (e.g., questions that cluster about a topic such as camouflage or questions that emerge from observations of a creekbed, from anomalies that arise during an experiment, or from analogies found in a favorite story), they may sometimes encourage different individuals and groups of children to simultaneously inquire into very different interests.

In the role of teacher-mentor who shares enthusiasm for railroads with the teacher-director in the earlier example, you might follow that teacher's example, telling students "stories" about your experiences with railroads, showing them artifacts, and suggesting that they watch the freight trains that pass through their neighborhood. But instead of designing the study around the history of railroads in the United States and defining the theme's study around the generalizations *Means of transportation change the way people live* and *People's needs and technology have influenced means of transportation,* you invite children's questions about railroads. And you add your own. Together, you and the students select those categories of questions that interest you most and decide on ways to research them. From their exploration, the big ideas emerge.

Cultural Heritage

One of the most widely used topics for special school studies that typically incorporate activities in the different areas of the curriculum is holidays. These can be studied as special events or as representations of human values and experiences. Most are recorded on calendars. Some may be defined through local folklife festivals and special community events. Local chambers of commerce can provide community calendars that designate celebrations that are especially meaningful to the community. Children and their parents are also excellent sources of information about cultural heritage activities.

A team of sixth grade teacher-directors chose to develop a theme study on Kwanzaa, the seven-day holiday between December 26 and January 1 that celebrates the African-American culture and the nguzo saba, or seven principles of human life: unity, self-determination, collective work and responsibility, cooperative economics, purpose, creativity, and faith. At this grade level, students are becoming more aware of these abstract principles and how they affect their own lives. The students studied each principle in each of their subject-area classes to better understand the concepts. Following are some questions used for study:

> *How does mathematics express unity?*
> *What kinds of unifying principles promote community?*

How do people express their feelings about unity?

What different kinds of unification have been developed by people in different times and places?

As each concept was studied, the students lighted the candles that symbolize the meanings of Kwanzaa. They performed African-American songs, dances, and chants and read poetry. To culminate the study, the students prepared and enjoyed a feast. According to their teachers, the students demonstrated understanding of these important generalizations:

There are universal principles that transcend ethnicity.

All seven principles can be related to our own lives.

When, in the role of teacher-guide, you explore cultural events, such as Asian New Year, Jewish New Year, Kwanzaa, Valentine's Day, St. Patrick's Day, Diez y Seiz, Juneteenth, Independence Day (Fourth of July), Columbus Day, Wurstfest, Dia de los Muertos, Halloween, Hanukka, Las Posadas, Christmas, or others that are meaningful to people of the local community, state, region, and nation, you select the big idea and suggest some questions. But you emphasize the importance of students' questions.

As teacher-mentor, you go a step further, encouraging the students to select the ethnic event, ceremony, or holiday to study and then begin wondering together about it until the most significant questions are selected for exploration.

Literature offers opportunities to study common elements of culture. Moss (1984) describes "folk-tale patterns" as a theme for third and fourth grade children. Carefully selected examples of folk tales from different cultures can start children on a journey to understanding the big ideas that *People in all cultures and times share the same hopes, fears, and drives* and *Oral traditions are embodied in all cultures, from the beginnings of human experience.*

As teacher-director, you select the folk tales and the explorations; as teacher-guide, you may offer some options to study so that the children make the selection as well as formulate the questions; as teacher-mentor, you allow free choice of the folk tales, drawing from those children suggest, and then participate with the children in inquiring into them.

A fourth grade teacher of Hispanic children living in the barrio decided to engage her students in developing the concept of culture through theme studies. Taking the teacher-director's role, he researched concept definitions for the term culture, selecting the components that he thought most meaningful to the students (as he uncovered very different and sometimes contradictory *definitions of culture). The teacher formulated some central questions and gathered resources for the children to consult. When his students raised questions about what they wondered most about their culture, other people's cultures, and culture in general, their issues clustered about sources of dysfunction in families and community groups. Switching to the role of teacher-guide, this teacher decided that the theme study might be better focused on helping the children inquire into social services—that is, the safety net for familial and community problems—than on defining culture. He reasoned that the children's interests spoke to immediate needs that deserve attention and that he could develop definitions of culture from studies that broadened children's understandings of options for help available to them and their families.*

Suppose that you detect an interest in oral traditions when your students discuss the performance of Los Pastores in their neighborhoods during the Christmas season. You are as intrigued as the children about where the play, its costumes, and its pagentry originated; when Los Pastores started; why Los Pastores is associated with Christmas and the Roman Catholic faith; and how the dialogue has been passed on from generation to generation and by whom. Enacting the role of teacher-mentor, you participate with the children in formulating the questions, finding and consulting resources, and gathering evidence for analysis. Together, you explore all aspects of this particular case of oral tradition, and, together, you compare your findings to the characteristics and origins of other oral traditions surrounding the nativity.

Through co-inquiry, you and the children articulate the multiple meanings of these traditions for understanding human hopes, fears, and drives.

Abstract Concepts

Highly abstract ideas, like *Discovery, Revolution,* and *Relativity,* can be sources of theme studies. In contrast to the more specific stimulators of inquiry that need broadening before they can support substantive theme studies, abstract concepts must be focused before they can be developed as meaningful curriculum for children in upper elementary grades. For example, the abstract theme *Patterns of Change* could be anchored in an examination of *Growth,* with a generalization that *All things change as they grow.* This could lead to a study of metamorphosis, germination of seeds, human growth and development, the growth of cities, astronomy, and mathematical concepts.

As teacher-director, you structure a theme study on this generalization by first examining adopted texts and the curriculum to identify related subjects and concepts. Throughout the students' study of these subjects, the theme of *Patterns of Change* is emphasized so that the children can find linkages and build a coherent understanding of the theme.

As teacher-guide, you present one or two familiar examples of things that change as they grow, such as seeds growing into plants or neighborhoods changing as a city expands. Then, individually or in groups, children make collections of things that change as they grow and present them in class to provide a list of possible topics for inquiry. You help them organize the information into mini-units of study and collect resources for each unit.

As teacher-mentor, you provide several examples of patterns of change and then invite the children to develop researchable questions about the generalization that emerges from their comparison of the examples. You help the children move from the more obvious areas of study to think about a broader range of examples. The major questions underlying the study might be these: How do different things change as they grow? and Why does this change take place? These questions can lead individuals and groups of children into rich areas of inquiry.

DEVELOPING THEME STUDIES

In summary, there are several critical ideas for developing theme studies for children's inquiry:

1. The literature contains different models for thematic studies by teachers and children. No one model is preferable to another. In fact, we recommend that individual teachers and teacher teams develop their own models. We encourage you to keep records of the ways you develop theme studies with your students, to note the successes and the failures, and to publish your descriptions and analyses of thematic teaching in order to contribute to the professional literature on this approach to curriculum development.

2. While there are different teacher roles in theme studies, one role is not better than another, though each is very different from the others. Teachers may begin a theme study enacting one role, but, as the study progresses, may find themselves moving along the continuum to take other roles. You select the role that best matches your personal teaching style, the needs of your students, the expectations of parents and administrators, and the characteristics of your instructional environment. As your experience with theme studies grows, you will find yourself enacting different roles in your work with different children. You may direct one child's or group's explorations, guide another's, and serve as mentor to the more self-directed inquirers in your class.

3. Most interests are first identified as topics. These become likely candidates for themes that define concepts and their interrelationships, most often stated as generalizations. No matter where or how a thematic study begins, it is your responsibility to find and support children's discovery of the truly large ideas that become guiding principles for understanding the natural world in which we live and the meaning of our humanness.

4. Starting points for thematic inquiries are unlimited. Find those that most intrigue your students and you, too, because inquiry is fueled as much by the teacher's curiosity as by the children's.

REFERENCES

Barber, J., Bergman, L., & Sneider, C. (1991). *To build a house: GEMS and the "thematic approach" to teaching science.* Berkeley, CA: Lawrence Hall of Science.

The LHS GEMS series includes nearly 40 teacher's guides for hands-on science and mathematics activities and handbooks on key educational topics. For more information, contact GEMS, Lawrence Hall of Science, University of California, Berkeley, CA 94720; (510) 642-7771.

Chatton, B. (1989). Using literature across the curriculum. In J. Hickman & B. E. Cullinan (Eds.), *Children's literature in the classroom: Weaving Charlotte's web* (pp. 61–70). Needham Heights, MA: Christopher-Gordon.

Dallas, D. (Producer and Director). (1993). *Richard Feynman: Take the world from another point of view* [Film]. Princeton, NJ: Films for the Humanities.

Doris, E. (1991). *Doing what scientists do: Children learn to investigate their world.* Portsmouth, NH: Heinemann.

Gamberg, R., Kwak, W., Hutchings, M., Altheim, J., with Edwards, G. (1988). *Learning and loving it: Theme studies in the classroom.* Portsmouth, NH: Heinemann.

George, J. C. (1972). *Julie of the wolves.* Pictures by John Schoenherr. New York: Harper Trophey.

Golden, C. (1986). *American history grade 11: Course of study and related learning activities.* New York: New York City Board of Education, Division of Curriculum and Instruction.

Heine, A. (October 1984). *Teaching the easy way (the multi-disciplinary approach).* Corpus Christi, TX: Corpus Christi Museum of Science and History.

John-Steiner, V. (1985). *Notebooks of the mind: Explorations of thinking.* Albuquerque: University of New Mexico Press.

John-Steiner, V. (1997). *Notebooks of the mind: Explorations of thinking* (Rev. ed.). New York: Oxford University Press.

Johnson, T. D., & Louis, D. R. (1987). *Literacy through literature.* Portsmouth, NH: Heinemann.

Kuhn, T. S. (1970). *The structure of scientific revolutions* (2nd ed.). Chicago: University of Chicago Press.

Moss, J. F. (1984). *Focus units in literature: A handbook for elementary school teachers.* Urbana, IL: National Council of Teachers of English.

Sebesta, S. L. (1989). Literature across the curriculum. In J. W. Stewig & S. L. Sebesta (Eds.), *Using literature in the elementary classroom* (pp. 110–128). Urbana, IL: National Council of Teachers of English.

Short, K. G., Schroeder, J., Laird, J., Kauffman, G., Ferguson, M.J., & Crawford, K. M. (1996). *Learning together through inquiry: From Columbus to integrated curriculum.* York, ME: Stenhouse.

Somers, A. B., & Worthington, J. E. (1979). *Response guides for teaching children's books.* Urbana, IL: National Council of Teachers of English.

Whitin, P., & Whitin, D. J. (1997). *Inquiry at the window: Pursuing the wonders of learners.* Portsmouth, NH: Heinemann.

Chapter Four

Implementing a Theme Study

I understand that I can take the role of a teacher-director, a teacher-guide, or a teacher-mentor, depending on my unique situation. I have a range of alternatives for selecting a theme. But how do I know which approach to use with my class this year? How can I make sure that the children get really involved in exploring the theme? How do I make sure that the children are learning what they are supposed to be learning in this grade? And will they meet the expected standards of our school's curriculum?

These are significant questions that teachers ask when they begin a theme study, especially when they are new to this approach. In this section, we discuss some ways for you to address these important issues: selecting a theme; conducting substantive brainstorming; thinking about available resources; helping children to develop sound, researchable questions; and meeting required standards. As we discuss these issues, we suggest criteria, strategies, possibilities, and limitations.

We view curriculum design as a closely integrated process in which objectives, content, learning activities, and assessment are interwoven. However, we also acknowledge that teachers and children work in the linear sequence of real time, that theme studies do have a beginning and an end, and that teaching and learning, however cyclical and recurrent they may be, happen one day after another. We also recognize the uniqueness of each classroom, of each interaction among teachers and children, of each learning period. We therefore encourage you to consider our suggestions and guidelines in the light of your own situation and think how you can use them with your students.

SELECTING A THEME

Any theme study is bounded by three major criteria:

▼ the interests of the learners
▼ the availability of resources
▼ curriculum standards

These three criteria must all be considered at the beginning of a theme study.

Developing a theme study is a fluid, continuous process of broadening and narrowing: generating ideas and categorizing these ideas, developing a large field of alternatives and selecting from those alternatives.

The initial selection of a topic may be the decision of a teacher, a team of teachers, or a teacher working with children, using any of the starting points described in the preceding chapter. What criteria can you use to make a selection? The following criteria may guide this process. A theme should be

1. appropriate to the developmental level of the children;
2. open to broad areas of inquiry;
3. familiar enough to preclude extensive preliminary study;
4. varied enough to appeal to different interests;
5. supported by various types of accessible resources, including primary sources;
6. explorable from a variety of perspectives; and
7. related to required content and skills goals and standards.

FROM TOPICS TO THEMES

In *To Build a House,* Barber, Bergman, and Sneider (1991) present the philosophy undergirding the Lawrence Hall of Science Great Explorations in Math and Science (GEMS) thematic approach to teaching science. Using the house-building metaphor, the GEMS staff places thinking processes at the foundation of thematic curriculum. Themes of study make up the framework of the curriculum. Content knowledge provides building blocks to fill that framework, which are mortared and nailed together by student enjoyment and curiosity.

A pile of rocks in a pasture or a stack of bricks on a city street cannot amount to much until they are given form. They are like inert knowledge: present and potentially useful, but having no power to move itself. Content knowledge offers us building blocks to construct our learning. But those stones or bricks need form—a framework or scaffold to help us connect them with other ideas and develop dynamic knowledge that can be transferred to other formats and applied in different contexts. Topics of study can provide great quantities of isolated information. But themes give them form because themes give rise to big ideas, which serve to integrate discrete bits of knowledge and help us make connections and new associations.

Themes are large ideas that define concepts or take the form of generalizations, principles, theories, and laws that interrelate several concepts. Themes can be *concepts,* such as *Adaptation, Survival,* or *Environment.* They can be statements of how concepts are linked to other concepts—*truisms* and multivariate causal statements that become generalizations, such as *Living things develop adaptations to their environments that enhance their ability to survive in those environments.* Themes may also be issues (Golden, 1986), such as *How can people's actions change our planet?*

The study of a topic can be interesting to an individual and offer opportunities for in-depth study and productive inquiry, but topics are limited in scope and usefulness. To return to the house-building metaphor, some topics may have little to contribute to students' development of meaningful associations. They are like loose bricks that need form before they can become dynamic knowledge. By contrast, big ideas or themes provide the scaffolding for comparative, causal, associational, analytical, inferential, and evaluative thinking.

Determining the Value of the Big Idea

There are several criteria that help determine whether a theme is important enough to warrant children's study. A meaningful theme should pass the test of these questions:

1. Is the big idea true over space and time?
2. Does it broaden students' understanding of the world or what it means to be human?
3. Is the big idea interdisciplinary?
4. Does it relate to students' genuine interests?
5. Does it support student inquiry?

As a teacher-director, you are likely to select a topic and check it carefully against the criteria. You think carefully about the students' capabilities and interests to make sure that the selected topic will engage the children in exploration and inquiry. You review the available resources in the classroom, in the school library, in the electronic media, and in outside sources, such as the public library, museums, and local field sites, to ensure that there is enough material for the students to use. As you select these resources, you consider the students' prior knowledge of the topic and their skill levels in reading, writing, mathematics, and research and inquiry to make sure that exploration of the topic will not be too easy or too difficult. As teacher-director, you also think about the subject areas to be addressed to ensure that the theme study addresses the content to be taught at this grade level and engages the children in the type of thinking and skills required in the curriculum. You are likely to ask yourself these questions:

- ▼ Will the children be interested in this topic?
- ▼ Does this study build on what we have learned before?
- ▼ Can I locate enough resources for the children to be able to explore a variety of questions and subtopics?
- ▼ How will the children expand their content knowledge and their skills in reading, writing, mathematics, problem solving, critical thinking, and inquiry through this study?

In the role of a teacher-guide, you work with your students as they begin an initial exploration of the topic. You might ask the children what they know and what they would like to know about the topic in order to judge the level of the children's prior knowledge, breadth of interest, and conceptual level. For example, if the children pose a number of varied questions that have potential for inquiry, you can proceed with more confidence than if the children's questions are limited in scope and seem superficial. As teacher-guide, you take responsibility for locating possible resources, but also ask the children to suggest what might augment these suggested resources. You look carefully at the children's ideas and questions and consider the content and skills that will be learned. As teacher-guide, you are likely to ask your students these questions:

- ▼ What do you know about this topic?
- ▼ What would you like to know about?
- ▼ How could you try to find out?
- ▼ What do you need to learn about this topic?

You also ask yourself what content, knowledge, and skills can be developed through the children's inquiry.

In the role of a teacher-mentor, you involve children at all steps in the development of a theme study. You encourage the children to suggest possible topics and then ask them to check their own prior knowledge and possible areas for exploration even before a topic is selected. You also give the children the responsibility for suggesting resources and how to locate them. You encourage the children to think about their potential learning in the proposed inquiry. As a teacher-mentor, you may discuss the following with your students:

▼ What do we know about the topic?

▼ What new questions would you like to explore?

▼ Where would you go to explore these questions?

▼ Do you know how to find and use these resources? What do you need to learn?

▼ What new knowledge do you think you will learn from this theme study?

▼ What new skills do you think you will learn from this inquiry?

BRAINSTORMING AND IDENTIFYING AREAS FOR INQUIRY

After selecting a theme that meets the criteria indicated above, you and the children begin to brainstorm about the theme. This brainstorming may lead to refinement and development of the chosen theme, it may indicate new paths for exploration that had not emerged in the initial consideration of the theme, or it might even lead the group to abandon that theme and pursue a different one, perhaps one that emerges from the children's ideas, questions, and discussions. It is much better to change directions early in the process than to persevere with a theme study that seems to be limited, seems to lack direction, or does not excite the learners.

In brainstorming, ideas tend to be generated by making connections and using categories. In a theme study, brainstorming can use discipline categories or conceptual categories. Each produces a very different product.

Discipline categories are derived from conventional subject areas or academic disciplines. One of the most precious and classic examples of this approach that we know was given by Aalbert Heine (1984), former director of the Corpus Christi Museum. Heine's ideas are reproduced in Figure 4.1 as a testimony to his creative contributions to children's expansive learning through exploration. It is possible to examine most topics through these lenses:

▼ the natural science disciplines: for example, biology, geology, chemistry, physics

▼ the social science disciplines: for example, political science, sociology, anthropology, psychology, education

▼ the literary arts: poetry, fiction, biography, nonfiction

▼ the fine arts: visual (painting, sculpting, printmaking), musical (classical or popular forms of vocal and orchestral music), performing (dance, drama)

It is very important to focus at this stage on thinking about the topic through the perspectives of a thinker in each field: How would a biologist view this topic? A psychologist? A painter or photographer? A composer or a choreographer? Using the lenses of the different disciplines helps to broaden possibilities for inquiry and at the same time helps the learners to appreciate a variety of viewpoints.

Figure 4.1
Understanding a rusty nail

Aalbert Heine, former director of the Corpus Christi Museum, reminds us that "just one object in a museum, a square nail, rusty and bent, is all that is needed to open up the world, to introduce the flow of knowledge." For instance:

History: to illustrate how houses were built in the old part of town; how the extreme paucity of nails hampered settlement of the prairie states; how important a blacksmith shop used to be.

Mechanics: to unravel the forces that bent the nail, the kinetic force of the hammer and the forces of friction that hold it in the lumber; to discuss the electromagnetics.

Chemistry: as an element and an example of oxidation.

Geology: to show the processing of ores to metal.

Anthropology: to discuss the Stone Age and the development of technology into bronze and iron; to discuss societies built without metals.

Astronomy: to discuss meteoric iron and to speculate about the core of the earth.

Economics: the value of nails to railroads and ship building.

Art: as a source of yellow ochre.

According to Heine, the nail can be seen as the center of the universe.

Teachers and children often tend to think in terms of school subjects, which may lead to premature concerns about activities: What would we do in art? In math class? But this approach tends to inhibit inquiry and exploration. For example, a class exploring the theme of *Calendar* might develop a variety of questions from the disciplinary points of view of a historian, a scientist, an astronomer, a philosopher, a mathematician, a sociologist, or an artist (see Figure 4.2).

Conceptual categories offer different views of the topic. Instead of formulating questions about the topic from disciplinary perspectives, it is possible to free associate, allowing questions to emerge from the associations you have with this topic. When the brainstorming is done by several people, this approach often yields a wide variety of questions. The various members of a brainstorming group have different associations with the topic, suggesting widely different conceptual categories. They often "piggy-back" on one another's ideas, producing sets of questions within a conceptual category. For example, brainstorming on the theme of *Calendar* might result in categories such as the origins of the calendar, units of measure, in-

Figure 4.2:
Questions about calendars: The disciplines

Historian:	▼ Who invented the calendar?
	▼ When did our calendar take the form we know? Why?
	▼ When did human beings begin marking time? How?
Physicist:	▼ What is the atomic clock? How does it work?
	▼ How accurate is the atomic clock? Why?
Astronomer:	▼ How does the calendar relate to the movements of the earth around the sun?
	▼ How are cycles of the moon reflected in the calendar?
	▼ Would the calendar be the same on another planet? Why?
Philosopher:	▼ What calendars are used in the different religions of the world?
	▼ Why are those calendars different from each other?
	▼ What events or people are celebrated in the calendar?
Mathematician:	▼ What units of measurement are used in a calendar?
	▼ What is leap year? Why do we need leap year?
	▼ How do computers know what date it is?
Sociologist:	▼ Do all cultures have calendars?
	▼ Why do people need calendars? How do they use them?
	▼ What would happen if someone invented a new calendar? How could a new calendar be adopted by everyone?
Artist:	▼ Why are many calendars decorated? Why do people buy calendars with pictures?
	▼ What types of art are used in calendars?
	▼ What types of artists work on designing calendars?

novation, types of calendars, characteristics of time, reasons for timekeeping, uses of the calendar, the atomic clock, regulation, phases of the moon and the sun, cultural concepts of time, and biological influences (see Figure 4.3).

It is interesting to see how people's backgrounds affect their choice of questions. People tend to use their own experiences to make sense of topics and to color the connections they make. It is therefore often very helpful to allow participants,

Figure 4.3
Questions about calendars: conceptual categories

Origins of the Calendar:
▾ Who invented the calendar?
▾ How has time been measured in the past?
▾ What do the names of the days and the months mean?

Units of Measure:
▾ What are the units of measurement that we use in the calendar?
▾ In what other ways do we measure time?
▾ Why are there 365 days in most years and 366 in leap years?

Innovation:
▾ What if someone invented a different type of calendar? How could it be implemented?
▾ How do computers know how long each month is?
▾ What calendar will people in space stations use?

Types of Calendars:
▾ What were the first calendars?
▾ How many forms of calendars exist today?
▾ Which type of calendar sells well? Why?

Characteristics of Time:
▾ Did time have a beginning? Will it have an end?
▾ Why do we organize our lives by watches, clocks, and calendars?
▾ In poetry, why do we speak of time as if it were a person?

Reasons for Timekeeping:
▾ Was the calendar's origin related to trade or travel?
▾ How did our observation of the natural world determine the need for a calendar?
▾ Who decides what calendar everyone will follow?

whether groups of teachers, teachers and children, or children, to take the time to do their own brainstorming before sharing ideas with each other. Premature sharing may inhibit some very fruitful lines of research simply because once a line of thinking is established, the group tends to branch out from it rather than following their own ideas.

Teacher-directors, teacher-guides, and teacher-mentors at this stage involve children in brainstorming. As a teacher-director, you may prefer to brainstorm first with other teachers and to present a possible set of categories to help the children focus and to have some ideas to build on. As a teacher-guide, you may encour-

Figure 4.3 continued

Uses of the Calendar:
▾ Why do we use the calendar to mark the events in our lives?
▾ How does the school calendar affect our families? How does it affect business?
▾ What industries and businesses are affected by the calendar?

Atomic Clock:
▾ What is the atomic clock?
▾ Is the atomic clock absolutely accurate? Does it ever have to be reset?
▾ What is the most accurate way of keeping time? Why?

Regulation:
▾ How were conventional measurements determined for a day, days in a month, and months in a year?
▾ How are holidays determined (e.g., national holidays, religious holidays, school holidays)?
▾ What is Greenwich mean time? What is the international date line?

Phases of the Sun and Moon:
▾ What does the calendar have to do with the phases of the moon?
▾ How does the lunar calendar differ from the solar calendar?
▾ What mythology, poetry, or music is related to the seasons?

Cultural Concepts of Time:
▾ Is the same calendar used in all parts of the world?
▾ Do all cultures have calendars? How are these calendars alike and different?
▾ What calendar days are special in our school, our city, and our state?

Biological Influences:
▾ How do trees know to drop their leaves at the same time each year?
▾ How do animals know when to hibernate and when to come out?
▾ How is our biological clock (sleep) affected by the calendar?

---

age children to brainstorm freely and may then suggest categories for the children that you think can lead to rich exploration and for which resources are available. As a teacher-mentor, you encourage children to brainstorm and then ask them to identify the categories and questions that emerge from the results of the brainstorming.

Brainstorming is another example of the alternative broadening and narrowing that are characteristic of inquiry. Many ideas are generated and then are sorted into a more limited number of categories. At this point, it is important to reconsider the significance of the study and to develop some "big ideas" that meet the following criteria:

1. The big ideas are true over space and time.
2. They broaden students' understanding of the world or what it means to be human.
3. They are interdisciplinary in nature.
4. They can lead to student inquiry.

These big ideas usually emerge from a careful review of the categories and ideas developed through brainstorming. Teachers and children can ask themselves, "What can we say about this theme?" and come up with a number of generalizations. At first, these generalizations are often true, but somewhat trivial. Asking questions such as "Why?" or "How?" may help to deepen the significance of the generalizations. Sometimes two or three simple generalizations may be combined to make a more substantive one. At this point, it is not always necessary to select only one big idea to work toward, but it is wise to limit the number of big ideas that become the major goals for student learning in the theme study. For example, in the study of *Calendar,* these big ideas may emerge:

Calendars reflect movements of the sun and moon, the seasons, and important times in human life.

While calendars are created by human beings, they are based on movements of the sun and moon.

Each of these generalizations meets the criteria for a big idea. Each is broad enough and substantive enough to incorporate examination of the questions raised in brainstorming. Each is a generalization that could be reached through inquiry into the major categories identified above. And each can give a purpose and focus to the theme study, which keeps it from becoming too diffuse, while still allowing for extensive and imaginative inquiry.

It is important to spend enough time on this step. It is tempting to move directly from the brainstorming and development of categories to the planning of activities, but this often leads to a series of learning experiences that may be interesting, but that have little focus or significance, and the learners may lose sight of the central thrust of the theme study.

For the teacher-director, the development of big ideas may be the responsibility of the teacher or a group of teachers. In this case, you as teacher-director must make a conscious decision whether to share the big idea with the learners at the outset of the study or to structure their inquiry in ways that lead them to discover the big ideas for themselves. In the role of a teacher-guide, you may ask the learners to suggest some generalizations that emerge from the results of the brainstorming and then may take these suggestions and develop them into one or more big ideas that appear to be substantive and significant. As teacher-mentor, you work with the children as they all generate possible generalizations and then as they all test these generalizations against the criteria for big ideas.

As we have indicated, teacher-director structures and presents; teacher-guide models and prompts; teacher-mentor participates and edits. These roles enable you to respond to the requirements of the curriculum, the school environment, and, above all, the learning needs of the students.

INQUIRY'S ESSENTIAL SKILLS

In Chapter One, we define inquiry as the search for information, knowledge, and truth. The operative word in this definition is *search* because inquiry is dynamic and driven by our use of several processes.

Theme studies should involve students with subject matter content pertinent to grade-level standards for their learning, provide for depth of study, contribute to students' understanding of a theme's big ideas, and develop their abilities for self-directive learning. These skills include questioning, finding resources, uncovering clues in resources, organizing and verifying data, and synthesizing findings.

Questioning

Knowing how to ask questions that start, develop, and deepen a search is a complex process. Students need to learn many component skills to become effective questioners. Some are developed as an inquiry proceeds; others require special skills lessons that provide guidelines, prompts, and guided practice exercises.

Finding Resources

Knowing how to look for and find resources that are meaningful to a search requires matching your questions to the most promising information you can find in print, in people, in places, in audiovisuals, in objects and artifacts, and in other sources. Creative associations between source types and your study focus can uncover the most reliable sources.

Searching for Clues

Understanding how to search for clues in sources is another, related inquiry skill. The creative inquirer is a good detective—looking for clues where most would expect them to be, and also in unlikely places. Finding and using resources will be discussed more fully in Chapter Five.

Recording and Organizing Data

Taking notes and knowing how to visually record, tabulate, and organize data are skills that many people never develop well. These are not usually learned incidentally. The fundamental principles of good note taking and data organization need to be modeled with clear examples for students to apply and then modify to meet the particular needs of their individual searches.

Finding Meaningful Patterns

Data interpretation follows naturally from its organization. Patterns found in collected clues that help to answer specific questions are revealed or hidden by the way the clues are organized. Knowing how to present information to answer particular questions that are garnered from different sources helps to determine the veracity of that information—all the more reason for teaching students many and varied ways of displaying the information collected for each question under study. Chapter Six will address in more detail the processes of inquiry.

Synthesizing and Presenting Findings

Methods for presenting the results of a search frequently help the inquirer synthesize the most important findings. These will be discussed more fully in Chapter Seven. All types of verbal, visual, auditory, and performance presentations—from disciplined writing to multimedia production—need to be added to students' individual presentation toolboxes from grade to grade, consistently introduced, used, and refined over their years of schooling.

Each of these skills is highlighted in different chapters of this book as we examine their role in developing theme studies. In this chapter, we give special attention to questioning, the process that permeates inquiry. Since inquiry begins, proceeds, and concludes with questions, we have chosen to showcase that central process in this discussion of how to launch inquiry-driven theme studies.

WAYS OF QUESTIONING

Questioning is an important part of daily living. We question for many reasons: to find out what others are doing and how they are feeling; to find out how to go somewhere; to learn where a product or service is found and what it costs; to find out where, when, and how something has happened and who was involved—we ask questions to learn, and we learn when we get answers. Questioning is a linchpin for learning: our questions express what we understand about the content of our explorations; their wording suggests how we make sense of our experiences. The types of questions we ask show how we direct our own learning. The form, style, and content of our questions reveal the role of language in learning and the influence of individual propensities, styles, and talents for constructing knowledge.

Young children exhibit curiosity from birth; their attentiveness to certain stimuli implies latent questioning. But research on children's questioning indicates that curiosity does not necessarily translate into articulated questions. In fact, most children need to be taught how to formulate their questions—using language to express precisely what they are wondering about. And there are levels of questioning that require cognitive development of intellectual and linguistic processes—development influenced by nature and by nurture.

As any good interviewer can attest, not all questions are equal. Some are better than others, influenced by the questioner's depth and breadth of knowledge about the topic of inquiry, understanding of related concepts, degree of interest in the topic, and linguistic proficiency in expressing queries.

Children must learn to ask questions that move beyond fact gathering to interpretation and analysis of experience. Success in doing this depends on teachers' proficiencies as questioners themselves because they must understand the difference between shallow questions and deeper ones, between simple queries and complex ones, between mundane questions and provocative ones. There is more to this than recognizing when a child asks a question the teacher has not asked or answered before—the "good" question in conventional dialogue. Teachers need to diagnose the levels of children's questions and be able to match their instructional response to the particular cognitive and linguistic needs of students in order to raise their levels of questioning.

Throughout this text, we define differences in the instructional approaches of teacher-directors, teacher-guides, and teacher-mentors. Each role meets different student needs; effective individual teachers move from one role to the other as student learning needs are manifest. Ease of instantaneous transition from one role to another is the mark of the master teacher. At no time during instruction is this proficiency more critical than when teachers are developing in their students inquiry's most fundamental process: questioning.

Your role as teacher-director in teaching for questioning matches the beginning questioner's needs to develop basic questioning skills. As teacher-director, you are likely to show students how to ask the specific questions they are trying to formulate.

For example, when a student indicates interest in finding out about dinosaurs by pointing to a picture of triceratops, but is unable to articulate a question, as teacher-director you offer some questions to see which ones match the student's interest. In effect, you are asking the student: "Do you want to find answers to questions like What's this dinosaur called? Where did it live? What did it eat? What animals attacked it? How did it protect itself?" You are supplying question forms that the student has not yet learned to formulate.

As a teacher-director, you model specific questions that apply directly to the students' studies. You may actually assign specific questions to students, both to focus their research and to model question formats. Most of us can recall the study guides teachers gave us, comprised of several questions designed to focus our reading and thinking about a topic.

For example, students are reading Milligan's (1990) *With the Wind, Kevin Dolan,* about Irish immigrants to Texas at the time of the Texas Revolution, and Martinello's (1992) *Cedar Fever,* about German-Americans in Texas during the First World War. In the role of teacher-director, you provide them with a set of questions to guide their reading and to model question asking for comparison of the human issues in these novels. These might include the following: What were the views of war held by the Irish and the German Texans in these stories? What similar traditions did both groups maintain even in troublesome times? What did maintaining those traditions contribute to the lives of the people?

The teacher-guide role is appropriate for students who know the syntax of basic questions and can independently formulate them. In the role of teacher-guide, then, you attempt to help students enhance their questioning strategies by modeling. One common way to model questioning is to show students how you would formulate questions about a focus that is different from their topic of study. Given the model, students are encouraged and helped to apply those same question formats to their own studies.

For example, as teacher-guide, you show students how questions were formulated from different perspectives to explore a topic. Heine's exploration of a nail, shown in Figure 4.1, illustrates this. It shows how different perspectives enlarge the study of so humble an artifact, making it, in Heine's view, "the center of the universe."

Using this approach, as teacher-guide you would show the students the questions that can be asked on the nail from each of Heine's disciplinary perspectives. But then, unlike the teacher-director, who would ask the students to research those same questions in order to better understand the question form and ultimately to be able to apply it to their own inquiries, you ask the students to apply the model to their own topics immediately. A teacher-guide would model questioning by asking questions about an object or artifact different from the nail, but using the same perspectives and wordings used when studying the nail.

Another example: As teacher-guide, you might introduce students to Alison King's (1991) question stems (Figure 4.4) and model the process of using the stems to create questions about a topic such as *Our Neighborhood* or *Whales* or *Simple Machines* or *Friendship as Depicted in* Charlotte's Web (White, 1952). Once these examples are shared, you encourage the students to emulate the process by using the stems to formulate questions about the topics they are actually studying.

King's question stems are interesting because her research found significant correlations between student use of the question stems to formulate questions about reading assignments and their reading comprehension and problem solving. All stems may not be useful for *every* topic or for *every* student, and the stems themselves do not guarantee that the questions they spawn will be meaningful in all contexts. However, the stems provide guidance in constructing questions that encourage comparison-contrast, explanation, interpretation, and evaluation.

Unlike in the other roles, as teacher-mentor you participate in the questioning process with the students from the outset. This participatory approach to inquiry—working as a co-inquirer with students—is used when students do not require many examples of questions or models of the questioning process. As teacher-mentor, you may occasionally introduce questions for study, but your main goal is to serve as catalyst to enhance the level of the students' questioning. This is a subtle

Figure 4.4
King's question stems

How is . . . related to . . . ?

What is a new example of . . . ?

In your opinion, what is the best . . . and why?

What are some possible solutions for the problem of . . . ?

Explain why . . .

What conclusions can you draw about . . . ?

What is the difference between . . . and . . . ?

How are . . . and . . . similar?

How would you use . . . To . . . ?

What do you think would happen if . . . ?

What are the strengths and weaknesses of . . . ?

Why is it important . . . ?

Do you agree or disagree with this statement: . . . ?

What do I (you) still not understand about . . . ?

What is the main idea of . . . ?

What if . . . ?

What is the meaning of . . . ?

Why is . . . important?

What conclusions can I draw about . . . ?

What is the best . . . and why?

method, introducing ideas and raising issues to make your students think about what they are exploring.

Ellen Doris (1991) describes her teacher-mentor approach in *Doing What Scientists Do*. Her dialogues with her students illustrate how she diagnoses their needs and helps them to refine their observations. Doris offers illustrative dialogues of her interactions with children about a classroom guinea pig, crickets, finches, and nests. As teacher-mentor, your purpose is to challenge the children to see what they can see and to know what they can't see and don't know, and hence to search for more.

For example, if upper elementary students are looking at a well-defined photograph of a historic house and see only the number on the front door, as teacher-mentor you could redirect their attention to the house's building material, the people standing nearby, the words and numbers on the lintel or cornerstone, the street signs, and the like, prompting them to inquire from and with the information they gather. Solicited questions would be of several different types.

Some Types of Questions

Questions have been typed in different ways, most often with an eye to cognitive level. Higher-order thinking is easily linked to higher-order questioning, and many of the same categories offered by Bloom (1956) apply. Sanders (1966) used Bloom's taxonomy to suggest question categories. Dillon (1990) offers schemes for identifying questions asked by people in different contexts and for different purposes, that is, the physician's questions, the lawyer's, the journalist's, the teacher's. Our purpose is not to reintroduce these frequently used categories. Instead, we focus our attention on different types of questions that are particularly useful in open inquiry because open exploration is the least well represented in the literature on questioning.

We recognize that in any exploration inquirers move back and forth among question types because the particular questions asked and the way they are phrased are determined by individual inquirers' content knowledge pertaining to the topic of study, facility with the jargon of the pertinent areas of study and related occupations, frames of reference for studying the topic, and points of view about particular topical components under study. We discuss here some types of questions that we believe apply to every open inquiry, no matter how basic or advanced the study. All are used by teacher-director, teacher-guide, and teacher-mentor, each applying them in the ways that are pertinent to the instructional purposes of each role.

Beginning Questions

Information-Seeking Questions.

We typically begin our study of something new and relatively unknown to us with the journalist's set of fact-seeking questions: Who? What? Where? When? How? Why? These standard interrogatives help us to get acquainted with the topic and determine our focus.

Questions derived from observations are also especially useful when starting a search. Whitin and Whitin (1997) illustrate the power of detailed and sustained observation of birds and their behavior near a feeder for fourth graders' inquiry. The children's observations of the birds over time caused them to search for details in the familiar, note unusual behaviors and unexpected events and spot the unfamiliar, make comparisons and contrasts, and become aware of what they *could* not see in addition to what they *did* not see.

For example, observing the characteristics of different beak shapes can lead to questions about how birds use their beaks and why beaks come in different shapes. Observing old photographs can spawn questions about the subjects' clothing, activities, and surroundings and, on the other side of the camera, the photographer's equipment, skill, perspective, and circumstances. Reading a descriptive narrative about a person, place, or thing can prompt questions about any and all qualities of the subject.

Multidisciplinary Perspectives for Questioning. Viewing your subject from perspectives of different fields of study suggests multiple ways to think about your topic. Like Heine (1984), you can look at a topic from basic and applied viewpoints in each field. The natural sciences offer the traditional disciplinary perspectives of biology, chemistry, physics and geology and those of newer multidisciplinary fields, such as biochemistry and neurobiology, as well as the applied perspectives of the physician and paramedic, pharmacologist, spelunker, and mechanic, to name a few.

The social sciences encompass such traditional disciplines as sociology, psychology, education, geography, and political science, among others, and applied areas of the pollster, teacher, politician, and so on. The literary arts include creative narrative and lyric writing, journalistic writing, literary criticism, linguistics, and related studies of language and literature. And the fine arts are concerned with music, dance, visual representations, drama, and acting.

For example, to raise multidisciplinary questions about something like a calendar, we might ask, "What would someone who works in the natural sciences, basic or applied, ask about the calendar?" Some suggestions follow:

▼ How are the movements of the earth around the sun related to the calendar?

▼ How do flowers of the season know when to bloom?

▼ How do the different seasons of the year affect human health and well-being?

Probing Questions

John-Steiner (1985) refers to analogies and anomalies as paths for discovery. Analogies link what we know to the unknown, imbuing the unknown with enough meaning to make it accessible for further study. Anomalies, because they are inconsistent with our experience, can cause us to take note of something that might otherwise be overlooked. Anomalies raise our level of curiosity and heighten our interest in an apparent discrepancy—something that is "out of true" for us.

Using Analogies. Questions that use analogies help us to find relationships among facts and ideas—the clues we are uncovering. Children will form analogies spontaneously because they don't have the language to name something or express an idea. They can be encouraged to use this method of bridging linguistic and knowledge gaps in their question asking by explicitly linking the unknown to the known.

For example, children who are exploring fossil growth in limestone find a piece of a fossilized crinoid and have no idea what it is. Therefore, it's difficult to ask questions about it—there are few words that help them. So they begin to think about what the unusual fossil reminds them of—a piece of a stem. Now they can ask: "Is this fossil like a plant?" "Does this tubelike structure act like a pipe?" "If so, what is conveyed through the tube?" "For what purposes?" One analogy-testing question leads to another and another, based on a line of reasoning that was prompted by the initial analogy.

Analogies can develop into hypothesis-testing questions. Ruef (1992) recommends that students learn to look and think by analogy on the way to theory formulation. In *The Private Eye,* Ruef describes how seeing how one thing is like another can lead to metaphors, which lead to theories. Ruef uses the fingerprint, likening it to whirlpools, tree rings, freeways, and crawling worms. When the "like" is dropped, metaphors emerge, and the fingerprint becomes a whirlpool or freeway, leading to finding other "fingerprints" in our environment. Hypotheses about the reasons for the shapes of those prints can surface.

For example, when Martinello (1987) found a medicine bottle from the early twentieth century that had a raised line in the glass with the words "trial mark" (designating the amount of the medicine a user could sample and still return the product for a refund), she likened the "trial mark" to a young bride's first tries at creating her own home. Trial marks became a metaphor that suggested hypotheses about homemaking by ordinary women living everyday lives at the turn of the twentieth century in the rural Texas hill country. The ensuing search became a test of those metaphor-founded hunches.

Exploring Anomalies.

Some things spark our curiosity because they are inconsistent with our experiences, beliefs, or expectations. They make us take notice because they surprise us—like a magic trick is surprising even when we know that the magician has special boxes to make it appear that a woman is being sawed in half or that a rabbit is being pulled out of a hat. The unexpected makes us ask, "Why?"—it never fails. Therefore, anomalies are sure starters for inquiry.

For example, one of the classic anomalies in scientific discovery was the one Alexander Fleming made. Returning to his lab from a weekend holiday, Fleming saw that bacteria were growing everywhere on the nutrient agar in his Petri dishes except in the area of a mold that had apparently "blown in" to contaminate his cultures. "Why?" "What was the connection between the mold and retarded bacterial growth?" That unexpected event prompted Fleming to ask questions that ultimately led to the discovery of penicillin.

A child might wonder why live oak trees seem to grow round seedlike structures on the underside of their leaves. At first glance, these structures might be thought to be acorns. But why are they attached to the leaf? Acorns are attached to the stem. Further study of this discrepancy—something that doesn't fit with our concept of an acorn or seed—will uncover oak galls, "tumors" created by the tree in response to the presence of an oak wasp's egg, laid on the underside of its leaves. From this, a substantive research project can grow.

Testing Hypotheses. Sometimes analogies and anomalies can suggest hypotheses. Just as "I wonder . . ." statements can raise questions for study of whatever is being wondered about, "I suppose . . ." statements can uncover hypotheses and hunches that can advance explorations. When observations come together to suggest meaningful patterns, hypotheses may develop. These are informed guesses at explanations.

For example, the same child who wondered what those growths on the underside of leaves could be, after observing a boring insect's hole in the smooth surface of several of these structures collected from different oak trees, might suppose that they are related to an insect. This supposition is the foundation of a hypothetical question: Is this seedlike object something that an insect grows in? The question now tests an explanation and fuels other questions, some of which test other interrelationships of variables and explanations (see italics): Which insect? *Does the insect make the structure, or does the tree?* What is the purpose of the structure? *Does it protect a developing larva?*

Asking Evaluative Questions. Questions formed from evaluative thoughts about the topic under study also advance inquiry. Evaluative questions often test the goodness or rightness of something. Editorials are usually written to explore an evaluative issue. So are provocative literary works.

For example, August Wilson has written several plays to explore questions about human choices. Throughout *The Piano Lesson,* Wilson (1995) asks his audience to grapple with the choice between maintaining tradition and pursuing change. He explores this universal dilemma through the sociocultural setting of an African-American family.

Through her bilingual poetry, Pat Mora (1986) engages her readers with tensions in the borderlands between Texas and Mexico, Anglo and Hispanic lifestyles, university and neighborhood environments, and professional and domestic situations.

Children raise evaluative questions about what the characters they read about do or don't do. After reading *Julie of the Wolves* (George, 1972), a child asks a question that shows her valuation of life with wolves over life with people: "Why didn't Julie stay with the wolves?" The question is loaded with opportunity for study of significant issues of human and animal lifestyles.

Question Sequences

One of the most sophisticated tasks in inquiry is learning how to build a series of interrelated questions that probe an idea. The best example of this is the well-done interview. Some adult interviewers know how to ask a question, listen for the answer, develop the next question from that answer, and continue in this way until the persons interviewed have thoroughly explained what they know or believe about a topic. This skill is not well developed in all interviewers or in most people. But it should be. And it can be.

With practice, children can learn how to ask questions that build on answers to earlier ones. They need to become good listeners, paying attention to what is being said and then turning the response into a question that meets their interests. For instance, an interview with a building construction worker might contain the following questions and answers:

Q: How do you make a door fit a house?

A: First, you have to build a frame.

Q: What is a frame?

A: It's like an outline of the door. You put the boards together to outline the place where the door will be.

Q: How do you put the boards together?

Or What kinds of outlines do you make for doors?

Or What types of boards do you use?

Or How do you support the corners?

Or . . . other questions that match the interest of the inquirer.

CRITERIA FOR EVALUATING STUDENTS' GROWTH IN QUESTIONING

Growth in questioning is easily measured when records are kept of questions asked during a search. Inquiry notebooks are good repositories of questions asked as theme studies proceed. Dated entries of questions recorded in individual and group notebooks can be compared with several criteria in mind:

1. Questions show attention to detail.
2. Questions clearly state what they seek to find out. They are unambiguous.
3. As the search develops, questions show more evidence of
   - ▼ comparison/contrast
   - ▼ hypothesis testing
   - ▼ use of analogy
   - ▼ exploration of anomaly
   - ▼ evaluation
4. As the search develops, a series of questions is formulated about particular subtopics, indicating intent to probe the subtopic and deepen understanding of particular issues.

MEETING REQUIRED STANDARDS

Classroom learning and teaching exist within a larger sphere. As teachers, you are held responsible for helping students to reach curriculum standards dictated by the school, the district, the state, or even the nation. These standards are usually developed within traditional subject areas, and they normally address knowledge, skills, and sometimes attitudes.

Any well-designed theme study will meet process standards appropriate for the grade level. Content standards, too, must be addressed as you plan theme studies.

Sources of Standards

There are a variety of sources for standards, which may form the basis for locally developed curriculum guides. Such sources could include

- ▼ national standards;
- ▼ standards developed by professional subject-area organizations, such as the National Council of Teachers of English and the International Reading Association (1996) and the National Council of Teachers of Mathematics (1989),
- ▼ state-adopted or locally adopted texts; and
- ▼ districtwide curriculum standards.

Such standards are usually based on current research, with input from a variety of interested persons, including teachers and parents.

Using Standards in Theme Studies

The pool of knowledge is expanding exponentially, and it is increasingly evident that in the modern world it is impossible to keep up with the constant flow of new knowledge. Content curricula are necessarily becoming more selective. For example, a fundamental premise of Project 2061 (Rutherford and Ahlgren 1990, p. xi) is that in science teaching "the schools do not need to be asked to teach more and more content, but rather to focus on what is essential to science literacy and to teach it more effectively." The notion of "less is more" undergirds much thinking about curriculum content, with an emphasis on depth of exploration rather than breadth of coverage. Theme studies can provide such depth.

No learning, however, is content-free, and so teachers have to look carefully at how content is taught within their own class, at their own grade level, and across the whole school curriculum. It is often tempting for teachers to select a topic for a theme study that is generally popular with students and well supported with resources and to teach it every year of a child's schooling. This can be counterproductive and repetitive for the learner. On the other hand, if it is a rich topic or theme, it can indeed be explored in depth at a variety of levels, with learners developing broader knowledge and deeper understanding of concepts over time.

For example, learning about families (both human and animal) can be approached from a variety of points of view at the various grade levels:

K: We live in families so that we can look after each other.
1:   Different members of families have different roles to satisfy the needs of each individual.
2:   Different kinds of families or groups behave in different ways according to their environment.
3:   Living things change throughout the life cycle.
4:   For survival, living things adapt to their environment.
5:   Change in any part of an ecosystem or community affects the entire ecosystem or community.
6:   All living things interact with and influence other living things.

Communication across grade levels is obviously essential. Some schools select a common theme, such as *Change* or *Diversity,* that is the focus for theme studies across the grades for a limited time period. Other schools draw up matrices to show how different themes become the focus for each grade level. In other schools, teachers or teams of teachers are free to select their own themes, but there is ongoing communication to ensure that each theme fits into the larger picture across the school and throughout a student's education.

REFERENCES

Barber, J., Bergman, L., & Sneider, C. (1991). *To build a house: GEMS and the "thematic approach" to teaching science.* Berkeley, CA: Lawrence Hall of Science.

Bloom, B. S. (Ed.). (1956). *Taxonomy of educational objectives: The classification of educational goals: Book 1. Cognitive domain.* New York: Longman.

Dillon, J. T. (1990). *The practice of questioning.* London and New York: Routledge.

Doris, E. (1991). *Doing what scientists do: Children learn to investigate their world.* Portsmouth, NH: Heinemann.

Gamberg, R., Kwak, W., Hutchings, M., Altheim, J. (with Edwards, G.). (1988). *Learning and loving it: Theme studies in the classroom.* Portsmouth, NH: Heinemann.

George, J. C. (1972). *Julie of the wolves.* Pictures by John Schoenherr. New York: Harper Trophey.

Golden, C. (1986). *American history grade 11: Course of study and related learning activities.* New York: New York City Board of Education, Division of Curriculum and Instruction.

Heine, A. (1984). *Teaching the easy way (the multi-disciplinary approach).* Corpus Christi, TX: Corpus Christi Museum of Science and History.

John-Steiner, V. (1985). *Notebooks of the mind: Explorations of thinking.* Albuquerque: University of New Mexico Press.

King, A. (1991). Effects of training in strategic questioning on children's problem-solving performance. *Journal of Experimental Education, 61*(2), 127–148.

King, A. (1994). Guiding knowledge construction in the classroom: Effects of teaching children how to question and how to explain. *American Educational Research Journal, 31*(2), 338–368.

Martinello, M. (1987). *The search for Emma's story: A model for humanities detective work.* Ft. Worth: Texas Christian University Press.

Martinello, M. (1992). *Cedar fever.* San Antonio, TX: Corona Publishing Co.

Milligan, B. (1990). *With the wind, Kevin Dolan.* San Antonio, TX: Corona Publishing Co.

Mora, P. (1986). *Borders.* Houston: Arte Publico Press.

National Council of Teachers of English & International Reading Association. (1996). *Standards for the English language arts.* Urbana, IL: National Council of Teachers of English; Newark, DE: International Reading Association.

National Council of Teachers of Mathematics. (1989). *Curriculum and evaluation standards for school mathematics.* Reston, VA: National Council of Teachers of Mathematics.

Ruef, K. (1992). *The private eye: Looking/thinking by analogy.* Seattle: The Private Eye Project.

Rutherford, F. J. & Ahlgren, A. (1990) *Science for all Americans.* New York: Oxford University Press.

Sanders, N. M. (1966). *Classroom questions: What kinds?* New York: Harper & Row.

White, E. B. (1952). *Charlotte's web.* New York: Harper & Row.

Whitin, P., & Whitin, D. J. (1997). *Inquiry at the window: Pursuing the wonders of learners.* Portsmouth, NH: Heinemann.

Wilson, A. (Producer). (1995). *The piano lesson* [Video]. Hallmark Hall of Fame Productions, Inc. Los Angeles: Republic Entertainment, Inc.

Chapter Five

Using Resources for Interdisciplinary Theme Studies: Print, People, Places, and Things

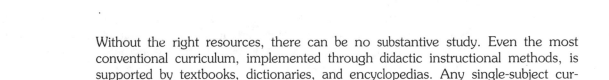

Without the right resources, there can be no substantive study. Even the most conventional curriculum, implemented through didactic instructional methods, is supported by textbooks, dictionaries, and encyclopedias. Any single-subject curriculum that is organized around questions requires at least teacher access to several data sources for students' exploration of those given questions.

Question-driven interdisciplinary theme studies demand much more. They require many and varied resources to support students' search for answers to questions that cross conventional disciplinary boundaries. The abundance and diversity of resources is often discovered during planning for theme studies because the interdisciplinary perspective allows teachers to see the potential for investigation in any source, no matter how closely it may be associated with a particular field of study. We present in this chapter several common categories of resources that are important contributors to children's exploration of interdisciplinary themes:

1. print resources,
2. interviews with people,
3. field sites,

4. artifacts and objects, and
5. experiments.

In Chapter Six, we extend this discussion to include resources for inquiry offered by

6. visuals, audiotapes, and audiovisuals; and
7. computer technology

Interdisciplinary inquiries accommodate different learning styles because their search for meanings encourages students to use many and varied resources. The several categories of resources that we discuss here appeal to one or more of the modes that differentiate our preferences and options for learning. While it is important to appeal to students' individual learning styles, a high-quality education guarantees that students enlarge their repertoire for learning. People should be able to direct their own learning in a wide variety of contexts and through widely different content. This is an inherent advantage of the interdisciplinary question-focused approach to curriculum development. Exploratory studies require students to search for clues in many sources, piecing them together to find meaningful patterns, moving students beyond the limiting goal of only finding specific answers to particular questions. The process of learning from diverse resources can encourage students to use many more than their preferred modalities. Students can enlarge their repertoires for learning as they interact with resources that invite multimodal learning. Learning how to gather information in different ways is like being multilingual.

According to recent neurological studies of memory and learning in the aged, experiences with multimodal learning early in life may be helpful in developing alternative neurological pathways for accessing and storing information that will serve the learner well into old age.

Regular use of the different types of resources discussed in this chapter can develop students' abilities to access information through aural, oral, visual, and tactile stimuli by establishing and reinforcing alternate neural networks for associational learning. The process of consulting various types of resources with questions in mind encourages students to rehearse the skills listed in Figure 5.1. Rehearsal builds toward mastery.

USING VARIED TYPES OF RESOURCES FOR STUDENT INQUIRY

There are four important considerations in selecting resources:

1. The resource is accessible to the students who will be using it; that is, the resource is locally available, and its difficulty level is appropriate to the

Figure 5.1
Habits of mind and thinking processes

Finding and keeping focus includes knowing how and when to ask questions and how to define problems in ways that can narrow or broaden the search for information. Comparing and contrasting and organizing or categorizing are important "skills" here.

Asking good questions is synonymous with clear thinking and its expression. Doing this requires thinking in multivariate and logical ways and expressing that logic through the syntax of questioning.

Simplifying questions and problems refers to skill in using symbol systems (words, numbers, or other symbols) to clarify the intent of questions and problems by isolating variables and stating predictions and hypotheses.

Being attentive is a habit of mind that modulates how we observe details, how we see wholes, and how we remember and imagine concrete and abstract images, sensations, and symbols. This habit of mind influences how we perceive and gather information.

Seeing anomalies is one of the most powerful tools for inquiry because it causes us to recognize and possibly question our assumptions. To see anomalous events or discrepancies, we must understand what we think we know and recognize challenges to that knowledge.

Thinking fluently and flexibly is open-mindedness in creative thinking that permits variations on the theme and paradigm shifts. Like the characteristic of attentiveness, this habit of mind influences abilities to look through different lenses to see from different perspectives.

Forming hunches is clearly concerned with predicting and hypothesizing and with sensing cause-effect relationships. This "if-then" anticipatory reasoning is mandatory in successful problem solving and decision making.

Designing tests and experimenting cannot be done without the ability to isolate and to test possible influences in physical events, in human performances, and in our thoughts. The act of "experimenting" in any medium involves data collection and analysis. It also enables the verification and evaluation of "findings."

Searching for patterns is the drive to see relationships, to find associations and to categorize, to infer and to generalize, and even to see the whole as more than the sum of its parts. Synthesis is an especially important process in this effort.

Using models and metaphors and *thinking by analogies* use imagic modes of inquiry to communicate and to explain the intangible or the incompletely understood. Associational and analogic thinking are processes that figure prominently in designing models and using metaphors.

Figure 5.1 continued

> *Finding elegant solutions* also demands the ability to synthesize and evaluate ideas in order to break through artificial complexities. This habit of mind values the aesthetic in thinking.
>
> *Taking risks* undergirds problem solving, decision making, and inventing, among a host of human activities too numerous to list. This affective dimension of thinking is present in all thought, to lesser and greater degrees, depending on the circumstances.
>
> *Cooperating and collaborating* and *competing* move to and fro in human thinking activities. Like risk taking, these emotional habits of mind can influence the way any thinking process or skill is used.
>
> *Persevering* and *having self-discipline* are at the heart of learning to learn. Without the exercise of these, a search cannot proceed far; only accidental learning is likely to occur.

students' abilities to use the resource. Generally, this means that the student can independently read, interact with, and interpret the resource. In other words, the resource is student-friendly.

2. The resource contains enough clues so that at least a few questions can be answered by gathering data from it.

3. Data gathered from the resource permit students to make informed inferences or hypotheses about the topic under study.

4. The resource suggests researchable questions. In addition to answering students' questions, the resource should cause students to formulate elaborative questions that build on the information gathered to deepen the search.

5. The resource may be combined with other resources to support student investigation of the theme study's big ideas and therefore to extend and expand student inquiry about the theme.

TEACHER ROLES IN THE USE OF RESOURCES FOR INQUIRY

One way to determine which role a teacher is enacting is to look at how resources for student inquiry are provided and used for theme studies: The teacher-director supplies all resources and tells students how to use them; the teacher-guide supplies initial resources and then helps students find additional ones, suggesting ways to draw information from them; and the teacher-mentor involves students in finding resources from the very beginning of their search, working with students to uncover the clues they contain.

The teacher-director role places the greatest burden on the teacher for finding resources and making them accessible to students. As teacher-director, you plan theme studies by formulating the questions students are expected to explore and by finding and assembling the resources needed to explore those questions—all or most of the resources that will actually be used by students. In this role, you are also responsible for making sure that students can use the resources supplied. When the only resources germane to a question are written at an adult level, you must choose whether to change the question to one for which there are available resources that are more accessible to the students or to translate the substance of the adult resources into language students can understand.

This dilemma was faced by a third grade teacher who wanted to develop a theme study on the origins of the Texas city in which she and her students lived. She defined the central questions for study and then searched for and found in local public, university, and research libraries an extensive collection of books written about San Antonio's native populations, the Spanish colonists, the establishment of early missions, and the establishment of the city's government; she found local historians who study different dimensions of the city's foundations who were available for interviews; and she obtained from the Bexar County archives official documents and personal papers testifying to the events pertaining to discovery of the place, the establishment of Catholic missions, the Spanish military presence, and the formation of the civil settlement. But none of these was appropriate to third grade levels in reading or comprehension. She tried reading some of the print material to her students, but they did not have the memory or organizational skills needed to retain the information, and she did not have the time to translate all the resources into written materials the students could revisit. She regretfully changed the topic of study from San Antonio to study of pioneers because she could find a wide variety of child-friendly resources on the latter topic.

Teacher-guides model methods for determining the types of resources needed, locating the resources, and extracting information from them that speaks to the questions students have raised about the theme. At the beginning of the study, as teacher-guide you provide a collection of initial resources that match the students' questions. But concurrently you ask the students to collaboratively determine what additional resources of different types may be used and where they might be found. While teacher-guides, like teacher-directors, frequently must secure most resources, as teacher-guide you also ask the students to obtain them wherever possible. The same progression in student assumption of responsibility for procurement of resources applies to their use: As teacher-guide, you may model ways to gather information from different types of resources, but then expect students to apply those models to the resources that they consult as they explore their questions.

Teacher-mentors may have the easiest role to perform in resource procurement. In the role of teacher-mentor, you expect students to determine the specific resources they need for their inquiries and to find the great majority of these. You may introduce students to additional resources that are more obscure, but the primary burden rests with the students to locate and obtain them. You work cooperatively with students in finding ways to draw information from these resources, frequently refining these methods as their inquiries become better focused.

For each of the resource types discussed in the following pages, all teacher roles apply. The selection of which role to enact is based on evaluation of student needs, including background knowledge pertinent to the theme and command of inquiry skills, and your own comfort levels with the theme, the resources, and the ways in which the resources will be used. It is possible and desirable for you to change the roles you perform as instructional situations change and especially as students become more proficient and self-directive in inquiry learning.

PRINT RESOURCES: TEXTBOOKS

For many years, textbooks have been the primary resource for student learning in classrooms. More recently, there has been a strong move to supplement or even replace class sets of textbooks with children's and adolescent literature, trade books, and other print and nonprint materials.

In interdisciplinary theme studies, textbooks are used as one important resource among many. Textbooks have many advantages:

- ▼ They present a large amount of material,
- ▼ The artwork and production are usually of high quality,
- ▼ They are written for a specific developmental and reading level,
- ▼ They contain a wide variety of suggested activities for teachers and students, and
- ▼ Supplementary materials are designed to accompany the text.

However, they also have disadvantages:

- ▼ Concepts and topics are often not explored in depth or detail,
- ▼ They do not usually engage students in inquiry,

▼ They are written for a very broad audience and therefore may not meet the needs or build on the experiences of specific groups of students, and

▼ Supplementary materials such as worksheets frequently test rather than teach.

With careful selection and focus, you can make textbooks a valuable and rich resource for student inquiry.

Selection and Focus

In many states and districts, certain textbooks are adopted for use in schools, and although teachers usually participate at some stage in the selection process, individual classroom teachers seldom have much choice in determining what textbooks will be available to them.

Teachers can, however, make choices as to how to use the textbooks. As we have seen in previous chapters, you can help students to select and organize materials from textbooks according to the main questions to be explored and the major generalizations to be learned.

A fifth grade class was engaged in a theme study in which the major generalization was Systems provide structure and organization. *As the students explored this theme, they found appropriate information in their social studies text, which addressed systems of government, and in their science text, which had sections on systems such as biomes, the solar system, the periodic table, and the control systems of the body (nervous and endocrine systems). The mathematics text provided information on Roman and Egyptian number systems, base five, systems of measurement, and various types of patterns.*

Learning to Learn through Textbooks

Students in the intermediate grades usually are familiar with the organization of textbooks and know how to find and use a table of contents or an index. They frequently do need help, however, in identifying the key words or concepts that will enable them to use an index effectively. For example, the key word *systems* may not appear in the index. If the children have been engaged in identifying the questions they wish to investigate or the areas they wish to explore, they can use the index more effectively. In the social studies text, they might look for key words such as *government;* in the science text, key words might include *biome* or *solar system;* in the mathematics text, students could look for key words such as *patterns, number systems,* or *measurement. Proficiency in word searching is equally applicable to effective and efficient internet use.*

PRINT RESOURCES: DOCUMENTS

In interdisciplinary theme studies, documents are an important primary resource that can complement and provide verification for secondary sources, such as textbooks, encyclopedias, and trade books.

Documents fall into several categories:

▼ *Personal documents:* letters, accounts, bills of sale, diaries, certificates, and so forth

▼ *Government documents:* Census reports, records, laws, rules and regulations, announcements, certificates

▼ *Business documents:* advertisements, catalogs, day books, accounts, correspondence, employment records

▼ *Church records:* baptismal, marriage, and death certificates; vestry minutes

▼ *Educational documents:* children's magazines such as *Ranger Rick,* National Geographic Society publications, informational leaflets, guides

▼ *Directories:* telephone directories, city directories

▼ *Newspapers and journals*

Documents may contain verbal, visual, and numerical information that students can use in their investigations.

Selection and Focus

Your responsibility as teacher is to work with the students to identify the sources for documents. This requires open-mindedness and creativity. Documents may be found in homes, schools, and businesses; in churches and hospitals; in stores and flea markets; and in government offices and service organizations. Some textbooks contain lists of resources that include documents. There are publications such as the *Educator's Guide to Free Materials* series (Educators Progress Service, 1996a–1996d) that list a wide range of resources, including documents. Libraries often have vertical files or special sections for documents. Often the best aid for locating documents is a willingness to look for information in likely and unlikely places.

In a study on Survival, *seventh grade students were investigating the question* How do weather and climate affect food production in different regions of the world? *They found a wealth of documents pertaining to the countries they were investigating not only from foreign embassies and tourist offices, but also from less likely sources, such as the United States Department of Agriculture. In their study of farming, they contacted food manufacturing and distribution firms that provided factual information about imports and exports and about food processing. Even the local supermarket was able to provide some written information about fruits and vegetables from different parts of the world, which contributed to the students' understanding of the relationships between climate and crops.*

Learning to Learn through Documents

Documents are usually written in adult language, and this can interfere with children's access to them. You can address this in several ways:

1. Read the document to the students. This may be useful as a short-term strategy, but it does not help students learn how to use documents.
2. Select parts of documents that are particularly relevant to the theme study, and provide additional supportive resources, such as visual aids, to help the students understand and use them.
3. Provide structured directions or study guides to enable students to find their way around the documents.
4. Teach students how to find information in documents. This should be taught in authentic situations where the students want to use the information to answer real questions. This is probably the most valuable approach in the long run because students can apply these strategies to other sources as they conduct their own individual or group inquiry.

The seventh grade students in their study of different geographic regions were impressed by the number of official-looking documents they received in answer to their letters to foreign embassies and tourist offices. They were also somewhat overwhelmed by some of the technical language and the statistics. The language arts teacher used these real problems to teach the students some word roots and suffixes that would help them to decode and comprehend unfamiliar vocabulary and reviewed strategies for using dictionaries effectively. The math teacher meanwhile used the documents as authentic data to be explored in the required study of statistics.

PRINT RESOURCES: LIBRARIES

Print sources other than textbooks are usually stored in some type of library, which often also provides access to electronic media. This may be as small as a class library or your own professional library. It may be a public library in the community, a government library, or a library attached to an institution such as a college or university, museum, historical site, or hospital. It may be part of a factory or business enterprise. It may be a national or international library, which is usually accessed through some type of electronic network.

Selection and Focus

Most classrooms have a limited class library, which often includes books from the teacher's personal library. Such a library is seldom adequate for a full interdisciplinary theme study. These resources need to be augmented either by bringing more resources into the classroom or by enabling the students to visit other libraries, either in person or through the electronic media.

Many public libraries have a policy allowing teachers to take out 30 or 40 books for a limited time for classroom use. Children's librarians at the local public libraries are often willing to identify appropriate materials in the children's and adult sections of the library and are also able to give valuable advice about electronic sources and search machines for student use.

Teachers may also find resources in local university libraries. Curriculum libraries, designed primarily for students in the teacher education program, often provide literature for young people and other print and nonprint materials that are appropriate for children's use. Local educational resource centers, which have good collections of print and nonprint materials, are another source.

It is not enough to bring books into the classroom. For one thing, the scope of the resources is necessarily limited by space and availability. More important, students who find all their information in teacher-provided books do not learn how to find their way around libraries.

For many children, the school library is often the first large library that they encounter, though families may introduce their young children to the public library as soon as they can enjoy books. The school librarian is an important member of the team for interdisciplinary theme study. It is a good idea to include librarians in early planning stages whenever possible, or at least to give them a copy of the broad scope and sequence of the theme study. The librarians can make sure that different grade levels do not need the same books at the same time. You might also invite the school librarians to attend the classes when the students brainstorm on themes and identify the questions they wish to investigate so that the librarians can identify appropriate library sources for the study. Some library books may be housed temporarily in the classroom for the duration of the theme study. Whenever possible, however, the students should go to the school library and learn how to locate the information they need.

Learning to Learn through Libraries

All libraries contain large amounts of information, usually cataloged in a variety of ways. Like any resource, it is necessary to learn how to use a library in order to retrieve information. These skills are best taught not in isolation, but as part of student research.

When working with students, you can help them to use libraries in various ways:

▼ by looking up material with your students;

▼ by collecting a limited number of books related to the focus of the theme study;

▼ by taking students to the relevant part of a library;

▼ by teaching students how to use catalogs, indexes, and electronic media;

▼ by working with students in a library situation and helping them to find specific information; and

▼ by teaching students how to get help in a library.

On occasion, it is valuable for students to go to libraries outside the school. In their study of different areas of the world, some of the students found a great deal of information at the public library, while one enterprising group contacted a local foreign-embassy official and gained access to the embassy library.

Any of these approaches may be appropriate at different times. Your main goal should be, in the short term, to enable students to find the materials they need to conduct their inquiries as efficiently as possible and, in the long term, to learn how to use libraries effectively.

INTERVIEWS WITH PEOPLE

People in all walks of life are usually willing to share their knowledge and their ideas with others. This human resource is perhaps the most readily available and least well used of all resources for inquiry.

Human sources on almost any subject include:

▼ professional experts,

▼ serious amateurs,

▼ people who have casual experiences with aspects of the subject.

Professional experts may be found in the Yellow Pages of the telephone directory and through local chambers of commerce, museums, reference libraries, and universities. Serious amateurs are usually located through clubs and volunteer organizations. People who have had casual experiences with many and varied subjects of interest for theme studies are all around us, in our communities, our neighborhoods, and our homes. To find them, ask, "Who do we know who might know something about this topic or be able to refer us to good sources of information?"

Selection and Focus

A key to finding human resources for an inquiry is found in the specific questions asked. The questions usually contain references to concepts. These concept labels are clues to categories of human resources. For instance, when the seventh grade students wanted to explore how climate affects food production, one of the questions they posed was *How are climate and weather interrelated?* The concept labels *climate* and *weather* are clearly associated with meteorologists. The students contacted the local weather broadcaster, and she agreed to be interviewed.

Learning to Learn through Interviews with People

Interviews can form the heart of an inquiry project.

A mixed fourth/fifth grade group of students was engaged in a Community Connections Project that focused on a local social service agency. Teams of children were set up, which included a team leader, a camera operator, a sound engineer who audiotaped the interviews, and two or three reporters. Each team was responsible for interviewing staff and clients in the daycare center, senior service center, or thrift shop. The teachers set up an initial interview with the center's director and took the team leaders along to make the first contacts. Then the teams had to take responsibility for scheduling visits and conducting interviews with staff, young children, and older adults, including some non-English speakers. The teachers provided support, but trusted the children to solve their own problems. Information gained through the interviews was later developed into HyperStudio© multimedia presentations. In reflecting on this experience, the teachers commented that

> *although the children grew tremendously over the course of this project, it was their teachers who learned the most. The sometimes frightening thoughts we had ("I don't know where this thing is heading! . . . Are we giving them too much to deal with?") were more than counterbalanced by the sense of pride and wonder we felt while watching them handle each situation with growing confidence and maturity. For students, it was a real-world experience that required very grown-up skills; for teachers, it was an exhilarating reminder that our real job is to teach them to get along without us (Junco & Cook, 1998, p. 30).*

Less formal interviews can be done by individuals or small groups of children who can talk with parents and other family members and neighbors in their homes. This encourages the students to develop skills of "visiting." To uncover the story of the life of a Texas farm woman, Martinello (1987, p. 211) found informal interviews useful:

> The people I interviewed preferred a conversational style, a style more appropriate to "visiting." Often, the person I was visiting would serve me food, and conversation would

continue over the table. Paper and pencil were my best ally for maintaining records of those conversations. The notes I made while conversing were cryptic, but as soon as I got home, I transcribed them. Then, to be sure that those notes were accurate, I sent the informant copies of the transcription with a self-addressed, stamped envelope and a request to review what I had written, make corrections and even additions as necessary, and return the notes to me. This proved to be a good way both to verify my understanding of what they had said and my recollection of how they had said it. It also sparked recollections that had not come to mind during our conversations. Several sets of notes were returned to me with significant additions.

Teachers who assign interviews for homework are pleased when students return to class with a sheaf of notes in hand. The notes are evidence of their ability to obtain information from human resources. Just as significant is the appreciation they express for the resource when they state, with the gleefulness of a brand-new realization and appreciation, "I didn't know my grandmother knew so much. I didn't think that she had so much to share."

FIELD SITES

Field sites offer rich opportunities for students to conduct investigations across the curriculum. At field sites, students can trace the history of a community, observe scientific principles in action, follow the workings of government, learn about the natural world, or develop an appreciation for art or music.

Field sites abound in any community. Think about the possibilities in your own community in each of these categories:

1. Sites designed to be used for educational purposes:
    Museums
    Nature and wildlife centers, including zoos
2. Sites that include an educational component:
    Public services (e.g., fire station, police station, courthouse, bus system)
    Businesses that have tours for schoolchildren
    Military bases
3. Sites designed primarily for recreation:
    Parks, including theme parks
    Sports facilities
4. Sites not primarily designed for educational purposes:
    Businesses (e.g., grocery stores, corner stores, specialty stores, department stores, offices, factories, farms, ranches)
    Neighborhoods (e.g., streets, houses, public buildings, recreation areas)
    Services (e.g., restaurants, medical services, auto repairs)
    Artisans (e.g., artists, musicians, potters, weavers, dancers)

Selection and Focus

As you plan field studies for your students, there are a number of important questions that should be considered.

How Do We Plan for the Field Visit?   Any field study requires careful preparation. Chicago's Field Museum of Natural History (Voris, Sedzielarz, & Blackmon, 1986) suggests the following steps in planning:

Get to know museums [or other field sites] in your area.

Decide why and where you are going.

Visit the [field site] before your field trip.

Make advance arrangements.

Introduce museums [or field sites] before the trip.

Practice perceptual skills.

Introduce field-trip subject.

Plan field-trip activities.

Review field-trip plans with chaperons.

Where Shall We Go?   The amount of choice and autonomy that a teacher has in selecting a field site varies from school to school. Some schools or districts specify the field trip for each grade level: the zoo for first grade, a museum for third grade, the symphony orchestra for fourth grade, a local historical site for seventh grade, and so on. This can make it difficult to use the field site for an investigative learning experience, but if you know in advance which field site you are required to visit, you can design interdisciplinary unit studies that incorporate the field site as a learning laboratory.

In other places, teachers have more choice, though choices are rarely unlimited. Early planning for the year allows for the selection of field sites that are the most appropriate resources for the theme study. In addition, popular field sites may become booked up early in the school year. Some field sites, such as local stores or nearby parks, can be used with minimum prior planning. They also have the advantages that there are no travel expenses and that the visits can be arranged on short notice to meet the needs of the students. The fourth and fifth grade students who conducted an investigation of a community social service agency were able to walk to the site. In another school, the housing project that was home for many of the students became a site for exploration of the murals that had been painted on the ends of each block and provided the students with new insights into their own culture and background.

When Should the Field Visit Take Place?   In some schools, there is an unfortunate tradition of scheduling field trips at the end of the school year. This may provide a pleasant day out, but minimizes the possibility of substantive learning.

Field studies should be organized to take place within a theme unit. It is particularly desirable that the field visit be scheduled far enough into the study for students to have sufficient background information and preparation to use the field site wisely, but early enough for the students to be able to use the information learned at the field site to illuminate and enrich other aspects of the study. The exact timing of a field visit within the theme study depends on its purpose. Sometimes a field study can come fairly early in the theme study, providing a starting point for investigation. Alternatively, a field visit later in the theme study affords opportunities for synthesis, extension, and application of earlier learnings. Ideally, any theme study should probably incorporate several field visits.

Who Should Go on a Field Study?   Anyone for whom it will be an appropriate learning experience should have the opportunity to make the visit, provided the trip is purposeful and a good use of the students' time. Frequently, all the students in a class or grade level go to the same field site at the same time. Where teachers work in teams, it may be more rewarding to take selected groups of students to a variety of field sites, even if limited time and money restrict each student to a single field visit. In the Community Connections Project described above, teams of fourth and fifth graders were assigned to various parts of the social service agency: the child care center, the senior center, and the thrift shop. Since the two grades were working together on this project, one teacher could accompany a small group to the agency, while the other groups stayed to work in the classroom with the other teacher.

Sometimes, particularly in the upper elementary grades and middle school, students are excluded from field visits because of behavior problems. Care should be taken to ensure that such students get other opportunities for field study, perhaps in more structured environments, and that while their fellow students are on the field visit, these students are engaged in rewarding and meaningful investigations at the school site. Such students often do well in a small group where they have a specific responsibility. In the Community Connections Project, a boy who had difficulty with self control was the only member of his team who could speak Spanish, and he therefore took a leadership role in his team's visit to the thrift shop, where most of the customers and many of the workers spoke only Spanish (Junco & Cook, 1998).

How Do We Get There?   This often depends on district policies. Sometimes school buses are chartered; at other times, students and teachers travel by public transportation. As we have seen, some field sites may be within walking distance. It is important to remember that the travel time itself should be an important learning time for the students as they go through an unfamiliar part of town or look at familiar sites through new "lenses" that provide different perspectives and added significance. Children who studied the murals in their housing project came back from their walking tour of the project where they lived saying, "I never saw that before!" and this suggested new questions to explore.

Learning to Learn through Field Visits

Field trips are probably one of the most popular and most misused activities in schools. While field study provides wonderful opportunities for students to engage in real research and relevant learning, a field trip is often perceived as passive entertainment, with learning being incidental.

Students need to be prepared so that a field visit becomes an interactive learning experience. This includes two types of preparation, which may be termed *logistical* and *educational*.

Logistical preparation includes setting rules and expectations so that the students know how to behave at the field site and on the way to it. When children are in unfamiliar settings, they feel insecure, and this insecurity often is displayed in inappropriate behavior. Students should be very clear about what to expect, what they will see, the schedule for the day, and how refreshments and bathroom breaks will be provided. You should discuss appropriate behavior, and students should have opportunities to ask questions about the logistics of the trip. Sometimes taking the responsibility for writing letters to inform parents or chaperons can help children to visualize the trip more fully and can allay some concerns they may not know how to articulate. Students can also be encouraged to develop their own standards for behavior so that they are clear about the expectations and can take some ownership and responsibility for the success of the field trip.

Educational preparation is part of the interdisciplinary theme unit. Before the students reach the field site, you should make sure that each individual or group knows clearly what questions they are investigating, how to conduct the investigation, and how to record their data.

An interdisciplinary team at an urban middle school in San Antonio, Texas, selected the San Antonio Missions National Historical Park as a focus for a theme study. Their central question was Why were the missions established? *This question led them to explore the theme of motivation. As they conducted their inquiries, they discovered a number of universal ideas:* Apparent motivations are not always the accurate ones; the design of buildings is related to their purposes; artistic design may emerge from deep conviction and dedication; religion and politics are often inextricably entangled. *The field trip they took to Mission San Jose was highly successful because the students knew exactly what they wanted to learn, the processes they would use, and the means for recording data. The field trip allowed them to explore mathematical problems (such as the dimensions of the compound and the height of the church towers), science concepts (such as the characteristics of natural and cultivated plants used by the mission Indians), and social science questions (such as how the Indians conducted their daily lives and why they chose to live at the missions). Every student was fully engaged in the investigation of his or her own questions, which had emerged from preparatory study so thorough that at times the students were even able to correct the park rangers, delighting both parties!*

ARTIFACTS AND OBJECTS

Artifacts and objects include just about anything that is tangible. Many people associate artifacts with times past. An old chair is an artifact, but so is one made by a living carpenter or in an automated furniture factory. Artifacts are generally defined as simple objects that show signs of workmanship or modification by humans, as opposed to natural objects (living and nonliving things not modified by humans). Whether natural or manmade, the things of our world hold clues to nonhuman and human life. They need not be old. A contemporary coin can tell as much about the culture in which it is used as an ancient coin tells about earlier people and their times. Artifacts and objects can spark inquiry by raising questions, and they can fuel inquiry when they are consulted specifically to find answers to questions brought to them.

Heine's elegant discussion of the interdisciplinary significance of a rusty nail, reproduced in Chapter Four, illustrates the power of objects and artifacts to spark inquiry. For decades now, museum educators have been encouraging people to learn how to "read" objects and artifacts to *detect* the information they hold. In the search for the story of an early-20th-century German-Texan farm woman's life, *The Search for Emma's Story* (Martinello, 1987), the author examined several *signpost* artifacts; the term denotes an artifact that guides a study by suggesting new directions for the inquiry. Several signpost artifacts in *The Search for Emma's Story* were interpreted: a wedding portrait, an empty medicine bottle, a list of home furnishings handwritten by Emma, and the house in which she lived. Each of these artifacts holds clues to understanding the woman, her community, her times, and her way of life. By attending to details, searching for patterns, and forming hunches, the inquirer was able to tease out those clues, form questions that led to other sources, and find interrelationships among the data obtained from the several sources. The habits of mind we term *being attentive, searching for patterns,* and *forming hunches* are critical to this process.

An old road can spark inquiry into its origins, the settlements along its route, its history of trade and transportation, the engineering that determined its construction, and the people who traveled its pathways or lived along its route, among a myriad of other factors that influence and are influenced by the built environment.

A middle-school theme study developed from inquiry into Los Caminos Reales in Texas, a network of Indian trails that became important routes for transportation and commerce during the Spanish Colonial period and have since merged with contemporary public highways. Some questions asked about that "King's Highway" include these:

- ▼ *Why was our community settled along the Camino Real, and how did it become linked to others along the route?*
- ▼ *What was the Camino Real used for?*
- ▼ *What caused changes in the modes of transportation and in the routes taken?*
- ▼ *Who were the people who settled our Camino Real community?*
- ▼ *What was the terrain and natural environment of the area like when the first settlers arrived? How did they adapt to it, use it, and change it?*
- ▼ *What effect has our area's climate had on its economy?*
- ▼ *How has the ecology of our area been altered by commerce along the road?*
- ▼ *What conflicts occurred when economic or cultural values clashed?*
- ▼ *How are these reflected in the myths and folklore of the cultures along the Camino Real?*

The clues that surface as the search proceeds lead to new questions, and each new question can impel inquirers to explore beyond the known and to consult additional sources.

Selection and Focus

Objects and artifacts for student inquiry are abundant and readily accessible in our everyday world. In addition to the natural life and manufactured items that surround us, there are artifacts in attics, closets, and flea markets, among the most obvious places. Replicas of artifacts can be purchased from museum shops and commercial distributors. Natural objects can be collected from the outdoors and obtained in quantities from scientific supply houses. Availability is not the issue—usefulness for inquiry is.

Whether working with living organisms, like the mealworms, butterflies, and grasshoppers discussed below, or artifacts, like Heine's rusty nail, the key process that enables learning from them is observation: careful, detailed, and precise. The better the observations, the more informed the questions. Therefore, when you use objects and artifacts, you must select them for the richness of the observational data that can be drawn from them. Following are some criteria for selecting objects and artifacts for students' inquiry:

1. Are there many observations that can be made by examining the artifact/object through the several senses?
2. Does the artifact/object encourage attention to detail?

3. Are there levels of observation supported by the object/artifact; that is, can the student look beyond the surface features to deeper features and, by so doing, enhance appreciation of the item?

4. Can the artifact/object be associated with students' experiential backgrounds?

5. Can the artifact/object be viewed through the lenses of different fields of study and occupations? Does each perspective uncover something new?

6. Can the artifact/object be complemented by other artifacts/objects to encourage students' comparisons/contrasts and detection of discrepancies or variations that prompt new questions about the item and its contexts?

Learning to Learn through Artifacts and Objects

Whitin and Whitin (1997) make the important point that observation is frequently given short shrift in discussions of higher-order thinking. Perhaps this is because sensory experience and knowledge, including visualization, are associated with animal behavior, whereas human thought is prized for the abstractions of linguistic interpretation. But observation is a core tool in many inquiries, whether in the sciences or the arts. Each of us observes the same thing in different ways, depending on our personal experiences, our individual perspectives, and our sensory acuity. Students need to know how to experience an artifact or object through different senses, what they can and cannot perceive about it, and how to unlock its mysteries.

Consider the following example of the use of objects in the fourth grade theme study:

"What better way to begin a study of animal growth and development in fourth grade than with living animals?" the teachers thought. They wanted the students to discover the concept of metamorphosis. The science textbook suggested observing mealworms to study the life cycle of the meal beetle, Tenebrio molitor, *illustrating metamorphosis. Mealworms can be obtained from pet stores and biological supply houses. The teachers had access to class quantities through their local teaching resource center.*

The reading textbook contained a story about frogs, another example of metamorphosis. Butterflies provided yet another example. Grasshoppers were selected to illustrate partial metamorphosis.

The teachers studied the mealworm's potential for observation by the students, gathering information about the insect and its life cycle from the textbook, from personnel in the pet stores that sold mealworms as food for pet birds and lizards, from literature provided by biological supply houses, from professional sources of ideas for science teaching, and from other teachers who had used mealworms for instruction. The teachers found an excellent source of ideas for using mealworms in the now classic Elementary Science Study teacher manual and kit entitled The Behavior of Mealworms *(1966).*

They filled large mayonnaise jars three-quarters full of bran, with apple or potato slices as moisture sources to encourage the mealworms to complete their metamorphic life cycle. They wanted the students to observe the exoskeletons that would pile on the surface of the bran as the mealworms shed them from 9 to 20 times during their larval stage. They also studied the opportunities for observation of monarch butterflies, tadpoles, and grasshoppers and planned to provide examples of these real organisms in the classroom for daily observation.

Their instructional goal was to stimulate the students' questioning about what was occurring as the mealworm metamorphosed into a beetle. When the students identified shared attributes of this life cycle with those of the monarch and the tadpole, they'd be close to defining metamorphosis.

Now they would present the students with a dilemma by having them observe the life cycle of the grasshopper as a metamorphosing insect. The children would observe that the grasshopper does not have a cocoon stage, although it does exhibit a marked change in its physical form during its development. This discrepancy would, the teachers thought, spark new questions about which changes are metamorphic and which are not.

When engaging students with artifacts/objects, several steps are worth holding in mind (though we ask you not to view these in a lock-step, linear order):

- ▼ Ask students to examine the item through as many senses as possible.
- ▼ Encourage students to look at the item through the lenses of many different disciplines and fields of study and occupations. Students may be led through an exercise that names a perspective and asks them to use that perspective for making observations and formulating questions.
- ▼ Once the surface qualities of an item are examined, ask students to look more deeply. This may require cutting or dissecting the item (if possible) or examining x-rays of it or paying attention to its context (e.g., where a fossil was found or the background figures in an old photograph) or its trappings (e.g., barnacles on an oyster or labels on a bottle).
- ▼ Develop question sequences with students, listing the first questions that were asked about an artifact/object and those that follow in a logical sequence. Record those "lines of questioning" to help students see how their ideas piggy-back and their questions become more probing as they see more and learn more about the item under examination.

EXPERIMENTS

Many experiments that are done in the elementary and middle school are usually done in science class as outlined by the textbook. Too often the answer is supplied, rendering the "experiment" an exercise and not a real investigation. Experiments can be done in social studies, the visual and literary arts, and mathematics, just as they are done in science studies.

Some experiments *test* the effects of isolating, manipulating, and controlling specified variables. Experiments in physics and chemistry are often associated with this approach to inquiry. When the purpose is to *identify* variables for later testing, more open-ended experiments are conducted. This type of investigation tends to be associated with qualitative studies in disciplines such as history and education. Qualitative experiments are also done in the arts, not with the language of numbers or words, but with the language of visual and tonal forms, designs, and styles.

Experiments in elementary and middle school classrooms typically appeal to students who learn well from the manipulation of equipment and the sensory experience of physical variables. Experiments are also meaningful to students who enjoy creating models and designing and testing inventions. These are often learners who prefer imagic modes of thinking.

A useful way to think broadly about "experiments" is to think about them as "learning activities" that encourage students to gather and interpret information. Many good "activities" that are offered in teacher's guides actually qualify as experiments, whether they ask students to gather survey data about some social issue, or make observations of animal or plant behaviors, or build a model paper airplane to test, or determine the mechanical advantage of a pulley. What distinguishes an experimental activity from nonexperimental activities is that the former always re sponds to an explicit question.

Selection and Focus

Questions determine the type of experiments you will help your students conduct. Some questions seek to simply determine facts: "How was this log house built?" Others test hunches: "Was this log house built to withstand the strong windstorms that are common to this region?" Both types of questions deserve attention, and you should encourage students to form questions that compare and contrast and search for interrelationships among identifiable variables.

Sometimes you need to help students restate their question so that it is possible to gather meaningful data. For instance, the question *Why does a plant have fruit?* needs to be focused through subquestions before answers can be discovered. As stated, the question offers no direction for isolating variables and collecting data. When asked in a more operational way, the question becomes researchable through direct experimentation. Some possibilities are as follows:

▾ Which plants form fruits?
▾ Where does the fruit come from?
▾ What happens to each part of the fruit as it ripens?
▾ What develops from moistened seeds? How long does it take?

These questions direct the inquirer to look at specific characteristics of plants and fruits. They will observe the plants they choose to study as they grow and form fruits, they can compare and contrast the fruit parts, and they can test the influence of time and moisture on new plant germination and growth, with increasingly sophisticated and controlled experiments.

Experiments that you demonstrate can produce data to help students answer their questions. Sometimes a teacher demonstration is the most efficient and safest way of gathering good data. But there is no substitute for students' active and personal involvement in experiments, where they take the role of experimenter.

You must also be aware of those experimental situations that require special precautions, skills, and equipment. When seventh grade students were involved in a theme study about the germ theory of disease in a microbiology laboratory course, the teachers had to prepare them to use the microscope. Special skills sessions were conducted in using this tool. The students also had to learn the skills of sterile technique, slide preparation, staining procedures, and general precautions for working with living microbes. Protective gear is needed even in the regular classroom during science studies. You need to prepare students to use protective clothing when necessary. Whether the gear includes goggles and lab coats for science experiments or smocks for experiments with art media, learning how and when to use them is prerequisite to inquiry that can proceed without distracting and potentially harmful accidents.

Learning to Learn through Experiments

Many of the ways of thinking that are most readily associated with inquiry are developed through experimentation. Almost every experiment requires students to

- ▼ formulate questions;
- ▼ make observations;
- ▼ compare and contrast;
- ▼ form hunches that will suggest predictions and become formalized as hypotheses;
- ▼ build models and use metaphors;
- ▼ isolate variables and, in some experiments, control and manipulate them;
- ▼ collect, record, and organize data;
- ▼ interpret data, making inferences from observations;
- ▼ evaluate hypotheses and form generalizations;
- ▼ report findings; and
- ▼ formulate new questions.

Use of probabilities by fifth graders during a study of deserts led to one group posing the question What are the chances of rainfall increasing in a desert area during the next decade? *Their teacher helped them use the data on conditions associated with rainfall in deserts and other areas and on weather conditions in the desert during each month of the year over the past ten years in order to make informed predictions.*

The stories the seventh grade students had been reading about how human beings deal with hardships caused one group to ask What kinds of hardships do students in our school have to cope with? *The group consulted the math and social studies teachers about ways to gather this information. The teachers suggested doing an experiment by conducting a survey on hardships experienced by their peers. The group set to work to develop a survey instrument that would provide quantitative and qualitative data. They trial-tested the instrument with their classmates. Their findings uncovered interesting information about hardships and also about flaws in their instrument. They redesigned the survey and trial-tested it again. When they were satisfied that it would gather the type of information they wanted, the students asked permission from the principal to administer the survey to all students in the school who were willing to complete it. The volume of data they collected was impressive and kept the students busy finding the most efficient ways of collating, analyzing, and reporting their findings. Their report revealed a number of severe hardship cases in the school that needed attention.*

The conventional resources of print, people, places, and things are readily available and easily accessible by teachers and children. Modern technology increases the variety and scope of available information, helping to broaden and deepen children's explorations in ways that were not possible in times past. These intriguing resources for inquiry that are offered by media and technology are the focus of the following chapter.

REFERENCES

Educator's Progress Service, Inc. (1996a). *Educator's guide to free health, physical education and recreation materials* (29th ed.). Randolph, WI: Educator's Progress Service, Inc.

Educator's Progress Service, Inc. (1996b). *Educator's guide to free home economics materials* (13th ed.). Randolph, WI: Educator's Progress Service, Inc.

Educator's Progress Service, Inc. (1996c). *Educator's guide to free science materials* (37th ed.). Randolph, WI: Educator's Progress Service, Inc.

Educator's Progress Service, Inc. (1996d). *Educator's guide to free social studies materials* (36th ed.). Randolph, WI: Educator's Progress Service, Inc.

Elementary Science Study. (1966). *The behavior of mealworms.* Nashua, NH: Delta Education.

Harcourt Brace Jovanovich. (1988). *The United States: Its history and neighbors* (HBJ Social Studies: Landmark Ed.). Orlando, FL: Harcourt Brace Jovanovich.

Hoffer, A. R., Johnson, M. L., Leinwald, S. J., Lodholz, R. D., Musser, G. L., & Thoburn, T. (1992). *Mathematics in action: Grade 5.* New York: Macmillan/McGraw-Hill School Publishing Co.

Junco, C., & Cook, G. (1998). Community Connections: The Madonna Center Project. *Primary Voices 6*(1), 24–31.

Kyvig, D., & Marty, M. A. (1982). *Nearby history: Exploring the past around you.* Nashville, TN: American Association for State and Local History.

Mallinson, G. G., Mallinson, J. B., Froschauer, L., Harris, J. A., Lewis, M. C., & Valentino, C. (1991). *Science horizons: Grade 5.* Morristown, NJ: Silver Burdett.

Martinello, M. (1987). *The search for Emma's story: A model for humanities detective work.* Fort Worth: Texas Christian University Press.

Voris, H. H., Sedzielarz, M., & Blackmon, C. P. (1986). *Teach the mind, touch the spirit: A guide to focused field trips.* Chicago: Department of Education, Field Museum of Natural History.

Whitin, P., & Whitin, D. J. (1997). *Inquiry at the window: Pursuing the wonders of learners.* Portsmouth, NH: Heinemann.

Chapter Six

Using Resources for Interdisciplinary Theme Studies: Media and Technology

Colorful and dynamic images, with good-quality sound, are delivered to us in our homes through televisions and personal computers. We find them just about everywhere we go, in almost everything we do, throughout the day and night. They are so plentiful and available that we tend to take for granted some of the richest resources for inquiry ever known. With these resources, children and teachers can greatly broaden their horizons.

VISUALS, AUDIOTAPES, AND AUDIOVISUALS

Still and moving images, with and without sound, are readily found and easy to use in the classroom. High-resolution still color images are abundant in magazines, books, and posters. For decades, photographs, maps, drawings, and filmstrips have been recognized as useful and inexpensive resources for teaching and learning. Additionally, videotapes offer moving images with narrative for student study. CD-ROM discs and videodiscs store great quantities of information in visual, audio, and audiovisual format.

By the age of 16, most children will have been entertained by television for more than 15,000 hours. The entertainment continues through their exposure to the sights and sounds of the movies, video games, videotapes, and audio record-ings. Children who have such multimodal experiences from their earliest days develop receptivity to audio and visual stimuli that prepares them for learning in dy-namic and multidimensional ways. These ways are dramatically different from the linear and print-oriented learning styles of earlier generations. Although the impact of audiovisual technology on children's cognitive development is often discussed and recognized by teachers, schooling continues to rely heavily on use of the printed text as the primary resource for student learning.

Visuals are so prominent in our communication media that we tend to take them for granted and do not always carefully evaluate the ones we use for instruc-tion. The same criteria that we suggest for any resource are applicable to visuals. In addition, visuals should:

- ▾ be unambiguous in their presentation of information;
- ▾ be large enough to be seen in the physical situation in which they will be studied;
- ▾ be rich in detail, displaying primary and secondary information;
- ▾ have aesthetic appeal; and
- ▾ engage the viewer's imagic thinking.

In his classic work simply titled *Visual Thinking,* Arnheim (1969) explains how visual thinking enables ways of knowing that are different from ways derived from thinking with words. McKim's (1980) innovative applications of visual thinking strategies to creative production describe images as vehicles for thinking that allow the solution of problems that cannot be solved with linguistic or numeric symbol systems. Visual thinking is a learning-to-learn process that requires early develop-ment along with the skills of reading text.

For dyslexic students and those with hearing disabilities, visuals take on added importance in learning. All students, but especially those with limited modalities for learning, need to develop the skills for probing the details and the full character of images. But they can learn how to use images for inquiry only when the visuals are good enough to support probing investigations.

Perhaps because television's audiovisual presentations are associated with en-tertainment, their use in the classroom has tended to be tangential—an add-on to the "regular" lesson. Whether in the classroom or living room, students have been invited to *witness* broadcasts or videotapes rather than to interact with their con-tent, to ask questions of their presentations, to discover patterns that enlarge con-cepts, and to critically explore their assertions.

Selection and Focus

When a living plant or animal or an inanimate object cannot be brought into the classroom, students can gain considerable information about the subject by study-ing its photograph or other graphic representation. The same is true of sounds and music and of moving images of dynamic actions and events that students cannot experience directly. Audiotapes, compact discs, films, videotapes, and laser discs bring exotic sounds and images to the student. These materials are frequently experienced in their entirety, partly because graphics, audio recordings, and audiovisuals are associated with entertainment. Most of us usually view photographs superficially, focusing on their central subject. People prefer to listen to an entire musical performance and to view a movie from beginning to end; the stage and movie theater continue in the age of television partly because they provide for relatively uninterrupted performances. At home we can mute the commercial intrusions into the sequence of events we are viewing. Rarely do people *study* parts of a recording, an image, or a selection from a film. The "entertainment" way of experiencing resources is inconsistent with education in general, and with interdisciplinary inquiry in particular.

An image may be full of details that contain clues to understanding its subject's context. Photographs, maps, diagrams, and other graphics can be studied for their background content as well as their obvious subject. For instance, a photograph of a picnic at the beach in the 1920s may contain visual information about the condition of the beach and its ecosystem and the ways people of the time dressed for swimming and played on the beach, in addition to information about who attended the picnic. You can help students to look beyond the obvious and to attend to details in any graphic. They also need time to read still images; the time needed to read a graphic may be substantially more than that needed to read a page of print.

At some point in the process of inquiry, audio recordings and audiovisuals need to be studied in segments. But some learners may prefer to hear and view them first in their entirety. The access style will be influenced by the learner's tendency toward analytic or holistic perception as well as by the material itself. But all inquiry requires attention to details within their larger context. The use of audiovisuals as resources for inquiry is no exception. At some point, the inquirer must search for clues that address particular questions and examine the most relevant parts of the resource.

Fourth grade students were investigating this question: How alike or different are the calls of birds of similar species who nest in different areas of the world? *When discussing ways to gather the necessary data, the children realized that they could record the calls of birds nesting in their own environment. The issue of how to hear the calls of birds nesting in distant areas of the globe required special reference material. Their school librarian found sources of audio recordings and videotapes that presented the types of birds the children were studying. Small groups assumed responsibility for selecting those parts of the audio- and videotapes that contained the sounds the class wanted to compare. They were able to record the appropriate reference for quick retrieval. During several whole-class sessions, each group presented its selection, and the teacher helped the class develop a comparative chart, noting the children's descriptions of the distinguishing characteristics of the bird calls they heard.*

Students with visual or hearing impairments are especially well served by audio or visual resources, respectively. Often people with sensory impairments have developed sharpened abilities to collect information through other senses. During theme studies that require the use of detailed audio or visual data, children with impairments may make valuable and unique contributions when asked to use their strongest sensory abilities to gather data for their classmates.

Bilingual students can make invaluable contributions to class inquiries that need information from non-English sources. For instance, when seventh grade students were studying similarities and differences between Spanish and Mexican cultures, they obtained documentaries on lifestyles in Spain and Mexico from Spanish and Mexican television stations. The English-speaking students were able to gather some data from the visual presentations, but their comparative study could go no further without Spanish interpreters. Bilingual Latino students in their class assumed responsibility for this; an important byproduct was peer-group recognition of the bilingual students' special expertise.

When fifth grade students asked about endangered species that could not be brought live into the classroom, their teacher immediately thought of still pictures and video. Sources of images on endangered animals are abundant in nature magazines such as Audubon, *in magazines published by the National Wildlife Federation, in the many trade books on animals for young and adult readers, and in posters and other oversized images that are readily available through catalogs, museum shops, and specialty stores. When the teacher and children had compiled all available sources, the teacher selected the images that were richest in visual information to encourage children's attention to detail and search for patterns.*

Transparencies for overhead projection can now be made in color, and 35-mm slides make clear and colorful large images when projected. A 35-mm camera can be used to produce slides or color prints that are usable in the classroom. The fifth grade teacher of our example was an amateur photographer who enjoyed visiting the zoo, her camera loaded with 35-mm color film, to make photos to complement the collection. Technological tools (discussed later in this chapter as resources for inquiry) allow transformation of visuals for different instructional purposes and for use in various instructional contexts. For instance, in addition to images made with digital cameras, color prints can be scanned, digitized, and modified, using programs like Adobe PhotoShop. These digitized images can be projected singly or in combination onto large screens or printed as color transparencies or large color prints. They are also useful in Hypercard stacks, in presentation programs, and on home-pages.

Some of the most useful images are made by the students because they pho-tograph subjects of study from their own perspectives.

A field trip to the desert conservatory of the local botanical gardens was sched-uled during the seventh grade study of climatic regions. The students used au-tomatic 35-mm cameras to make color slides of desert plants with observable adaptations for life in arid environments. Those images were later compared with pictures of desert plants in the trade books the teachers had borrowed from the library to search for commonalities and differences. The students dis-covered variations in the characteristics of spines on succulents that generated new directions for inquiry that the teachers had not anticipated. New sources, including Audubon Society videos, supplied some answers.

As the study of climatic regions progressed, National Geographic Society videotapes were found on climate in several illustrative regions of the world. The images were outstanding, and the narration was clear. Because not all of the regions the students were studying were represented, the teacher decided to have only those groups whose climatic regions were represented actually view the videotapes. They reviewed with the students the questions about cli-mate to keep in mind during the viewing and reminded them to record infor-mation that was pertinent to each question to share with classmates who did not view the videos.

Frequently, videotapes contain only segments that are pertinent to a set of questions students are exploring. Although viewing the entire video may be enter-taining, student inquiry is more productive if only the most meaningful excerpts are viewed—perhaps several times to uncover their full information. You may select those sections of the videos for student viewing. In some cases, you may prefer to have students determine for themselves the most useful sections of a video, to de-velop their abilities to cull the "wheat from the chaff" in a resource.

Audio recordings of various types of natural and manufactured sounds in our environment, musical forms, and the spoken word are also valuable resources. They have particular relevance for students who are visually impaired or who learn best through tonal modalities. The same types of considerations that apply to se-lecting visuals apply to audio recordings. They should:

▼ be unambiguous in their presentation of information;
▼ have auditory quality appropriate for hearing in the physical situation in which they will be studied;

▼ be rich in detail, offering primary and secondary information;

▼ have aesthetic appeal; and

▼ engage the listener's imagic thinking.

Audio recordings and complementary photographs offer means for teachers and students to collect data for their inquiries. Where camcorders are available, student-made videotapes that document a trip or an interview are invaluable for reviewing and verifying the data collected.

Learning to Learn through Audiovisuals

Visual literacy refers, in part, to the skills of observing and interpreting images. The best way to interpret a visual is to look at more than the subject of the image; the idea is to view the image as the image maker might have perceived it and to look beyond the subject to explore its depicted surroundings and the environment in which it was made.

During a fourth grade study of deserts, special emphasis was given to exploring changes that humans have caused in the environment. One group of students had access to dated photographs of similar locations in several desert environments. The photographs offered opportunities to compare and contrast observable changes in those locations over time. The population densities in one area had grown substantially more than in another, and the impact of human population growth had dramatically affected the natural environment. The students asked questions of these photographs that led them to understand what had happened in each location and why. By examining the details of each picture, the students were also able to infer why, when, and how the photographs had been made. Some of these inferences raised questions that led them to search the library for demographic and topographic maps of the regions and for newspaper accounts of events in the areas when the photographs had been made. By the time they were done, the students had discovered many of the changes that accompany the economic development of an area.

Being visually literate is more than knowing how to observe and interpret visual images. It means knowing and using graphic language. Kyvig and Marty (1982) describe the expressions of visual language as light and shadow; color and texture; line, shape, and pattern; similarities and contrasts; and movement.

Tufte's *The Visual Display of Quantitative Information* (1983) explores the "pictures of numbers"; his *Envisioning Information* (1990) examines "pictures of nouns," and *Visual Explanations* (1997) is about "pictures of verbs." Tufte explains informational graphics as having a vocabulary of its own. Ability to "read" that visual language is critically important to drawing information from visual resources.

As the fifth grade students continued their study of endangered species, they were able to visit a local art museum where they could view a special exhibit on paintings, photographs, and sculptures of wildlife. The teacher guided the students to gather information about the characteristics of each depicted endangered animal—a skill of seeing details—and also to view the artworks in terms of the artists' use of light and shadow; color and texture; line, shape, and pattern; similarities and contrasts; and movement—elements of the visual vocabulary.

In addition to visual language, the language of sound influences our ways of learning and knowing. Audiovisuals are as much an auditory medium as a visual one. Listening for pitch, volume, and timbre can heighten our sensitivity to a piece of music. Sensitivity to those tonal elements in a movie's background music can increase the listener's understanding of the meanings the music contributes to the images it accompanies. Attentiveness to nuances in spoken language helps us to detect the implied as well as the explicit meanings of human talk.

We mentioned earlier in this section how important it is for students to interact with a video or audio for learning, rather than being passive viewers. Learning is an active process that requires work. The mentality of students who interact with video presentations in order to find answers to their questions is entirely different from the attitude of those who want entertainment. Teacher-directors, teacher-guides, and teacher-mentors all work toward the same purpose of encouraging students to learn from video presentations by selecting segments to experience (teacher-director) or helping students select segments to experience (teacher-guide) or reviewing videos with students to cooperatively select the most meaningful excerpts (teacher-mentor). In all of these roles, you can also help students organize their methods of culling information from audiovisuals by using graphic organizers.

We have found that students frequently lose sight of the questions they want to study when they are distracted by the multidimensional content of audiovisuals that were designed to entertain and not to answer students' questions. But students respond well to anchors. And the best anchors are their questions. The skill they must learn is to view and listen for information that matches their questions. A simple divided page with questions on the left side of the centerfold and space to record clues on the right works well and is easy to prepare. Like any skill, extracting pieces of information from audiovisuals takes practice, but the principle is simple: Keep your question front and center no matter what sensory diversions a videographer uses to distract your attention. Advertisements are excellent training aids. Students who learn how to avert the grip of those who want to sell a product will become intelligent consumers as well as successful inquirers.

COMPUTER TECHNOLOGY

The *Educational Testing Service 1997 Annual Report* (1997) makes several stunning predictions about students and their use of technology in the 21st century:

- ▾ By the year 2000, three million students will take a portion of their instruction over the Internet.
- ▾ By the year 2005, it will be possible to navigate the entire college application process by computer, including interactive communications with the campus.
- ▾ By the year 2020, virtual reality simulations of professional environments will be standard instructional tools in most universities.
- ▾ By the year 2025, global universities will provide instruction via computer and television, and students will be able to access a tutor by computer or take any subject from teachers and professors all over the world.

These predictions, by themselves, argue for developing student abilities to use computer technology effectively. When you consider the ability of technology to exponentially increase the resources that teachers and students can access to support their inquiries, its value is compounded for interdisciplinary theme studies as we define them.

A persistent instructional problem has been the unchanging sequential form of the most common audiovisual materials. It is usually more difficult to access a section of a videotape than a page in a book. It is often harder to obtain a sustained and repeating view of a moving image than to examine a printed graphic in a textbook. But developing technology is changing that. Enter the personal computer as a powerful tool for learning.

Computer technology has many and varied applications and forms. In this chapter, we discuss only a few of the technological tools that have special significance for students' interdisciplinary theme inquiries. Each tool is examined in broad contexts on the assumption that their particular forms will change dramatically as research and development efforts succeed in producing more efficient, more powerful, and more economical resources based on intuitive and user-friendly design principles that substantially simplify the interface between the user and the machine. These qualities of the computer should make it a particularly valuable learning tool for intuitive learners. Computer programs may be able to engage students who have been disadvantaged by their intuitive preferences (notably girls) with the study of subject matter such as mathematics and the physical sciences that traditionally is not taught in ways that appeal to the intuiting mind. The tools we believe will have continuing relevance for interdisciplinary theme studies include word processing and spreadsheet programs, CD-ROMs, multimedia and interactive multimedia, networking, and the Internet.

Selection and Focus

Several decades ago word processing, graphics, and spreadsheet programs; CD-ROMs; multimedia and interactive multimedia; and networking were recognized as opening new vistas for learning. The possibilities for their development in the 21st century could drastically change schooling and unquestionably enhance and expand the processes of inquiry. These remarkable resources can connect students with the larger world to make their explorations more substantive and more challenging. The tools offered by personal computing, if used with imagination, can even help students exceed many of the curriculum standards that have been formulated in times of more limited resources for teaching and learning.

Word processing programs encourage different ways of composing. Most people who do "electronic" writing differentiate the "feel" of composing on the computer from writing with paper and pencil or with the typewriter. Format preferences, multiple fonts and print styles, layout and editing options, and spell-check programs offer the writer a full desktop of tools, easily found and used. Their availability frees the writer to concentrate on the expression of ideas. Students can make many drafts of their written work, saving each to floppy disks for editorial review and comments by many different readers, such as peers, parents, and teachers. Word processing programs make it possible for students to keep, organize, collate, and share notes on their explorations, create several drafts of their writing, and produce clean and professional-looking final copies of individual and group work. When combined with graphics programs, students may add their own illustrations and clip art to enhance the presentation of their findings. Spreadsheets offer students ways to do the same things with quantitative data and their graphic expression. The implications for learning to learn are many, as discussed below in "Learning to Learn through Computer Technology."

The enormous reserves of print and visual information that are contained on CD-ROMs literally bring the libraries of the world into the classroom, including many archives of special collections that were once reserved for use by scholars. Students conducting an inquiry into almost any theme can gather information from diverse primary and secondary sources through CD-ROM technology.

When eighth grade students who were studying World War II wanted to know the different points of view about the war, they asked their school librarian to help them find resources. The librarian first acquainted the students with CD-ROM encyclopedias to help them focus their search and frame their questions. The students phrased a number of researchable questions: How did the people in different parts of the United States view the reasons for the impending war in 1939? How did this compare with people in Germany? Great Britain? France? How did attitudes change in 1942? What changes in opinion were occurring in 1945? What about today? The librarian was able to obtain CD-ROM collections of American newspapers from major metropolitan areas for the years the stu-

dents had selected. He also began searching for similar resources for British, German, and French populations. As the students' inquiry continued, other resources were found in audiovisuals, extending the exploration to other groups in the class; the inquiry continued for the full school year.

A particular value of CD-ROM resources is their combination of audio, visual, and print data. Technology makes it possible to experience phenomena on demand. CD-ROM encyclopedias can present movie clips, including cross-section and x-ray views, that illustrate the written text.

Patrick Lynch (1991), of the Yale University School of Medicine, makes a case for the computer's abilities to meet individual learning needs because students interact with the applications, directing each according to their unique interests and preferences. Lynch refers to the terms *hypertext* and *hypermedia,* coined by Nelson in 1974 (Nelson, 1987), as "nonsequential documents," containing audio, print, and visual material that the computer can search for, retrieve, and interlink to form a "web of information." Interactive hypermedia programs invite students to select foci for study from arrays of questions. Through a system of linked "cards," students may access print, graphic, and audiovisual resources for their study in any combination and sequence they choose. Students may add resource options as they discover them, enhancing the program during their inquiries. There is a striking parallel here to our concept of interdisciplinary theme studies. The interdisciplinary inquiries that we are recommending are specifically designed to guide students through the exploration of questions and ideas in nonsequential ways by consulting diverse resources through varied learning modalities. Throughout the process, students should discover meaningful patterns in the webs of information they construct and interpret. Computer technology can aid this process, helping students to develop the habits of mind we describe as critical to self-directed, lifelong learning.

An increasing variety of commercially produced interactive multimedia programs can allow students to interact with persons, places, things, and phenomena that are not typically available to ordinary people. Some multimedia programs invite students to conduct experiments that formerly were done only in uniquely outfitted research laboratories having highly sophisticated and costly prototype equipment. For instance, interactive multimedia programs permit students to explore the action of an object in zero gravity, alter the variables in an ecosystem to determine their effects on the inhabitants and the habitat, test proofs of mathematical theorems, apply principles of design to invent solutions to problems such as architectural and mechanical problems, perform simulated dissection and surgical procedures, experiment with models of dangerous substances, and even experience some characteristics of life in different places during past, present, and future eras. Many of these programs invite students to take the role of detective to research questions about human experience, all forms of life, and the physical world.

Sally Narodick and the Education Team of the Edmark Corporation (1992) offer a clear set of criteria for selecting software for students, which they compiled from studies of educational software for young children. The criteria have equal relevance for older students and, indeed, for all people who use educational software for learning. Formulated in the early days of educational software development for children, they remain pertinent and helpful:

1. *Can the individual use the software easily and independently?* Narodick and her associates prefer graphic and spoken instructions for children so that reading skill is not a prerequisite for computer-assisted learning.
2. *Is the software open-ended and exploratory?* The idea here is that the user should be able to control the software's pace and path. Further, the software should invite students to experiment and to think creatively about what they are doing.
3. *Can the software "grow" with the student?* Software programs that are developmentally appropriate permit students to explore varied concepts in different ways and on different levels of complexity.
4. *Does the software provide quick reactions to selections?* Students should be able to use the entire screen, exploring different components of the visual presentation and receiving responses that are immediate.
5. *Is the software technically sophisticated?* Programs should appeal to students' multisensory ways of learning. The computer's capabilities to make presentations in print, sound, still graphics, and moving images should be used fully to capture and hold the user's attention.
6. *Is the software appropriately challenging?* Programs that are worth using invite sustained exploration. Ideally, they should impose no ceiling on the potential for learning through their use.
7. *Is the program lively and entertaining?* This criterion refers to the program's ability to encourage students "to use their imaginations, to explore, and to laugh" (Narodick et al., 1992, p. 7).
8. *Does the program build self-esteem?* All learners need to feel successful and to experience empowerment through learning. The best programs *guide* students to find answers to questions, rather than giving them the answers, and always meet student responses with positive and constructive feedback.

The hypertext and hypermedia authoring tools that commercial producers use to create the types of multimedia programs referred to above are also available to the teacher and student. They are becoming increasingly easy to create and to use. Their special value is their ability to make resources accessible in forms that students can understand. When teachers create hypertext and hypermedia programs for their students, they select and focus the presentation of resources to reduce students' frustration in dealing with quantities of data that may be overwhelming to the novice researcher, while still providing enough challenge to motivate the students' drive to wade through extraneous information. For instance, in an eighth grade theme study of *Ethnic Conflict* in the United States during World War I, a well-designed hypermedia program might offer students several articles about German-Americans from different newspapers around the country circa 1917–1918, a selection of letters and diaries written by German-Americans during that time, and film clips from audiovisual documentaries about the U.S. involvement in World War I that deal with issues of distrust of Germans (e.g., the official renaming of German measles as "liberty measles" and dachshunds as "liberty pups"). The same type of selection and focus would present accessible primary sources to students searching for patterns of ethnic distrust in the treatment of Japanese-Americans during World War II.

Teachers who want students to consult sources on a theme like *Migration* might construct a HyperCard stack that includes some of the main questions and subquestions that they and the students have identified, with access to resource files including film clips, maps, data tables, oral histories, legends, drawings, and other resources that contain clues to the migratory patterns of the people or animals under study. In effect, hypermedia allow teachers and students to compile and access any of the resource types discussed in this chapter.

Virtual reality further expands the opportunities for extraordinary experiences that are available to ordinary people. Students may visit places that once were reserved for the most affluent and elite or were unapproachable by human beings, entering those environments with full sensory stimulation. So, for instance, students may walk through a technological simulation of the Palace of Versailles or the Taj Mahal; they may visit a Brazilian rain forest or the Sahara Desert; they may enter the human circulatory system, moving through arteries, veins, and vital organs with the blood flow; or they may look inside an erupting volcano or experience an earthquake. Immersion in these simulated environments can effectively offset the limitations imposed by learning disabilities or physical handicaps.

There is, of course, no substitute for students' direct experience with a resource in real time. But by bringing distant, unique, and precious resources within the reach of every student, technology can effectively equalize the opportunities of all students to use resources that once were not available to even the wealthiest and most privileged.

Networking connects people electronically across large distances around the world. Technology makes it possible for students in villages, towns, cities, the barrios and ghettos of large metropolitan areas, and even remote areas of the world to communicate instantaneously and over time with others. The implications of interstate, interregional, and international networking for interdisciplinary theme studies are enormous. Networked students can collaborate, contributing their questions, resources, and ideas to one another's theme studies. Through their "electronic conversations," participants can share their knowledge, resources, questions, and perspectives with one another. The use of technology to link people for collaborative learning in this way may serve to develop multicultural insights, values, and appreciations as a natural outgrowth of students' shared experiences during the search for knowledge, information, and truth that is the process of inquiry.

Of all the tools made available by computer technology, the most useful to inquiry is the Internet, and especially the World Wide Web (WWW). Educators often decry the way electronic tools tend to drive teaching and learning when they should be helping us to solve instructional problems where conventional methods have failed. In the realm of cyberspace known as the Web, we have a promising means of solving a long-standing problem in inquiry: accessibility of resources.

Successful inquirers are quick to remind the novice that, no matter how much a question intrigues you, it is futile to inquire about it if you cannot access meaningful resources that pertain to the issue. Not very long ago the only people who could pursue exotic studies were funded researchers who could physically travel to distant libraries, archives, and laboratories to find needed materials, equipment, and people to inform their explorations. But now, thanks to the WWW, there are many places, including libraries, archives, laboratories, and more, that any traveler can visit on the magic carpet supplied by an Internet-linked desktop computer. For teachers and students, this tool increases exponentially the types and quantities of resources available for almost any study. Of course, in the free speech environment of the Internet, unsavory, unethical, and even vile sites are present, but they should not distract from the larger value of innumerable sites that are laden with useful information and ideas. Teacher and parent oversight of student travels on the Internet may be easier, with electronic monitors, than control of their travels through, for instance, pornographic literature.

If intelligently used, according to the highest ethical standards, computer technology can become an aid to the democratization of educational opportunity. As a resource for interdisciplinary inquiries, this increasingly sophisticated technology can increase the depth of students' interdisciplinary inquiries.

Learning to Learn through Computer Technology

As indicated in the preceding section, computer technology has the ability to appeal to symbolic, imagic, and affective modes of thinking. Its multimodal qualities allow the student to determine which mode to use; it also enlarges the learner's opportunities to develop other modalities. Technology can help us "see" sound by presenting tonalities in graphic representation and "hear" visuals through the electronic representation of sounds associated with still or moving visual images. Virtual reality enables kinesthetic-sensory and audiovisual stimulation. "Electronic conversations" across political and cultural boundaries cannot fail to involve the affective dimensions of cooperation, competition, interpersonal relationships, and cultural interactions. The very character of computer technology appeals to and encourages intuitive thinking, even when the content may be presented in analytic ways. As all these abilities develop, the learner becomes more proficient and, in many ways, "smarter."

Developing these abilities is becoming as important as developing students' reading, writing, and computing skills. Beyond the basic skills required to use a mouse and keyboard, to work with the computer's operating system, to use various application programs (including word processing, presentation, and Web site development programs), and to operate the ancillary equipment (such as printers, external drives, and scanners, among others), some critical skills for successful use of technology in conducting, recording, and reporting inquiries are those of searching and navigating and of visually organizing. Their underlying abilities include verbal logic and visual thinking.

Searching and Navigating.   Teaching students to search the WWW means helping them learn to make associations and to link ideas in conceptual hierarchies and acquainting them with helpful search engines, directories, and reference tools.

One group of fourth graders was exploring the produce section of a neighborhood supermarket chain. One of their first questions was What kinds of produce are sold at our neighborhood market? *Their first inclination—a very appropriate one—was to search for the supermarket's Web site, which they found. It supplied information about produce specials advertised for a particular week and a couple of veggie recipes to encourage purchase of the specials. This prompted questions the site didn't answer, such as* Why is the cost of strawberries so much higher than the cost of any of the other fruits on sale? *The students' dilemma was where to look next. Now their teacher needed to supply descriptors (the teacher-director role) or help them name descriptors they might use to find other informative sites (the teacher-guide and teacher-mentor roles). Acting in the teacher-guide role, their teacher asked the students to list what words they thought they could use to find information on strawberries. The students suggested "strawberries" and recorded it. Then the teacher asked if they knew where strawberries are grown: They associated the fruit with California and recorded the state name. Then the teacher asked them what could influence the growth of a fruit. The students responded, "The weather," and listed that. The teacher asked what the weather had been like in California over the past few months. This stumped the students, realizing that they needed to find out about weather in California. But how?*

Rather than giving them the Web site address for NOAA (the National Oceanic and Atmospheric Administration), <www.noaa.gov> , as a teacher-director might do for students who need to find the source of their information quickly and easily, the teacher, as teacher-guide, suggested some search engines to try:

Alta Vista <www.altavista.com>
Excite <www.excite.com>
HotBot <www.hotbot.com>
Infoseek <www.infoseek.com>
Lycos <www.lycos.com>
Webcrawler <www.webcrawler.com>

The teacher also suggested expanding the list of descriptors by searching *Roget's Thesaurus* at <www.thesaurus.com> and finding information on strawberries in the *Encyclopedia Britannica* at <www.eb.com>.

Now the students had many options for searching: strawberries, California, weather. As they gained information about what strawberries need to grow and the climatic influences of the equatorial currents associated with high atmospheric pressures, called El Niño, they began to interrelate variables of climate, growing conditions, availability of foodstuffs, and market prices. At this point, their teacher suggested that they organize their ideas into a hierarchical flowchart (this is discussed in the following section on visual organization). In the spring of the school year, a class of sixth grade students visited a local wilderness trail that some of the students had visited the preceding June. The returning visitors noticed that something was missing: "Where had all the hummingbirds gone?" they asked. The students found that hummingbirds spending the summer months in central Texas migrate south to Mexico and other parts of Central America in the winter. This led to wondering about how these little birds are able to make such long trips. So they used the obvious search term, "hummingbirds," and found <www.derived.com/~lanny/hummers>, where there was information about the aerodynamics of the hummingbird's wing. The next question became How are hummingbird wings and flight patterns different from those of other birds? This comparative thought required moving to a larger category: bird flight. This descriptor led to the Audubon Web site, <www. Audubon.org>, where they found additional references to the aerodynamics of bird wings and migration patterns. By articulating their questions, the students were able to define the conceptual categories they needed for searching the Web in a productive way.

It's easy to get lost on the Internet. Just by clicking a button that looks interesting, students may find themselves detoured to a place distant from the source of answers to your questions. Questions can serve as anchor, so it's helpful to keep them out front, so to speak, written down for ready reference, and to be able to remember the variables contained within the topic being studied.

In a sixth grade study of education in rural America of the 19th century, teacher and students formulated a series of questions into question sets, with central questions and subquestions, as follows (Babb, 1998):

1. *How did physical characteristics of the one-room schoolhouse influence its past and present use?*

   Where were the one-room schools located in central Texas?

   Who built and maintained the schoolhouses?

   How were the schoolhouses constructed and appointed?

   What has become of the one-room schoolhouse structures today?

2. *What characterized a day in the life of a student in a one-room school?*

   Who came to school as students?

   What was the daily schedule?

   Where did students have lunch and what did they eat?

   How did students entertain themselves?

   How did the students' responsibilities compare to those of students today?

3. *Who taught in the one-room school?*

   What were teachers' credential requirements and how were teachers compensated?

   How were teachers expected to act and live in the community?

   What were the teachers' responsibilities both in and out of the classroom?

   How and why did the profile of the one-room teacher change over time?

4. *How does historical one-room schooling compare to education today?*

   What lessons were the students taught?

   What methods were used to teach the students?

   How did the teacher manage several grades in a single classroom?

   How did the teacher discipline and punish the students?

   Was the school work more challenging than lessons are today?

5. *What role has the one-room schoolhouse played in the history of education in Texas?*

   When did one-room schooling begin in Texas and why?

   How did governance of one-room schools change over time?

   Why do one-room schools exist today and how successful are they?

   In what ways, if any, can present educational practice benefit from the study of historical one-room schooling?

By keeping these questions in high prominence while searching for resources, students were able to remain focused on the variables that were central to their study, the variables that their questions sought to test: school construction, school populations, teacher characteristics, curriculums, and so on.

Visually Organizing.   Students can benefit from being taught how to visually organize the information they gather to show connections between and among ideas. The conceptual web is one tool frequently used to show the many connections among ideas. Another is the Venn diagram, which helps to find the critical mass of a set of categories—the shared features of the things compared. Less frequently used is the conceptual flowchart, which differentiates smaller from bigger from biggest ideas.

The students who were studying the reasons for the unavailability of strawberries in their supermarket's produce section were able to keep track of their ideas by visually recording the hierarchy of their concepts. They jotted down associations as they continued to explore their issue. But they did not record them randomly or by simply listing the ideas. They placed them in relation to one another to show their hierarchical categories of meaning. Therefore, they saw for themselves that while they started with strawberries, this built to a higher-order category linking weather and produce supply, which, in turn, led to an even higher-order category linking produce supply with pricing. The students were, in effect, uncovering big ideas as they developed their flowchart, some of which helped them to form informed hypotheses to test.

As mentioned earlier in this chapter, word processing programs empower students to create many drafts of their written work, editing them with one another's help as the writing process proceeds. In networked situations, students share their creative productions with others and serve as critics for one another, offering reactions and raising questions for constructive feedback.

Graphing programs allow students to enter data from direct experimentation or secondary sources that are instantly converted to graphs and charts that would take considerable time to construct by hand. The clear advantage is the reduction in time between the actual collection of data and an opportunity for its interpretation.

Perhaps the most long-lasting contribution that technology can make to students' ability to learn derives from its invitation to create. Animations may be made and edited by individuals or small groups working cooperatively. Photographs and graphics may be scanned into a printed text. Moving video clips can be imported into hypertexts. Computer technology offers many possibilities for creative synthesis and presentation of research findings.

Whether students make audio recordings of an interview, take snapshots of an event, videotape an experiment, construct a hypertext, or use any combination of technological tools to collect data during their inquiry or to synthesize and present their findings through a culminating project, they will be using increasingly complex thinking processes. Students' use of technology to construct materials that communicate their learning requires them to plan as teachers do, bearing in mind the needs of their audience while they work with the language and ideas of their selected content. When well done, student products have a professional, "high-tech" appearance that can be a reward in itself for the producers. The skills learned can also be used to help others, thereby teaching social responsibility and the value of giving.

A group of first grade students had enjoyed talking with an author of picture books they had read with their teacher. One of the parents recorded those conversations with a camcorder and showed the children the videotapes. Excited by these images, the children asked for help in making a "movie" of their "Talks with Writers." One child thought that most people wouldn't know what the talks were about unless they had read the books. She suggested that the interviews be added to a presentation of the stories themselves. Another child recalled the storybook programs they had been using, in which particular illustrations serve as "buttons" to reveal additional contextual information. So, with the help of several fifth graders who had created multimedia programs, the children and their teacher created their own version of living books. They scanned selected illustrations from the books themselves, decided which segments of the illustration to program, created additional illustrations to enlarge the text, and added video clips from the children's interviews with the author. As one child observed, the program looked like the ones he had seen on TV, where the author talks about the story after the story is told. These first graders shared the completed program with other children in their school. Its presentation, with large-screen projection, was the highlight of a local school board meeting.

Projects that use the electronic tools of technology to present student work need not be as ambitious as those described above. The key to learning to learn through technology is its use to construct and communicate meanings. It makes little sense to improperly use electronic equipment to do what a paper and pencil or chalkboard does sufficiently well. But when instantaneous, multidimensional, and multimodal service is needed to clarify varying types of data, large quantities of information, complex content, or abstract ideas, computers are tools with special advantages for teaching and learning.

REFERENCES

Arnheim, R. (1969). *Visual thinking.* Berkeley: University of California Press.

Babb, L. (1998). *Teacher's guide to the Van Raub Schoolhouse.* Unpublished manuscript.

Educational Testing Service (1997). *Educational Testing Service 1997 Annual Report.* Princeton, NJ: Educational Testing Service.

Kyvig, D., & Marty, M. A. (1982). *Nearby history: Exploring the past around you.* Nashville, TN: American Association for State and Local History.

Lynch, P. (1991). *Multimedia: Getting started.* Sunnyvale, CA: PUBLIX Information Products for Apple Computer.

McKim, R. H. (1980). *Experiences in visual thinking* (2nd ed.). Monterey, CA; Brooks/Cole.

Narodick, S., & the Education Team. (1992). *Parent's guide to educational software for young children.* Redmond, WA: Edmark Corp.

Nelson, T. (1987). *Dream machine/computer lib.* Redmond, WA: Tempus Books.

Tufte, E. (1983). *The visual display of quantitative information.* Cheshire, CT: Graphics Press.

Tufte, E. (1990). *Envisioning information.* Cheshire, CT: Graphics Press.

Tufte, E. (1997). *Visual explanations.* Cheshire, CT: Graphics Press.

Chapter Seven

Engaging Children in Inquiry

PRINCIPLES OF INQUIRY

Interdisciplinary theme studies are designed from the belief that the most meaningful education, especially for life in the 21st century, is

- ▼ integrated, finding meaning in the ways that the content of the several fields of study is interrelated;
- ▼ holistic, focusing on principles, theories, laws, issues, and questions that have universal significance;
- ▼ inquiry-oriented, inviting students to explore questions through varied types of research, to use diverse resources, and to develop their thinking processes; and
- ▼ constructivist, enabling students to derive their own meanings through the studies they are given and those they are encouraged to develop for themselves.

These premises are elaborated in the 14 principles of learning that the American Psychological Association (1998) has drawn from empirical research on learning. Each principle applies as much to the teacher as to the student engaged in the inquiries that drive interdisciplinary theme studies. No matter which of the roles on the teacher role continuum you enact, you are learning about the content of a theme along with your students. As you engage children in inquiry, you, too, are learning how to become an increasingly effective inquirer.

The American Psychological Association's (Learner-Centered Principles Work Group, 1997, pp. 4–8) principles are as follows:

1. The learning of complex subject matter is most effective when it is an intentional process of constructing meaning from information and experiences.
2. The successful learner, over time and with support and instructional guidance, can create meaningful, coherent representations of knowledge.
3. The successful learner can link new information with existing knowledge in meaningful ways.
4. The successful learner can create and use a repertoire of thinking and reasoning strategies to achieve complex learning goals.
5. Higher-order strategies for selecting and monitoring mental operations facilitate creative and critical thinking.
6. Learning is influenced by environmental factors, including culture, technology, and instructional practices.
7. What and how much is learned is influenced by the learner's motivation. Motivation to learn, in turn, is influenced by the individual's emotional states, beliefs, interests and goals, and habits of thinking.
8. The learner's creativity, higher-order thinking, and natural curiosity all contribute to motivation to learn. Intrinsic motivation is stimulated by tasks of optimal novelty and difficulty, relevant to personal interests, and providing for personal choice and control.
9. Acquisition of complex knowledge and skills requires extended learner effort and guided practice. Without learners' motivation to learn, the willingness to exert this effort is unlikely without coercion.
10. As individuals develop, there are different opportunities and constraints for learning. Learning is most effective when differential development within and across physical, intellectual, emotional, and social domains is taken into account.
11. Learning is influenced by social interactions, interpersonal relations, and communication with others.
12. Learners have different strategies, approaches, and capabilities for learning that are a function of prior experience and heredity.
13. Learning is most effective when differences in learners' linguistic, cultural, and social backgrounds are taken into account.
14. Setting appropriately high and challenging standards and assessing the learner as well as learning progress—including diagnostic, process, and outcome assessment—are integral parts of the learning process.

Interdisciplinary theme studies should be true to these principles. Those that are in-quiry-driven certainly will be. Perhaps one of the most convincing arguments on the educational integrity of interdisciplinary inquiries is how clearly and naturally they speak to the principles, discussed here by their major categories.

Cognitive and Metacognitive Process (Principles 1, 2, 3, 4, 5, and 6)

A theme study that is inquiry-oriented will encourage students to use a variety of thinking processes to gather information from diverse resources and to make sense of that information and the learner's experiences with the content of the study. Making sense of that content includes discovering concepts and the interrelationships among concepts that form big ideas. Making sense of the process requires learning how to talk about thinking and consciously thinking about your own thinking.

Theme studies are selected by teachers and students for their pertinence to their linguistic, cultural, and social contexts. Inquiry cannot proceed if the resources that support its explorations are not accessible in the learner's context.

Motivational and Affective Factors (Principles 7, 8, and 9)

Learner interest is of paramount importance in selecting theme studies. Your children's questions and your own speak to personal interest, which supplies intrinsic motivation to find out and to persevere when learning becomes difficult.

Developmental and Social Influences (Principles 10 and 11)

Interdisciplinary inquiries for theme studies are designed to draw from and develop student interests, which determine the direction inquiries take. Team research efforts encourage collaborative explorations of subquestions.

Individual Differences (Principles 12, 13, and 14)

Interdisciplinary inquiries, by definition, require the use of varied strategies, approaches, and skills. Different learners perceive subtopics of theme studies differently, select different ways to explore them, and naturally bring their linguistic, cultural, and social differences to bear on searching for answers to their questions.

The individual differences of teachers are also well served by interdisciplinary inquiries, as the continuum of teacher roles attests. You select those ways of engaging children with inquiry that best match your preferences for teaching practice, the needs of your students, and the characteristics of the content you are studying.

The same may be said of assessment: The search processes of interdisciplinary inquiries offer many opportunities for diagnostic, process, and outcome assessment as a study proceeds. Most occur naturally as you and your students, in detectivelike fashion, take stock of the clues you've uncovered, what you have learned, and what else you need to do to find answers to unanswered questions.

ESSENTIAL COMPONENTS OF INTERDISCIPLINARY INQUIRIES IN THEME STUDIES

The several components of interdisciplinary inquiries that make them theme studies have been presented and discussed earlier in this book. They are summarized here for emphasis because how they contribute to a theme study greatly determines how well that study meets the principles of learning discussed by the American Psychological Association. So we ask you to keep these in mind as touchstones for deciding how you will engage your students in inquiry.

Big Ideas

The inquiries provided by interdisciplinary theme studies must support student discovery of big ideas: generalizations, principles, laws, theorems. Each big idea that a curriculum purports to develop should meet the following criteria:

1. It is true over space and time.
2. It can broaden the students' understanding of the world and what it means to be human.
3. It is interdisciplinary.
4. It can lead to student inquiry.

Those big ideas will be discovered by the inquirers as they explore their questions, sort out their clues, and figure out how the meanings they're uncovering fit together to explain what the findings mean.

Questions

Questioning drives inquiry. Therefore, the substance of any interdisciplinary inquiry can be measured in direct proportion to the depth of the questions asked. The entire range of thinking processes—lower and higher order—contributes to question asking, as described in Chapter Four. So does the use of logic, which links questions and answers and builds new questions from what is known or has just been learned.

Resources

Accessible resources are essential for any inquiry to proceed beyond the superficial. You will sometimes determine resources for inquiry before you formulate or ask your students to formulate questions for study. In Chapters Five and Six, we discussed several types of resources that can engage students in meaningful explorations. Our categories include the following:

▾ print resources;
▾ interviews with people;
▾ field sites;
▾ artifacts and objects;

▼ visuals, audiotapes, and audiovisuals;

▼ experiments; and

▼ computer technology.

The number and type of resources used in an inquiry are limited only by the imagination of the inquirers. Therefore, we recommend that you help your students to think broadly about sources of information for their questions. Good resources invite students to search for the less obvious clues and answers to their subquestions. As subquestions are answered, the collected answers should help the inquirer better understand the full meaning of the central question that is built from those subquestions. As each central question is answered, the collected answers to all central questions should help students better comprehend the generalization or big idea.

UNIT STUDIES

A fourth grade teacher chose to develop his students' concept of *Adaptation* with the big idea stated as follows: *All living things adapt to their environment.* This generalization meets the criteria for a big idea:

1. *It is true over space and time.* It is possible to study adaptation over eras of human experience. It is also possible to study the evidence of adaptation in plants and animals that is presently observable.

2. *It can broaden the students' understanding of the world and what it means to be human.* Adaptation is an essential part of all life and of the human condition. Children have already experienced adaptation in their own lives as they grow and develop and as they enter new environments like school or a new class.

3. *It is interdisciplinary.* The study of adaptation can pertain to humans and to plants and animals, dealing with social as well as biological and ecological content.

4. *It can lead to student inquiry.* Children are intrigued with the ways that living things adapt. They wonder about the responses of animals and other living things to different environments.

In addition, the generalization also meets established curriculum requirements:

▼ *Adaptation* is a content standard in the *National Science Education Standards* (National Research Council, 1996, 155). This important concept frequently appears in science textbooks and local school district curriculum guides.

▼ *People, Places, and Environments* is one of the ten major themes in the *Curriculum Standards for the Social Studies* (National Council for the Social Studies, 1994). Textbooks in the social studies describe the ways people adapt to different physical and social environments.

▼ The *Standards for the English Language Arts* (National Council of Teachers of English & International Reading Association, 1996, p. 3) propose that students "develop an understanding of and respect for diversity in language use, patterns, and dialects," again providing opportunities for students to explore the ways by which people adapt to their linguistic and literary environments.

The design process now turns to developing the unit studies in more detail. In a question-driven, inquiry-oriented curriculum, these units are headed by questions. Our example uses *central questions* and *subquestions* to compile sets of activities designed to engage students with resources in which they can find clues and answers to the subquestions. This should put them on the road to developing better understanding of each central question.

Questions may be formulated in sets or sequences. A *question set* is comprised of a central question with subordinate questions, all of which are interrelated and intimately connected to the central question. A *question sequence* is a series of questions that are derived one from the other, representing a chain of reasoning—sometimes branched, sometimes linear—that develops as the inquirer's knowledge of the topic grows from consulting increasingly informative resources.

When teachers plan units for inquiry learning, they typically start with question sets because these may be logically defined and related to specific resources. Question sets represent a journalistic approach to inquiry and require some knowledge of the topic. Question sequences, on the other hand, do not require background knowledge of the topic to ask the initial question. They may start with elementary fact-seeking questions or with more advanced questions and then build more informed questions as the inquiry proceeds.

At the start of a unit, question sets can be developed by the teacher, by the students, or by the students and teacher in collaboration. In the role of teacher-director, you define most, if not all, of the question sets and identify all of the resources prior to the start of a study. As a teacher-guide, you involve students in identifying initial question sets, provide some resources at the start of the study, and ask students to formulate additional question sets and sequences as the study proceeds. By contrast, as a teacher-mentor, you are least likely to start a study with question sets, even those posed by students, with or without teacher consultation, opting instead for question sequences formulated by students as their knowledge of the theme increases. Question sequences occur only after students become engaged with resources—they are products of that engagement. Therefore, only question sets will appear in initial written plans. There is no standard number of question sets or sequences in an interdisciplinary theme study. Most unit frameworks for inquiry would have at least five, and some may have ten or more, depending on the length of the unit, the skills and needs of the students, and the availability of meaningful and accessible or student-friendly resources.

A sample unit framework for the generalization about *Adaptation* with two initial question sets appears in Figure 7.1. Note that the question sets are *initial* ones. As students develop their inquiries, additional subquestions will be formulated, and

Figure 7.1
Initial question sets for unit on theme: Adaptation

Unit Study: Adaptation

Unit Concept: All living things adapt to their environment.

Central Question 1: Why do some animals live in our area all year long and other animals don't?

Subquestions:
1.1. What is the place where we live like?
1.2. What are the characteristics of animals that live here (in South Texas) all year round?
1.3. What are the characteristics of animals that live here (in South Texas) only part of the year or not at all?
1.4. How are animals that live here all year long different from those that don't?

Central Question 2: How do people in different times and places obtain the food they need?

Subquestions:
2.1. What are the nutritional needs of human beings?
2.2. How did people in South Texas obtain the food they needed in prehistoric times?
2.3. How did people living in South Texas around 1900 obtain the food they needed?
2.4. How do people living in San Antonio today obtain the food they need?

---

new resources will be found to deepen the study. Most important, new question sets must be added to broaden the search. Variations will result from the role you select to best meet your students' needs and your comfort levels with the subject matter, theme studies, inquiry learning, and learner capabilities, interests, and needs.

LEARNING ACTIVITIES

After central questions, subquestions, and resources are in place, you decide how to engage students with resources to explore the questions. These *methods* become the bases for several lessons during the unit study and offer you options for lesson planning, keeping in mind several guidelines for interdisciplinary instruction:

1. Provide for different ways of knowing and thinking.
2. Maximize interdisciplinary connections among the subjects.
3. Stay true to the standards of the regular curriculum.
4. Use various resources for student inquiry.

Figure 7.2 shows examples of question sets and resources for a theme study on *Adaptation* with resources.

Figure 7.2
Initial question sets, resources, and sample activities
for unit on theme: Adaptation

Unit Study: Adaptation

Unit Concept: All living things adapt to their environment.

Central Question 1: Why do some animals live in our area all year long and other animals don't?

Subquestions:
1.1. What is the place where we live like?
1.2. What are the characteristics of animals that live here (in South Texas) all year round?
1.3. What are the characteristics of animals that live here (in South Texas) only part of the year or not at all?
1.4. How are animals that live here all year long different from those that don't?

Sample Resources and Activities (for inquiry-learning, activities are ways of engaging students with resources to find answers to their questions and to develop understanding of their questions):
1.1 What is the place where we live like?

Resources:
- ▼ Seasonal weather maps
- ▼ Local meteorologists
- ▼ www.NOAA.gov (National Oceanic and Atmospheric Administration)
- ▼ Science textbooks
- ▼ Geological survey maps
- ▼ Geological descriptions of the area
- ▼ Local geologists (from company, college, university)
- ▼ Street maps of the locale
- ▼ Local developers and real estate agents
- ▼ State wildlife and parks department rangers

Activities:
- ▼ Chart the climate of the region or make a yearly time line or map showing climatic zones.
- ▼ Make topographical maps of the area.
- ▼ Explore how much land in your region remains natural, how much contains homesites, and how much is used for industrial and commercial purposes.

Figure 7.2 continued

1.2 What are the characteristics of animals that live here (in South Texas) all year round?

Resources:
- ▼ State wildlife and parks department rangers
- ▼ Local nature trail or wildlife preserve
- ▼ Guidebooks to native animals
- ▼ Local bird watcher
- ▼ Ornithologist
- ▼ Reference books on the mockingbird
- ▼ Mockingbirds that live nearby
- ▼ Videos on mockingbirds
- ▼ Legislation that named the mockingbird as the Texas state bird
- ▼ Zoo education director
- ▼ State parks department consultant
- ▼ Reference books
- ▼ National Wildlife Federation materials
- ▼ Specialists who study specified animals
- ▼ Nature videos that depict the living needs and conditions of each animal studied
- ▼ www sites

Activities:
- ▼ Create list of native animals that are year-round dwellers. Select several to study.
- ▼ Inquire into the life cycle, characteristics, and needs of a native year-round bird (e.g., mockingbird), a native mammal (e.g., bobcat), a nonmigratory insect (e.g., moth species), a native reptile (e.g., horned toad).

1.3 What are the characteristics of animals that live here (in South Texas) only part of the year?

Resources:
- ▼ Maps of flyways
- ▼ Local hummingbird enthusiasts
- ▼ Reference books on the hummingbird
- ▼ Hummingbird feeders
- ▼ Migratory routes
- ▼ Zoo consultants
- ▼ The local zoo
- ▼ Reference books
- ▼ World Wildlife Fund
- ▼ Nature videos on big cats, butterflies, reptiles, as appropriate
- ▼ www sites

(continued)

Figure 7.2 continued

Activities:	▼ Study the life cycle, characteristics, and needs of a migrating bird (e.g., hummingbird), and native to the area (e.g., tiger), insects that migrate (e.g., monarch butterfly).

1.4 How are animals that live here all year long different from those that don't?

Resources:	▼ Local consultants who are specialists on each of the animals under study who can critically evaluate information collected and organized by students and who can respond to students' new questions
Activities:	▼ Chart the characteristics of local nonmigratory and migratory birds. Make time line of life cycle and qualities. Map locations at different times of year.
	▼ Chart the characteristics of selected native and non-native mammals.
	▼ Chart the characteristics of migratory and nonmigratory insects. Make time line of life cycle and map locations at different times of year.
	▼ Chart characteristics of native and non-native reptiles.
	▼ Analyze charts to determine
	▼ how natives are different from non-natives
	▼ how natives are suited to climate, terrain, and qualities of your habitat
	▼ List all the reasons for success of natives in your area.
	▼ List questions that remain unanswered about why natives remain in your area and non-natives or migratory species do not.

Central Question 2: How do people in different times and places obtain the food they need?

Subquestions:

2.1 What are the nutritional needs of human beings?

2.2. How did people in South Texas obtain the food they needed in prehistoric times?

2.3. How did people living in South Texas around 1900 obtain the food they needed?

2.4. How do people living in San Antonio today obtain the food they need?

Sample Resources and Activities

2.1. What are the nutritional needs of human beings?

Resources:	▼ School nurse
	▼ Dietician
	▼ American Heart Association

Figure 7.2 continued

	▼ Local hospitals, cancer societies, etc.
	▼ Science texts, reference books
	▼ Doctor, family medical encyclopedias
	▼ Magazine articles on famine
	▼ Seeds, small plants, carrot tops, potatoes
	▼ Calorie/fat charts and other nutritional information

Activities:
- ▼ Interview the school nurse or a local dietician.
- ▼ Write to organizations for free materials on nutrition.
- ▼ Develop a chart showing how the body uses food: proteins, carbohydrates, fats, vitamins, etc.
- ▼ Interview a doctor, read magazine articles on famine, and look up symptoms of deficiency diseases to discover what happens if people do not get the nutrition they need.
- ▼ Grow food plants and experiment with feeding them with different types of plant food to explore effects of nutrition on food plants.
- ▼ Keep records of children's own diet and nutritional needs and that of family members of different ages (babies, adults, old people).

2.2 How did people in South Texas obtain the food they needed in prehistoric times?

Resources:
- ▼ Witte Museum: exhibit on prehistoric people of the Lower Pecos Valley
- ▼ Archeologists from local universities or historical societies
- ▼ Plants and rocks typical of the Lower Pecos Valley

Activities:
- ▼ Visit the Lower Pecos Valley exhibit at the Witte Museum to identify types of food, food collection (hunting, gathering), and means of food preparation.
- ▼ Interview archeologists and explore books and the Internet to discover what types of edible animals and plants lived in the Lower Pecos Valley.
- ▼ Experiment with tool making from materials available in the Lower Pecos Valley.

2.3 How did people living in South Texas around 1900 obtain the food they needed?

Resources:
- ▼ Sauer-Beckmann Living History Farmstead; Lyndon Johnson State Historical Park
- ▼ *The Search for Emma's Story* (Martinello, 1987) (Teacher's resource)

(continued)

Figure 7.2 continued

	▾ Historians in Johnson City and Fredericksburg
	▾ Local natural food stores; scales, measuring cups, etc.
	▾ Old recipe books from libraries, bookstores, relatives
Activities:	▾ Visit Sauer-Beckmann Living History Farmstead to identify types of food grown and livestock raised on the farm.
	▾ Write letters or interview authorities by telephone to identify types of food not available on the farm.
	▾ Experiment with means of food preparation at the farmstead using basic ingredients.
	▾ Experiment with ways of preserving foods at the farm by making simple ice boxes and jams, jellies, and preserves.

2.4 How do people living in San Antonio today obtain the food they need?

Resources:	▾ Local supermarket
	▾ Local distribution centers or wholesale markets
	▾ Maps showing food production; road, rail, and air transportation routes
	▾ Local dairy farms and produce farms
	▾ Local farm cooperatives, local ranchers associations
	▾ Food packers
Activities:	▾ Visit local supermarket and interview manager to identify sources for meats, produce, groceries.
	▾ Interview managers at local distribution centers to find out about transportation routes, financial operations, scheduling, etc.
	▾ Construct a map to show local sources for dairy products and produce.
	▾ Interview local farmers and ranchers to find out where and how they distribute their products.
	▾ Make a chart showing the nutrition value of modern packaged foods.

Now you have a foundation for learning activities. In our view, learning activities provide the structure for student interactions with resources. The teaching methods used determine how students actually consult resources to explore their questions. Depending on the resources to be used, the pedagogical questions become the following:

▾ How will students gather information from print materials?

▾ How will they interview people?

▼ How will they gather data from field sites?

▼ How will they observe and interpret artifacts and objects?

▼ How will they read visuals, listen to audiotapes, and gather information from audiovisuals?

▼ How will they experiment?

▼ How will they use computer technology?

In order to answer each, you determine what prerequisite skills and knowledge your students must have to profit from the resource, how long they can be expected to stay engaged with the resource, and what the expected outcomes are. A plan for a learning experience includes the statement of the theme, unit concept, central question, subquestion, learning outcomes, learning activity, and follow-up.

Learning Outcomes

If you think about all the things you can explore starting from almost any learning activity, the likelihood is that you'll find boundless possibilities for individual learning by students, depending on their prior experience, their developmental level, their abilities, and their interests and aptitudes. However, teachers are accountable for knowing what students are expected to learn, and statements of anticipated outcomes help to provide direction and criteria for the learning activity. As the theme study develops, student inquiry will indicate new directions for exploration. These emergent outcomes need to be recognized by the teacher, who will then select and relate them to the major focus of the study.

There are three main types of outcomes, which address

▼ the factual content to be learned,

▼ the processes and skills to be developed, and

▼ the intellectual and affective mentalities to be nurtured.

These are closely interrelated in any activity. It is unlikely that students will learn content without using cognitive processes or experiencing the impact of attitudes, interests, and appreciations. However, for the purpose of accountability and clarity, it is helpful when you articulate the specific projected learning in each category.

Notice that these outcomes are not written in terms of exactly what the students will *do,* as is the case in some behavioral objectives. This difference arises from the philosophical and pedagogical basis of the inquiry-driven curriculum. The focus is on the students' understanding of

▼ concepts and significant "big ideas,"

▼ modes of inquiry skills, and

▼ habits of mind that lead to continued exploration and investigation.

The learning outcomes structure the way students will work with the resources and therefore engage in inquiry processes. For example, Figure 7.3 is an outline of a learning activity for inquiry about the theme *Adaptation*. One of the unit's central questions is *Why do some animals live in our area all year long and other animals don't?* This lesson plan is designed to engage groups of children (organized by seasons of the year) in exploring *What is the place where we live like?* (subquestion) by consulting weather maps (resource) and compiling found data into a chart (graphic organizer). The question, resources, and means of involving students in collecting data from those resources are determined by the specified learning outcomes, which propose to develop students' knowledge of the climate and terrain of their geographic area and skills in reading and interpreting weather maps. All components of this learning activity for inquiry are logically interrelated: Learning outcomes are specifically matched to the question under exploration, and the question is matched to a particular type of resource. Especially important here, the learning outcomes specify both knowledge (concepts and big ideas) and process skills (modes of inquiry). This keeps the activity closely tied to the question because it anticipates some of the "answers" children will find and the map-reading and -interpreting skills they must use to find those answers.

It seems self-evident, but many an inquiry has gotten off track because the resources were not well matched to the questions. Whether in the role of director, guide, or mentor, you serve your students well by reminding them to keep referring back to their questions, so that, when resources entice them to take interesting detours, they won't lose sight of the course they originally set for their studies.

Concepts and big ideas.   A learning outcome related to concepts and big ideas may be worded as *The students will know that. . . .* This phrase is important. Note that the teacher is required to state with precision the content that will be learned. For example, a content objective for one of the learning activities in the activity cluster described above might be *The students will know that people adapt to geographic challenges by relocating, by diversifying, and by using technology.* Note that this is more specific than saying *Students will know how people adapt to geographic challenges.*

The amount of detail depends on the scope of the learning activity. Content objectives may be very specific; for example; *The students will know that there are 12 inches in a linear foot.* Or they may be broader; for example; *Students will know that objects may be measured using standard or nonstandard units.* The scope of the content outcome is related to the scope of the learning activity.

Modes of inquiry.   In Chapter One, we discussed three major categories of thinking modalities: symbolic, imagic, and affective. These represent different ways of constructing and expressing meanings. Individuals differ in how they use these modes. In *The Unschooled Mind,* Gardner (1991) underscores the importance of planning instruction that engages special intelligences to maximize learning. When teachers consider the types of activities to include among sets of options for stu-

Figure 7.3
Outline of learning activity for inquiry on theme: Adaptation

---

Unit Concept: All living things adapt to their environment.

Central Question: Why do some animals live in our area all year long and other animals don't?

Subquestion: What is the place where we live like?

Learning Outcomes:
Students will *know* that our area is considered arid, with hot summers, warm fall and spring months, and temperate winters during which freezing temperatures can occur for short times.

Students will develop their map-reading *skills,* being able to *read* and *interpret* weather symbols, including areas of high and low pressure and front lines, temperature ranges, and degrees of precipitation.

Learning Activity (engagement with resources to find answers to the question):
1. Students group according to seasons of greatest interest.
2. Provide each with recent weather maps for their season. The maps should show high and low pressure areas and front lines, temperature ranges, and degrees of precipitation.
3. Provide each group with weather maps for the same months of their season, from earlier periods: 5, 10, 15, and 20 years ago.
4. Ask each group to determine what data they would contribute to a class chart to show the pattern of temperature and rainfall trends over time for all seasons.

Follow-up "lessons" would develop the composite chart, check it against the information provided by the local chamber of commerce and in almanacs, and interview a meteorologist about the veracity of the chart, among other climatic issues.

---

dents' exploration of any subquestions, they must consider how well these options promote student use of the different modalities. Even as we talk about preferences, however, we have to remember that people learn in multimodal ways. It's dangerous to think of students as those who are only symbolic learners, or those who can learn only in imagic ways, or those who need only affective stimulations for learning to occur. The troublesome word here is "only" because it suggests monomodal learning. Instead, we suggest that you plan for all modalities so that students may have multimodal opportunities to engage in inquiry. Some questions to guide your thinking for planning include the following:

▾ *What types of learning activities require thinking with words, numbers, or other symbol systems?*

▾ *What types of learning activities require visual, spatial, tonal, or kinesthetic-sensate thinking?*

▾ *What types of learning activities engage students with feelings and emotions that can color, direct, and drive an investigation?*

The roles of these modalities should be considered in every phase of planning for interdisciplinary theme learning.

Learning outcomes related to modes of inquiry may be stated as *The students will use these cognitive processes. . . .* It is sometimes difficult to put names to the types of cognitive processes that are the objectives of a learning activity. Kovalik and Olsen (1991) developed an Inquiry-Builder Chart (see Figure 7.4) that incorporates and synthesizes several models of thinking:

▾ Benjamin Bloom's (1956) taxonomy of cognitive objectives: knowledge, comprehension, application, analysis, evaluation, and synthesis;

▾ five of Gardner's (1983) "frames of mind": logico-mathematical, linguistic, musical, bodily-kinesthetic, and spatial; and

▾ science as inquiry described in the *National Science Education Standards* (National Research Council, 1996).

Kovalik and Olsen's synthesis provides a model for identifying the cognitive processes to be taught. It is impossible to identify all the cognitive processes that may be learned through an activity. The outcome should identify those processes that are the major focus of the activity. Thus, an activity that involves students in open-ended research might be designed to help students *identify, locate,* and *describe,* while the compiling of a report might require students to *organize, compose,* and *assemble.*

Habits of mind.   In Chapter One, we also described the habits of mind that appear to be shared by inquirers in all fields of study:

1. finding and keeping focus;
2. asking good questions;
3. simplifying questions and problems;
4. being attentive;
5. seeing anomalies;
6. thinking fluently and flexibly;
7. forming hunches;
8. designing tests and experimenting;

Figure 7.4
Inquiry-builder chart

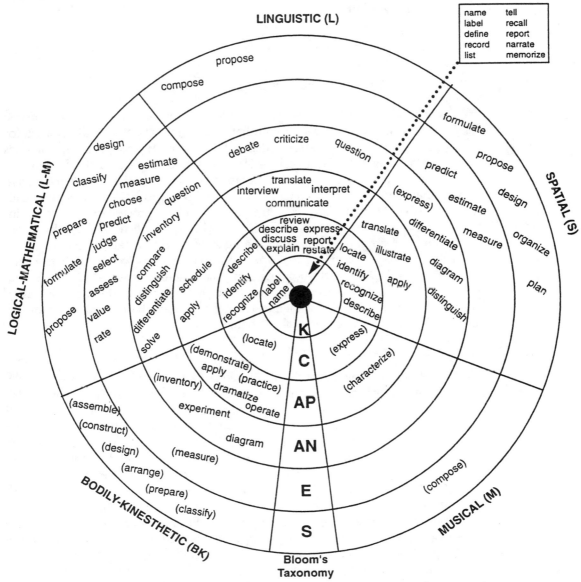

( ) indicates verbs that would be appropriate for this intelligence if specifically designed to be so

Source: *S. J. Kovalik & K. D. Olsen. (1994).* Kid's eye view of science: A teacher's handbook for implementing an integrated thematic approach to teaching science, K–6, *Second edition. 17051 SE 272 Street, Suite 18, Kent, WA 98042. For more information about the ITI Model (Integrated Thematic Instruction), contact Susan Kovalik & Associates, Inc., 253/631-4400.*

9. searching for patterns;
10. using models and metaphors; thinking by analogy;
11. finding elegant solutions;
12. taking risks;
13. cooperating and collaborating;
14. competing; and
15. persevering and having self-discipline.

These intellectual habits incorporate the processes that are often called "thinking skills" in the educational literature and that appear in state and district curriculum standards as process objectives for student achievement. Any curriculum that intends to develop students' learning-to-learn skills must attend to these habits of mind.

The students will develop these habits of mind. . . . Also in Chapter One, we said that the productive thinkers of the world seem to have developed "habits of mind" that include both cognitive and affective processes. The affective processes include finding and keeping a focus, being attentive, taking risks, cooperating and collaborating, competing, persevering, and maintaining self-discipline. As students engage in inquiry, it is important that they, as well as their teachers, experience the feelings and emotions that make inquiry possible and rewarding. Not all of these will be learned in a single activity or even in one activity cluster. However, over the course of a theme study, there should be opportunities for students to develop affectively as well as cognitively.

Descriptions of Learning Activities

The format and the amount of detail you require for a specific learning activity depend on a large number of factors. For example, the less familiar the learning activity is, the more detail you may wish to include. Some teachers can do much of their planning in their heads and like to record a brief summary of major points; other teachers find that the process of writing out a detailed plan helps them to clarify their thinking and planning. Sometimes the amount of detail needed depends on the audience for the plan. If only the teacher who designed it will use the plan, less detail is needed than if it will be used by a number of different people.

Even during open inquiry, individual student research requires planning; so does small-group work or a whole-class activity. Field trips and visits from people in the community need to be organized with as much care as a teacher-directed lesson. Appropriate degrees of structure, according to the teacher's assessment of student needs, provide the predictable environment in which investigations and inquiry can take place. Individual and group explorations in an inquiry-driven curriculum often require more planning than a traditional teacher-led discussion.

Student inquiry across the fields of study.   At this point in the planning, you should check learning activities to find opportunities for student inquiry in the different subject areas. For example, a seventh grade science teacher might find ways for the students to apply the knowledge and skills they have developed during their study of a subquestion such as *How are weather and climate interrelated?* by gathering data on climate and weather conditions in the respective regions. These data could be found in international indexes, atlases, and almanacs. The social studies teacher can make connections to political and topographic maps for student study of relationships among population densities and physical features and political boundaries. Using some of the same data, with appropriate additional raw data, a math teacher can seize opportunities for calculations of ratios and proportions, varied statistical treatments of quantitative information about populations and food production, and perhaps price indexes for traded produce. A language arts teacher can involve students in recording data in written form. Alternative ways of recording data might be offered by the art teacher. Tufte's (1983) *The Visual Display of Quantitative Information* suggests how students can make maps and graphs that use symbol, shading, color, visual metaphors, representational and abstract designs, black-and-white and color drawings and photographs, and two- and three-dimensional images of aesthetic presentations of numerical data.

SCHEDULING

It isn't easy or wise to plan learning activities without taking into account the time frame that can be allotted to each activity. This involves some scheduling.

In a self-contained elementary classroom, you often have some freedom to decide how to schedule the activities. In some schools, part of every day is allotted to interdisciplinary theme studies. In others, there are time allotments for the different subject areas, but you can determine how these requirements are met. Some schools like to maintain a fairly structured time schedule, with all classes at a certain grade level engaged in the same subject area at the same time. Such a situation calls for careful team planning to ensure that the interdisciplinary theme unit is appropriately incorporated into the curriculum.

For example, an extensive activity that incorporates mathematics, science, social studies, and language might be scheduled for an entire morning or a whole day. This allows students to get involved in their own inquiry without constant interruptions and changes of focus. Journal writing that is related to the study might be scheduled for 30 minutes each morning, perhaps during the time allotted for language arts. Of course, activities that are taught across the school by specialists, such as physical education and music, must be honored; where possible, these specialists should participate in the planning of the interdisciplinary theme study and develop learning activities related to its "big ideas."

In a departmentalized situation, especially in the middle school, schedules may be less flexible, and you may focus particularly on activities related to your own specialization. Team teaching and flexible grouping of the students within a grade level can allow for joint planning and teaching when the learning activities require the expert guidance of more than one specialist. For example, in a seventh grade exploration of the question *In what ways do weather and climate affect food production?* a teacher team found that one activity involved the students in language arts, science, math, social studies, and fine arts as they investigated types of food production across the world. They decided that for one week they would keep the students in their homeroom groups during the time allotted for math, science, social studies, language arts, and fine arts and would allow the small groups studying each major area of the world to visit the subject-area specialists whenever they had particular problems related to that subject area.

There are many possibilities for flexible scheduling to meet the major goals and specific objectives of the interdisciplinary theme study. The major consideration is, of course, how to provide the best possible learning situation for the students, bearing in mind that students learn in many different ways.

Four sample schedules present alternative ways of organizing theme studies in the classroom (Figures 7.5, 7.6, 7.7, and 7.8). These are merely suggestions, of course. There is virtually no limit to the ways in which theme studies may be integrated into the regular curriculum. You may begin with one type of schedule and then modify it as you and the students develop the theme study.

Figure 7.5 illustrates a time schedule for one day built around the extensive use of a theme. Students are working individually and in groups on theme-related explorations, and the teacher plans carefully to work with different individuals and groups over the course of the day. Sometimes groups may join with other groups; at other times, a group may split up for the students to work individually or in pairs. The class comes together for common experiences.

Figure 7.6 presents a time schedule for one week in which the teacher has allocated several blocks of time to work on theme studies. These may be expanded or adapted as needs arise and as the theme study develops. The Tuesday and Thursday schedules allow for a 2½-hour block of time for theme studies, with a break for lunch. The specific subject-area slots may be used to reinforce and teach particular concepts and skills as the teacher deems appropriate or may be used for work related to the theme study.

Figure 7.7 demonstrates a more traditional schedule, where a 1½-hour block of time each day is allocated to theme studies. During the rest of the time, students follow the regular curriculum, although connections with the theme are made wherever possible.

Figure 7.8 offers the most dynamic and organic type of schedule. In this example, theme studies are the core of the curriculum, and inquiry occurs when, where, and how children and teachers choose.

Planning for instruction is a complex, interactive, and dynamic process in which you always take into account a wide variety of factors. Within the broad scope of the curriculum guidelines established by your school, district and state and other local requirements or conditions, you strive to meet the instructional needs of students, using as touchstones those principles that are drawn from empirical research findings about learning. Inquiry-oriented interdisciplinary theme studies help you to do that because they require the use of logic in their planning and implementation and because they provide for both student construction of multidisciplinary knowledge and their attainment of the core learnings needed to become self-directed learners.

Figure 7.5
Time schedule for one day

8:00–9:00	*Work with whole group to discuss new ideas →			
9:00–10:00	Susie and Jose read and prepare for report	*Groups 3 and 6 work on measuring	Groups 1, 2, and 5 view film on animal adaptation	Mike and Gloria work on model habitat
10:00–11:00	→	Share results with each other	*Discuss film and continue individual work	→
11:00–12:00	*Reading aloud to whole class — LUNCH →			
12:00–1:30	*Groups 2, 3, and 4 work on science experiments	Groups 1 and 5 work on research about animal adaptation	Pete and Maria prepare questions for interview with Mr. Li	Marilyn and Sergio finish their letters to Ms. Wilson and write their interview report
1:30–2:15	P.E. *Conference period: meet with grade-level team —			
2:15–3:00	Groups 2, 3, and 4 write up science experiments	*Groups 1 and 5 share research findings and decide how to record them	Group 6 works on measuring and cutting paper for the model	→

*Indicates with whom the teacher is working directly.

Figure 7.6
Time schedule for one week

	Monday	Tuesday	Wednesday	Thursday	Friday
8:00–10:00	Theme Studies	Language Arts	Theme Studies	Language Arts	Theme Studies
10:00–11:00	Mathematics	Theme Studies	Mathematics	Theme Studies	Mathematics
11:00–12:00	Lunch ——————— Reading aloud to whole class ——————————→ →				
12:00–1:30	Social Studies	Theme Studies	Social Studies	Theme Studies	Social Studies
1:30–2:15	P.E.	Music	P.E.	Music	P.E.
2:15–3:00	Theme Studies	Science/Health	Theme Studies	Science/Health	Theme Studies

Figure 7.7
Time schedule for one week

	Monday	Tuesday	Wednesday	Thursday	Friday
8:00–10:00	Language Arts ———————————————————————→				
10:00–11:00	Mathematics ———————————————————————→				
11:00–12:00	Lunch ——————— Reading aloud to whole class ——————————→				
12:00–1:30	Theme Studies ——————————————————————→				
1:30–2:15	P.E.	Music	P.E.	Music	P.E.
2:15–3:00	Science/Health	Social Studies	Science/Health	Social Studies	Science/Health

Figure 7.8
Time schedule for one week

Monday	Tuesday	Wednesday	Thursday	Friday
Teacher and students schedule theme study activities in the classroom and school and at remote sites, incorporating music, art, physical education, and other special subject areas. Time allocations will vary from day to day and from group to group. Special needs will be met through special lessons. Skills will be taught as needed.				

REFERENCES

Bloom, B. S. (Ed.), *Taxonomy of educational objectives: The classification of educational goals: Book 1. Cognitive domain.* New York: Longman.

Gardner, H. (1983). *Frames of mind: Theory of multiple intelligences.* New York: Basic Books.

Gardner, H. (1991). *The unschooled mind.* New York: Basic Books.

Kovalik, S. J., & Olsen, K. D. (1994). *Kid's eye view of science: A teacher's handbook for implementing an integrated thematic approach to teaching science, K–6.* Second edition. 17051 SE 272 Street, Suite 18, Kent, WA 98042.

Learner-Centered Principles Work Group of the American Psychological Association's Board of Educational Affairs. (1997). *Learner-centered psychological principles: A framework for school reform and redesign.* Washington, DC: American Psychological Association.

Martinello, M. (1987). *The search for Emma's story: A model for humanities detective work.* Ft. Worth: Texas Christian University Press.

National Council for the Social Studies. (1994). *Curriculum standards for the social studies.* Washington, DC: National Council for the Social Studies.

National Council of Teachers of English & International Reading Association. (1996). *Standards for the English language arts.* Urbana, IL: National Council of Teachers of English; Newark, DE: International Reading Association.

National Research Council (1996). *National science education standards.* Washington, D.C.: National Academy Press.

Texas Education Agency. (1991). *State Board of Education rules for curriculum: Essential elements.* Austin: Texas Education Agency.

Tufte, E. (1983). *The visual display of quantitative information.* Cheshire, CT: Graphics Press.

Chapter Eight

Accountability and Assessment

Evaluative processes are continuous, pervading all learning and teaching. When we consider assessment carefully, we are also considering the reliability and validity of what we teach, and even the development of curriculum.

Evaluation is primarily designed to give information about learning to a variety of audiences—the learner, the teacher, the school and school district, the parents, the local community, and the general public. Each of these audiences has a different reason for seeking evaluation of learning. The learner needs feedback, the teacher needs information about the results of the learning-teaching process, the school and school district need evidence of the extent to which educational goals are being met, the parents need to know how well their children are matching up to standards, and the general public demands accountability for the tax dollars invested in education. Evaluation and reporting procedures frequently attempt to meet all these demands simultaneously—and frequently fail to meet any of them adequately. While it is certainly possible for the same evaluation procedure to serve several purposes, it is also important to keep in mind the primary purpose of any assessment.

FORMATIVE AND SUMMATIVE ASSESSMENTS

Formative assessment and *summative assessment* are educational terms that refer, respectively, to assessment that is ongoing during learning and assessment of a completed segment of learning. The terms are relative: The summative assessment of one learning activity may be part of the formative assessment of a unit; the summative assessment of a unit may be part of the formative assessment of a larger theme study. Formative and summative evaluations tend to serve different purposes. While formative assessment is designed primarily to give feedback to the learners (and teachers) that will help them to improve their future learning, summative assessment provides some measure of what has been learned by a certain point in time or in the curriculum. As an analogy, an athlete in training receives formative evaluation from the coach or other sources (including self-assessment), while the results of a race or contest provide summative evaluation. Summative evaluation tends to involve a comparison with standards and with the achievements of others, while formative evaluation tends to focus on comparison with one's own learning.

Thematic studies, like all learning, incorporate both formative and summative assessments. It is helpful for learners, teachers, parents, and the larger community to understand the relationship between these two concepts.

Formative assessment is essential throughout the theme study. The children's growing understanding of the big idea should be monitored at all times to ensure that neither learners nor teachers are moving into unrelated or trivial lines of inquiry. Question sequences need to be assessed by both learner and teacher to make sure that new questions are building on the knowledge gained from resources. Resources themselves must be evaluated for their intrinsic integrity and worth and for their relevance to the theme study.

Summative assessment is also an extremely important part of theme studies. At various points in the theme study, those involved must stand back and review progress so far. What new content has been learned? What new skills have been developed? What is understood about the big idea at this point in time? What new questions have been engendered? This type of summative assessment of part of the theme study does become formative assessment to guide further study, but it also provides valuable opportunities for reflection, for self-evaluation, and for new understandings of the processes of learning, which are applicable in many other situations.

Summative evaluation is also a critical element in the closing of a theme study. Culminating activities, which will be discussed later in this chapter, can take many forms. They allow the learners to celebrate their achievements, to report their progress to a variety of audiences, and to look back and assess what they have learned in terms of content, process, and self-knowledge.

ASSESSMENT PROCESSES IN THEME STUDIES

Through theme studies, children can develop all the types of content, skill, and affective learnings that are objectives of the standard curriculum. We should not need to supplement theme studies to ensure that our students learn to read, write, compute, and think. Well-designed and -developed theme studies can cover the entire curriculum, and through them, evaluation of all types of learning is possible—

evaluation that is integral to, not separate from, teaching and learning. Having said that, we must also recognize that theme studies, as we define them, are most intimately associated with inquiry. And inquiry learning is best suited to student achievement of inquiry skills.

We believe that evaluation is an ongoing process of regular teaching and learning activities and that, given the wide variety of assessment methods available to teachers and students, those used in every teaching and learning situation should be chosen to match that situation. Therefore, in this single chapter on evaluation and assessment—an area of study in its own right—we do not try to explore all possible assessment methods. Instead, we limit discussion to assessment that is intimately linked to children's learning of inquiry processes and to their comprehension of big ideas.

Any discussion of assessment must speak to each component of a theme's unit study and the interrelationships among those components: the big idea, questions and subquestions, resources, and new questions that arise as an exploration develops. If we think of each component as a touchstone for evaluation, the primary assessment issues are easy to state:

▾ How well do the children understand the big idea?

▾ How logically interrelated to one another and to the big idea are the questions and subquestions that students explore?

▾ How well are the children forming sequences of questions that are built from the clues uncovered in the resources they consult?

▾ How appropriate are the resources for exploring the unit's questions?

▾ What are the qualities of the new questions that are drafted during the exploration? How well do the new questions advance the theme study?

Understanding the Big Idea

While many useful facts will be uncovered as students explore the central and subordinate questions of their study, the most important knowledge outcome is understanding the big idea—the concept, generalization, principle, law, or theory to which all those questions point.

Knowledge outcomes. A learning outcome for knowledge development in a theme study on *Adaptation* expects children to be able to express the critical attributes of adaptation by the completion of their study. In adult language, that outcome might read:

> The children will know that adaptation is necessary for survival in any living thing and that adaptation is demonstrated by physical characteristics and behaviors that enable the organism to successfully adjust to circumstances within its environment.

To assess children's understanding of this concept definition, the outcome can be measured by criteria for levels of understanding. Sometimes these levels are identified by national or local statements of standards for learning, but frequently they must be defined by the teacher. Each level can be viewed as a criterion measure for knowledge development. Some might call a set of leveled criteria a rubric. For instance, the following criteria show progression in children's understanding of adaptation. Some students may achieve comprehension at level 1, others at level 2, still others at level 3, and so on:

1. The child identifies specific examples of adaptation in specific plants and animals.
2. The child explains how specific adaptations enable particular plants and animals to survive, given life-limiting and life-enabling factors in their environments.
3. The child is able to compare/contrast adaptations in specific plants and animals in environments having different life-limiting and life-enabling characteristics.
4. The child can predict which animals/plants can survive in specific environments and what adaptations will need to occur before survival is assured.
5. The child can identify those qualities and characteristics of organisms that are generally essential to survival in specific environments.

Process outcomes.   The learning outcomes for process skills are often couched in terms of thinking. Learning outcomes for process skills may be worded as follows:

▾ *The children will demonstrate the ability to observe and describe with precision the adaptive characteristics of plants and animals.*
▾ *The children will compare and contrast the adaptive characteristics of plants and animals.*
▾ *The children will discover the interrelationships of plant and animal characteristics and the specific qualities of their environments.*

Children's achievement of these process objectives, and others like them, can be inferred by reviewing the quality of their work products (writings, drawings, presentations, etc.) and by talking with them about the content of their studies. So, for instance, a learning outcome that is concerned with the skill of categorizing might read:

The children will clearly match plant and animal adaptations to the specific conditions of their environments.

The evidence you would seek in work products demonstrates this matching. If your students are studying adaptations in plants, you might look for their written and pictorial matching of, for instance, the water-saving waxy surfaces and moist, fleshy interiors of succulents with desert conditions. Or, on a bit more multivariate level, if animals are a focus of study, you might look for the matching of bird beak size and shape with foods available in each of the environments a particular species visits during its seasonal migration patterns.

The specific types of evidence for learning are many and varied. You decide which work products meet the objective by thinking about that objective in terms specific to the content of the children's studies.

Obviously, many thinking processes apply in inquiry learning. The learning modes discussed in Chapter One, symbolic, imagic, and affective, are clearly important in inquiry learning. We need to assess children's growth in the use of symbol systems: linguistic, mathematical, musical, and other discipline-specific languages. We also need to assess their growth in imagery. And we have to try to evaluate their development of those affective qualities that include the interplay of feelings like intuition and self-discipline, among others, with cognitive processes used for inquiry. Some researchers have made the study of these processes their life's work. We refer you to classic studies of thinking and knowing reported in the works of such authors as Dewey (1938) on instrumental thinking, Gardner (1983) on multiple intelligences, Arnheim (1969) on visual thinking, Perkins (1981) on creative thinking, and Margolis (1987) on judgment theory, among others.

We encourage you to consult those sources that are most meaningful for your teaching. That frees us to focus on the processes in inquiry learning that we are most qualified, by our research and teaching, to explore: questioning, using resources to explore questions, and analyzing the data collected, including the qualities of answers found.

Interrelationships among the Big Idea, Questions, and Subquestions

Children's questioning. Children's questions are good indicators of their knowledge about a topic. Naive questions asked by children are "cute" because of their innocence. From a teacher's perspective, those naive questions reveal the starting point for the child's development of content knowledge. The child who asks, "Why is rain wet?" clearly does not understand the water cycle. At the start of a weather study, this question is full of promise because it offers direction for what needs to be explored. But at the end of a weather study that inquired into the water cycle, that same question reveals lack of learning in its ignorance of a central big idea.

The questions that children ask at the start, during, and at the end of their inquiries are powerful indicators of learning. Inquiry notebooks help to keep track of them, especially if questions are recorded as dated entries. We can examine the content of children's questions at each step along the way of their inquiries to infer what they do and don't know about the topic, as, for instance, with "Why is the rain wet?" We have to ask ourselves, "Why is the child asking that question? What do children need to know to understand the answer? And what do they need to know to better understand what they're asking?" If, in this case, we recognize that the child is not making a connection between rain and water, probably doesn't understand the physical processes of evaporation and condensation, and doesn't know what precipitates condensed water, we can find the many subordinate questions that must be explored before an explanation of how water becomes rain can be understood. When the same child is able to formulate pertinent subordinate questions, we have a record of conceptual growth.

When visiting a nature trail, where a canopy of bald cypress shields the plants along a creek from light, one student asked a naive question that grew into a series of better-informed questions. She first asked: "How do plants living along the creek, where there is very little sunlight, stay alive?" The assumption underlying this question is that direct sunlight is required for plant life. The following became subordinate questions in this actual inquiry:

▼ What kind of light do plants need?
▼ What do they do with it? What parts of the plant actually use the light? How much light do they need?
▼ What methods have plants developed to concentrate the light that gets to the parts of their leaves that photosynthesize?

The questions speak for themselves. The student has learned that it's not sunlight that's important, but light, and that there are certain parts of the spectrum that are more important for plant life than others. The student's questions also indicate a growing awareness of the photosynthetic process—which wasn't there at the start —an understanding that not all parts of the plant photosynthesize food for plant growth. She also learned that some plants are able to concentrate very small amounts of light to make the most of what they get.

Another student started her inquiry at the same nature trail with "Where have all the hummingbirds gone?" This question struck her when she visited the nature trail in February, having spent some time there during the preceding June. The question shows her initial ignorance of hummingbird migration. It also started her on an exploration of hummingbird types, migratory patterns, and size. As she learned about migrations, she raised questions about different hummingbirds, their flyways and destinations, and their methods of flying and feeding while enroute. The more specific a student's questions, the greater the evidence of acquired knowledge and of growth in ability to frame new questions from foundations of information.

We can also categorize children's questions by type to determine whether they are learning to ask higher-order questions, which require more knowledge about a topic than do the lower-order types. There are many categories of thinking that teachers can use to classify questions by level of thinking. Bloom's taxonomy (1956) provides well-known categories for critical thinking. Ennis (1987) offers another way to categorize critical thinking. Taba (1962) analyzed inductive thinking. Eberle (1987) suggests categories for creative questioning. Krathwohl's taxonomy (1964) examines questions about feelings. Marzano (1992) offers question types to elicit eight process components of analytic thinking. Hunkins (1995) discusses many of these frameworks for questioning.

When we examine children's queries, we look for a variety of question types. A few of the most common examples are questions that as follows:

1. Seek a specific fact or examine a specific detail; for example, *Who were the people who first discovered our area?*
2. Suggest a comparison or contrast; for example, *How is Mexican food different from Spanish food?*
3. Examine interrelationships between/among variables; for example, *How important was the type of rock that's in our schoolyard for building the first houses in this town?*

While it is useful to look at questions in these categorical ways, doing so doesn't always uncover the depth of student learning or reveal the student's abilities to better formulate questions. A question that asks for a specific detail may be as much an indicator of learning as one that examines relationships among variables. Questions have to be evaluated in context to be fully understood. And the value of a question's wording is less in its complexity than in its clarity, its accurate use of the language or jargon germane to the topic, and its relationship to its preceding questions.

Questions from clues.   Most important in an inquiry-oriented theme study is the logical interrelationships of

▼ subordinate questions to central questions,

▼ central questions to one another, and

▼ central questions to the big idea.

The clearer those relationships, the better the students' *lines of questioning.* In Chapter Seven, we introduced the concept of the question sequence as a series of questions that present a line of inquiry in which the first question is refined, developed, and/or focused by the next question, and each succeeding question further refines, develops, or focuses the preceding questions. Assessing children's question sequences may be one of the best ways to determine growth in the substance of their knowledge and their investigative abilities. To do so, you have to track children's questions, the resources they consult, the clues they think they have uncovered, the new questions they ask, and the ideas they formulate about the meaning of the big idea. That sounds daunting. How is it done in ways that protect the teacher's sanity?

Children can be taught to keep track of their inquiry processes with flowcharts like the one in Figure 8.1, developed by the teacher who studied bald cypress trees along a creek (Traynor, 1988). It shows her wording of increasingly informed questions, from a very general *Where are cypress trees found?* to a more specific question drawn from observation of the real tree: *Why do roots grow out of the water?* and ultimately to a question that suggests a hypothesis, *Were the trees planted along Cibolo Creek to control flooding?* As the inquiry developed, the resources become more varied. The first references are to the Internet and one consultant. But then other consultants are noted, as are field guides, actual observations, and brochures. As resources increased, more clues were uncovered, leading to better, more informed questions. When the teacher learned that there are seven species of cypress trees that grow in swamps and soil with low oxygen, she asked *Why do they flourish along the Cibolo Creek?* Her source led her to understand the importance of a ready supply of water for the trees—they were abundant along the creek, but none could be found anywhere else in the area. As she looked at the trees in the creek, she wondered why the "roots" grow out of the water. She found out that those "roots" were not roots, but knees that supply oxygen to the roots underneath and also help stabilize the trees. The recorded progression of her inquiry shows how the additional information she gathered taught her how cypress trees contribute to the health of the creek and, from this, grew her wondering about how the bald cypress might actually help to control flooding.

Just as Figure 8.1 testifies to one teacher's learning about the interrelations of bald cypress and the creek and the development of her inquiry, so, too, can similar records of children's question sequences offer evidence of their content and process learnings. Records like these, kept in inquiry notebooks, can be examined for each of the following qualitative and quantitative attributes:

- ▾ number and type of questions and their logical interrelationships,
- ▾ variety of resources consulted,
- ▾ relevance of clues to the questions asked,
- ▾ number of clues obtained from different sources, and
- ▾ characteristics of last questions in comparison to initial questions.

Use of Resources

A particularly revealing method of assessing process skill development is how well students select and actually use resources to explore their questions.

Reliable sources. That phrase is especially meaningful in investigative reporting—and also in any inquiry. When looking at a student's inquiry notebook, we can ask, "Are the resources various and numerous?"

Some students may be content to consult many books from an extensive library search. That's a good start, but not satisfactory for a thorough inquiry. We might ask these students what people, what documents or papers, what audiovisual resources, and so on might be consulted.

Other students may consult a variety of resource types, but only one of each: one book, one person, one document, and so on. We might ask these students where additional sources of each type might be found.

Figure 8.1
Notes showing development of question sequence during inquiry about
Bald Cypress along a creek

What is cypress's scientific name?

|

Resources: Vines, 1994; Perry Guide to Cibolo Wilderness Trail (CWT);
Simpson's Field Guide

|

Clues: Seven species of cypress trees; 20 million found in East Asia, North America.

|

Where are cypress trees found?   *Why so few along Hwy 46?*
Resource: Web site on cypress   Resource: CWT Guide
Clue: Cypress tree grows in swamps   Clue: Trees in Boerne were cut and
and soil low in O_2.   milled; replanted only at CWT.

|

Why do cypress trees flourish at CWT?
Resource: CWT Guide
Clue: Abundance of water important.

|

In what conditions do cypress trees flourish? Why are they found near bodies of water?
Resource: Web site on cypress trees
Clues: Dispersion of seeds in moving water; seeds germinate on saturated soil.

|

Why do roots grow out of the water?
Resources: CWT Guide; Simpson Field Guide; Web site on cypress trees
Clues: Roots swell and cause "knees" to form; knees supply O_2 to roots, provide
stability; observed trees with roots underwater and knees above surface.

|

Did cypress trees play a role in the development of surrounding towns?
Resource: Brochure, Riverside Nature Center
Clue: Cypress is responsible for founding of Kerrville.

|

How was this so?
Resources: Kerrville Web site; CWT Guide; Vine's book; Mark Peterson, Texas
Forest Service
Clues: Shingle manufacturing industry in Kerrville began 1846. Shingle maker
named town after his friend James Kerr. Shingles are made from cypress wood.
Pioneers looked for rows of cypress trees as indicators of water source.
Some communities started that way. Settlers used cypress wood to build many
things.
There are ecological benefits of cypress trees. Cypress trees soak up floodwater
and trap sediment; provide wildlife habitat.

|

My hunch: *Were the trees planted along Cibolo Creek to control flooding?*

All students need to be pressed to seek alternative points of view on their questions. These need not be contradictory points of view, but they should represent different perspectives on the same subtopic or issue. We want students to think about corroborating their findings—how many different sources say that same thing? We also want them to learn how to assess the validity of their sources—figuring out how well qualified their sources are to provide the information they seek. This can be determined by asking this simple question: "How well do the resources match the question being explored?"

It goes without saying that inquiry can be successful only when there is a logical connection between resource and question. But it is possible for naive inquirers to select resources that don't match their questions well. By this, we mean selecting resources that are superficially connected to a topic. The classic example is student reliance on the encyclopedia. Although encyclopedic summaries are often useful during first explorations of a topic, by design they are not suited for deepening investigations. Also, the better the children's grasp of a topic, the more *resourceful* they will be. In addition to doing the obvious, such as locating a book about butterflies during a study of butterflies, they will find more exotic sources, like the segment on butterflies included in a video presentation on camouflage or, for a study of slavery in America, the slave narratives offered by Smithsonian archives on the World Wide Web. The criteria to assess levels of children's resource selection might include the following:

1. The resource is tertiary—presenting summary generic information about the topic of study.
2. The resource is secondary—offering syntheses of specific information about certain components of the topic of study, components that appear in the question under investigation.
3. The resource is primary—giving raw data meaningful to the question under study, data that is open to interpretation.

Qualities of New Questions

Just as we might compare early written work with later written work, or early tapes of reading skill with those made later, or math papers completed early and later in the school year, so we should compare questions asked over time in the course of an inquiry. By comparison with questions that are formulated early in a theme study, later ones should

- ▼ be more specific,
- ▼ contain more detail,
- ▼ suggest comparisons and contrasts,
- ▼ question interrelationships among variables,
- ▼ search for clarifications, and
- ▼ test big ideas.

Advancing a theme study means getting closer to finding patterns of meaning that help to clarify big ideas. Therefore, the last item in the above list helps to determine whether new questions students are framing are helpful in understanding one or more big ideas. Teachers might look for evidence of insight into the main ideas of a theme study in students' questions. For instance, in a theme study on *Adaptation,* initial questions might ask *What kinds of beaks do birds have?*

A later question that shows increased understanding of how beaks are related to food sources in the environment might ask *What type of beak is needed to gather food that is available to birds in the place where we live?*

This second question is clearly more specific and expresses relationships among the variables of beak characteristics and food in a particular environment. It also suggests that the student who phrased the question is understanding the interacting factors for natural selection. Questions at even deeper levels of understanding of adaptation as the means by which living things ensure their survival in particular environments might be *What kinds of beaks do birds who remain all year in our area have and what kinds of food do they need? How do the beaks and food needs of our year-round bird residents compare with those of birds that migrate, staying here only during specific seasons?*

Elements of big ideas are contained in advanced questions. Teachers can look for those elements in question statements during the course of inquiry and evaluate student achievement of important understandings over time.

Thinking about Thinking

Children can be involved in assessing their own growth by reflecting on what they have learned and the ways of thinking that they are aware of using. Through reflection on the strategies you use during a study, it's possible to expand and fine-tune techniques for self-directed learning.

In Chapter One, we described different ways of knowing. Teachers will keep those in mind when assessing learning. However, it's important that individual students learn to assess their thinking for themselves because the act of doing this teaches intellectual self-discipline. Children can be encouraged to ask these questions:

- ▼ How do I know what I know?
- ▼ What thinking am I doing? How do I think?

Being able to find answers to these questions, to think and to talk about thinking, requires a special vocabulary: a language of thinking. Most teachers are familiar with the standard terms: observing, comparing/contrasting, inferring, hypothesizing, synthesizing, and so on. But a language of thinking is more comprehensive than that and actually is more a part of conversational language than we may know. How often do you casually state "I wonder. . ." or "I thought . . ." or "He implied . . ." or "I sensed . . ."?

Tishman, Perkins, and Jay (1995) recommend that teachers consciously use thinking terms in their classroom speech. They offer a list of words associated with thinking to show that the terms are commonly known and that their daily use enriches talk about thinking in classrooms. These authors recommend that the classroom culture include a "culture of thinking," which is advanced through specialized language. One good way to develop your own language of thinking is to free associate on the terms that come to mind about thinking processes, check dictionary and thesaurus listings for synonyms for thinking, and listen to the language you and your students use when referring to thinking. When children get used to hearing their teachers talk about "asserting, considering, discovering, finding evidence, inquiring, probing, questioning, remembering, suspecting, verifying" (Tishman, Perkins, & Jay, 1995, 11–12), they are likely to follow suit. As their thinking vocabularies become enlarged, their reflection on how they think will improve.

During an inquiry, students accepted information from one resource as "truth," failing to verify their "answer" with corroborative sources. After consulting one newspaper article on the issue of how to augment and protect water resources for their growing metropolis, they accepted the author's point of view that the aquifer, the sole provider of water for their city, contained more water than the city, even in high growth, could ever use. During reflection on their research strategy, the children were encouraged to think about whether they had verified the "answer" by consulting other reliable sources. During a discussion of what sources they could consult and where they would be most likely to uncover alternative points of view, the students learned their initial method was inefficient. They now realized that a more comprehensive research strategy demands that more information for the same question be collected before "answers" are considered.

We can assess the efficacy of our own thinking and that of others by listening to how we describe our thought processes. Teachers can help children evaluate their thinking by talking with them about how they actually worked through a problem: the reasoning they used, the methods of data collection they followed, the ways they interpreted the information they collected, and the ways they made sense of it all. Children's inquiry notebooks are places for reflection on how the search was done. Children and teachers can look for evidence of growth in their use of various search methods and in their abilities to describe and to improve those methodologies.

REPORTING ABOUT CHILDREN'S LEARNING

Very few teaching situations are unaffected by the expectations of parents and the general public that some evidence of children's progress and achievement will be provided in familiar terms. For most, this means evaluative letter grades or percentages that are equated with "A," "B," "C," "D," and "F" or other designations. Most of us think that we know what those letters signify, even though, when pressed to define them, we must acknowledge that their meanings are often vague and unstandardized. In response, teachers, administrators, and evaluation committees have devised a wide variety of ways to evaluate and report levels of student knowledge and skill attainment in finite time frames. In this chapter, we will not attempt to discuss all those methods or debate the merits or limitations of each. Nor will we attempt to explore all possible types of learning that should be evaluated as children progress through a theme study. Instead, we will address the most frequently raised issue of working with evaluative letter grades or their equivalent because, no matter what aversion we may have to the letter or numerical grade tradition for reporting student achievement, teachers are typically asked to use them. As we have done earlier in this chapter, we focus here on applying these conventional grades to the task of reporting (1) student understanding of the big ideas that serve as themes for study and (2) student use of those processes that are essential to good inquiry.

At this point, a caveat is in order: In the pages that follow, we offer ideas about how reporting can satisfy the desire for letter grades, while remaining true to principles of evaluation that demand (1) the inclusion of all stakeholders, (2) clarity of communication, (3) integrity of criteria, (4) fairness in the application of criteria to all learners, and (5) emphasis on how evaluation is integral to learning and how learning can be guided by evaluation processes. We do not intend to present our examples as models of the only ways to deal with reporting issues. They are offered to illustrate how we might implement a philosophy of evaluation that has all the above stated elements, even given the limitations of evaluative grades. We ask you, our reader, to bring your creative energies and professional knowledge to bear on developing these ideas in your own educational contexts.

Communication and Standards

One of the challenges in assessment is to report children's learning and progress in terms that interested parties will understand (Schwartz, 1996; Wiggins, 1996). These interested parties, whether they are students, parents, administrators, or the general public, need some frame of reference in order to make sense of the results of student learning. A letter grade, a numerical score, a portfolio, or an exhibition is meaningful only in comparison with standards or with some other pieces of work. A student wants to know, "How well did I do?" A parent wants to know, "How does my child's learning and development compare with others of the same age?" Principals need to know how children in one class compare with those in another or how their schools compare with others in the district. The general public looks to national standards and norms as yardsticks for measuring children's learning in local schools.

In theme studies, as we have suggested, current performance can be compared with previous performance by collecting samples of children's questions, field notes, experiments, and other products over time. Portfolios can provide an excellent means for demonstrating progress.

Exhibitions can celebrate the achievements of both individuals and groups. Children can demonstrate their own unique strengths and abilities as they contribute to the learning of the group.

External standards and norms are also important in theme studies, as we have indicated in Chapter Four. Educators have the responsibility for preparing learners for the complexities of the larger society. Current national standards reflect these complexities. Standards developed by national associations, such as the National Council of Teachers of English and the International Reading Association (1996), the National Council of Teachers of Mathematics (1989), the National Research Council (1996); state organizations; and major testing agencies, such as the Educational Testing Service, are designed to be compatible with the expected demands of life in the 21st century. Assessment procedures at all levels are beginning to reflect these standards, standards that incorporate diverse, higher-level thinking and a variety of types of performance.

These standards can guide assessment in theme studies by indicating benchmarks for age or grade levels. For example, the content standards in the *National Science Education Standards* (National Research Council, 1996) provide detailed explanations of the abilities and understandings about scientific inquiry that students in grades 5–8 need to develop and give specific examples of such inquiry.

Reporting on Attainment of Big Idea Learnings

How often have you heard children ask what the grades on a report card mean? How many times have you realized during parent conferences about children's school progress that the meaning of grade reports you were sending home was not understood by the recipients? Even the parent of the child whose grade in a subject is "A" doesn't know what that really means—no more than the child understands, or even the teacher who is about to receive that child into the next grade level. There's not much to be learned from a vaguely defined letter or number. The solution is to define what each grade means in terms that everyone understands. Ideally, all parties should be involved in the defining process. But in the absence of time, energy, and resources to accomplish the ideal, teachers can offset this problem by communicating with all interested parties often and with clarity. If everyone understands what the expectations for learning are and the language in which those expectations are expressed, grade symbols lose their mystery.

In a theme study on Adaptation, the big idea might be stated as *The children will know that adaptation is necessary for survival in any living thing and that adaptation is demonstrated by physical characteristics and behaviors that enable the organism to successfully adjust to circumstances within its environment.*

The purpose of the theme study is to guide children to inductively arrive at this generalization through discovery, that is, by interpreting and synthesizing the findings drawn from exploring the theme's central and subordinate questions.

It goes without saying therefore that the generalization is not given to the students ahead of time. But the criteria for understanding the generalization should be discussed with children and shared with parents even before the theme study begins.

The following criteria for understanding the concept of adaptation were introduced earlier in this chapter. Although couched in adult language, they contain the expectations for student achievement of levels of understanding of the big idea. Therefore, they can be converted to a rubric that speaks to levels of comprehension.

1. The child identifies specific examples of adaptation in specific plants and animals.
2. The child explains how specific adaptations enable particular plants and animals to survive, given life-limiting and life-enabling factors in their environments.
3. The child is able to compare/contrast adaptations in specific plants and animals in environments having different life-limiting and life-enabling characteristics.
4. The child can predict which animals/plants can survive in specific environments and what adaptations will need to occur before survival is assured.
5. The child can identify those qualities and characteristics of organisms that are generally essential to survival in specific environments.

Let's assume that the teacher of a fifth grade class about to study adaptation believes that the background knowledge and developmental levels of students in the class make it possible for them to achieve understandings that are specified in criterion 5. The grading rubric might become

Perfect level of achievement = meeting criteria 1–5

Solid, if not perfect, level of achievement = meeting criteria 1–4

Moderate level of achievement = meeting criteria 1–3

Limited level of achievement = meeting criteria 1–2

If, on the other hand, a fourth grade teacher was developing a theme study on adaptation, the criteria would be altered to be more consistent with what is reasonable to expect of students at that grade level. The point is that the teacher must decide, drawing direction from local and national standards, what constitutes the various levels of achievement and their evaluative grade designations and how to explain those achievement levels to other stakeholders.

Children should be involved in helping to define the criteria in terms they understand. So, for instance, the above criteria would be formulated during class discussions about what the students and teacher hoped students would learn during the theme study. This could result in the following:

1. I will pick out specific examples of what makes it possible for specific plants and animals to live in specific places.
2. I will explain what makes it possible for specific plants and animals to survive where they live.
3. I will show how specific plants and animals that survive in particular places are alike and how they are different from plants and animals that live in other places.
4. I will predict which animals and plants can live in specific places and what they need before they can live there.
5. I will tell what qualities and characteristics plants and animals must have to be able to live in specific places.

Then the children, with teacher guidance, can work out the grading rubric:

A grade of "A" means that I have evidence of being able to do 1–5.
A grade of "B" means that I have evidence of being able to do 1–4.
A grade of "C" means that I have evidence of being able to do 1–3.
A grade of "D" means that I have evidence of being able to do 1–2.

Grading codes may vary according to local preference. The particular criteria also may vary, depending on standards, teachers, students, and parent expectations, but no matter what variations they show, all will be true to the fundamental qualities of the concept or generalization to be developed as the big idea of the theme study.

Reporting on Attainment of Inquiry Process Learnings

The same method of linking qualitative criteria to evaluative letter grades can be used to assess children's inquiry process learnings. Rather than assess questioning alone, or resource use alone, or ability to analyze and interpret data alone—all important component processes for formative evaluation—summative evaluation of children's inquiry skill development could look at the following components:

▾ number and type of questions and their logical interrelationships,
▾ variety of resources consulted,
▾ relevance of clues to the questions asked,
▾ number of clues obtained from different sources, and
▾ characteristics of last questions in comparison to initial questions.

In children's language, the criteria might be stated as follows:

1. I have written several questions [number may be specified] of different types that are connected to one another.
2. I have used several different types of sources to explore my questions.
3. The clues I have found in my sources help to answer my questions.
4. The clues that I have accepted are verified by different sources.
5. My last questions build on my earlier questions and show that I have learned about my topic.

A grading rubric might be the following:

I will earn an "A" if my inquiry record meets the requirements of 1–5.
I will earn a "B" if my inquiry record meets the requirements of 1–3.
I will earn a "C" if my inquiry record meets the requirements of 1–2.
I will earn a "D" if my inquiry record meets the requirements of 1.

Again, grading codes may vary. The specific criteria also will vary with the inquirers, the standards, and the interests of all stakeholders. But they will always be true to basic premises about what defines good inquiry.

When the clearly stated criteria and grading rubric are made public, children, teachers, parents, and administrators will know how evaluative grades will be determined and, when assigned, what they can tell each about the child's level of comprehension of the theme's concept/generalization and inquiry processes. Knowing the other possible levels of attainment helps each stakeholder view the "grade" as a benchmark and therefore a guide for future learning.

ALTERNATIVE MEANS FOR DEMONSTRATING PROGRESS AND ACHIEVEMENT IN THEME STUDIES: THE PORTFOLIO

In the preceding section, we have addressed ways of using conventional grading codes to assess and report student achievement in interdisciplinary studies and inquiry learning. In this section, we discuss some alternative methods for communicating and reporting children's learning.

Alternative assessments are described in many publications, including those "dedicated to furthering constructive discussion about assessment and to providing concrete directions for change" (Perrone, 1991, p. vii), practical guides (e.g., Herman, Aschbacher, & Winters, 1992), books linked to particular models of teaching (e.g., Marzano, Pickering, & McTighe, 1993) or specific subject areas (e.g., Assessment as Inquiry, 1997), books focusing on one aspect of assessment (e.g., Guskey, 1996), and issues of journals that present a variety of viewpoints.

National testing movements and current literature provide teachers with important perspectives on assessment, but here we focus primarily on those forms of assessment that are particularly appropriate for communication of children's learning within theme studies. Here two common forms of communicating and reporting are *portfolios* and *exhibitions,* both of which provide visible evidence of children's learning (Watt, 1996). Evaluation procedures include the collection of information over time, the analysis of data, and the search for meanings about learning. For years, architects, models, and photographers, among others, have used portfolios to chronicle their best work. The portfolio is equally applicable to the documentation and evaluation of student learning (Wiggins, 1992). When using portfolios, students can claim ownership in the evaluation process through self-evaluation and critical reflection about their work samples and the learning they represent. Teachers using student portfolios in their classes can monitor children's development and can make changes in curriculum and instruction to meet individual student needs. Parents can look at their children's portfolios in order to follow their progress.

A portfolio is a purposeful collection of dated student work that highlights the individual or group efforts of students in one or more areas of classroom study. Students and teachers are active participants in the selection of the content of the portfolio and in the identification and application of criteria for judging the merit of the portfolio's contents. An added dimension of the student portfolio is that it can show evidence of students' reflection about their work.

A number of potential purposes for portfolio assessment include the following:

▼ to examine growth over time;

▼ to involve students in self-evaluation;

▼ to help students and teachers set goals;

▼ to validate how students learn;

▼ to help students connect process and product;

▼ to provide student ownership, motivation, sense of accomplishment, and participation;

▼ to look at the development of process skills and thinking;

▼ to assess curriculum needs; and

▼ to improve communication.

In interdisciplinary theme studies, the portfolio documents learning and provides an ongoing record of development in exploration and inquiry. The organization and presentation of portfolios can also serve as a culminating activity for a theme study.

Selection of Materials

How will material be selected for the portfolio? Teachers need to help children choose samples of work that represent the knowledge, processes, and affective abilities fostered in the classroom. Students need guidance and time to learn how to select the items that demonstrate their learning. For instance, a teacher might ask students to identify the items that represent their greatest challenges, best work, or most satisfying learning experiences. Materials selected for a portfolio used during an interdisciplinary theme study might provide evidence for the learning outcomes indicated above:

▾ knowledge outcomes,

▾ process outcomes,

▾ forming questions from clues,

▾ using resources, and

▾ thinking about thinking.

As portfolios are developed, the quality of the work is assessed according to criteria related to the prior experience of the students, their developmental levels, the planned learning outcomes, and the task itself.

Portfolios can be used in both formative and summative evaluation of student learning. While they are being developed, portfolios allow students to review, assess, revise, and reorganize their work products and records. Students should be encouraged to select materials for their own portfolios, and as the portfolios expand, students can examine their collections and can reorder and discard previous materials as necessary to produce a coherent record of learning.

A group of fifth graders was investigating adaptation of animals to the environment. At first, they were locating and recording a large amount of largely unconnected data. As a group and individually, they selected what they considered to be the most interesting and well-written reports to include in a group portfolio. As the inquiry progressed, they decided to focus primarily on food cycles in mammals living in their own geographic area. A review of the portfolio allowed the students to identify earlier relevant data that enhanced their understanding of the topic and to remove and put on one side materials irrelevant to the narrower focus they had selected. At the same time, they became aware of how their own learning was progressing from broad and rather simplistic ideas to much more sophisticated understanding of the concept of adaptation. Their teacher, overhearing them comment on this, encouraged them to write briefly about the process of their inquiry and to include this meta-analysis in their portfolio. Later, the teacher commented to a colleague how the process the children were going through paralleled her own research efforts as a graduate student.

USING CULMINATING ACTIVITIES IN EVALUATION

A culminating activity is one that allows the students to synthesize their learning in an interdisciplinary theme unit and to present this synthesis to an audience. The culminating activity enables the students to shift from recording data to the next important step of reporting learning. Every unit should have some type of a culminating activity:

- ▾ to bring closure to the unit,
- ▾ to provide opportunities for students to reflect on their learning,
- ▾ to enable them to share their products with a real audience, and
- ▾ to assess the learning that has occurred during the theme study.

Bringing Closure to the Unit

Inquiry has no end. An investigation can open up new questions that lead to new investigations. This does not mean, however, that there should not be closure to a unit. The length of a unit is determined by a number of variables, including the school calendar, with its reporting periods; students' interests; availability of resources; and the necessity to address other aspects of the larger theme. As human beings, we look for beginnings and endings: the week, the year, the seasons, the stages and cycles of our lives. Students and teachers gain a sense of satisfaction from experiencing the beginnings and endings of units of study.

Reflecting on Learning

Dewey was an advocate of reflection as a significant and integral part of learning. In schools, we often deny students opportunities to engage in reflection. To bring closure to a lesson, we may reiterate the objectives or ask students to tell what they learned, but we seldom allow students the time or opportunity to think deeply about the concepts they have internalized, the processes and skills they have developed, or the attitudes they have adopted. A culminating activity can offer students with opportunity.

Sharing Products with a Real Audience

If learning is to be meaningful and long-lasting, it cannot be divorced from real life. Curriculum developments in all of the subject areas stress the importance of relevance and of real experiences. Students read literature, create real mathematics problems, conduct scientific experiments, and investigate social issues. How they report their new knowledge, however, often tends to take the traditional forms—essays, book reports, pages of practice exercises, and tests—designed primarily for one audience, the teacher. When students engage in real investigations, they need to report their results in ways that are true to the spirit of inquiry and that can be shared with wider audiences.

Assessing Learning

Culminating activities are an effective form of summative evaluation. They allow learners, teachers, parents, administrators, and other stakeholders to view the children's work in a holistic way and to celebrate the learning that has taken place. While completed portfolios are likely to provide a record of learning throughout the unit, culminating activities demonstrate what has been achieved by the end of the unit. Like portfolios, culminating activities should reflect the learning outcomes of the unit: knowledge, process, questioning, using resources, and thinking about thinking.

Types of Culminating Activities

Students growing up in contemporary society are constantly exposed to sophisticated methods of sharing news, ideas, and entertainment. They learn from an early age to use symbolic, imagic, and affective modes of thought to understand the world and to express themselves. As we have seen in Chapter One, these are the same modes of thought that are used by thinkers in the various fields of study.

Culminating activities can be designed to use these modes of thought as students synthesize their learning and present it for new audiences. Culminating activities can encourage students to contribute in different individual ways. A variety of means of presentation should be used so that all modes of thinking are represented.

Symbolic modes of thought. These include thinking with words, numbers, or other symbol systems. Culminating activities that use this mode of thought include:

▾ writing and publishing books: class books, group books, individual books;
▾ producing dramatic works;
▾ making oral presentations;
▾ creating new mathematics problems and solving them;
▾ writing reports, letters, diaries, and so forth; and
▾ designing timelines, charts, and maps.

The symbolic modes of thought are those most commonly represented in traditional schoolwork. Care must therefore be taken that the culminating project does involve the students in meaningful and relevant uses of symbolic thought.

Imagic thinking. This includes visual, spatial, tonal, and kinesthetic-sensate thinking and representation. Many students are very comfortable with these ways of thinking and enjoy using them. Students can use these preferred ways of thinking to create products such as:

▾ murals and pictorial displays;
▾ models, dioramas, and other three-dimensional artifacts;

▼ movement and dance;

▼ musical productions; and

▼ videotapes, audiotapes, and films.

For students who are raised in environments rich in imagic stimulation, including television and computer technology, this type of culminating project is particularly meaningful.

Affective modes of thought.   Much schoolwork depends heavily on rational thinking. Investigations tend to follow a sequential, reasoned, scientific process. We teach students to use models and strategies. Intuitive thought, the largely unconscious processes that lead to flashes of inspiration, is rarely acknowledged or encouraged in schools. Yet all great thinkers, scientists and artists alike, pay tribute to the significant role that intuition plays in their work.

Most culminating projects are rational, ordered, organized syntheses of student learning. Yet synthesis can also be an intuitive flash of understanding, a vision that makes sense of unrelated ideas. Students should be encouraged to use and value intuition as one mode of thought. Culminating projects that incorporate and value intuitive thinking might include:

▼ inventing new ways of solving problems,

▼ creating models or visuals out of unconventional materials or media,

▼ presenting data in imaginative ways (e.g., poetry, comic strips, songs, and skits), and

▼ developing surrealistic ways of writing or drawing or moving.

Children and young people are much more comfortable with intuitive thinking than are many adults. Interdisciplinary theme studies can provide many opportunities for students to use this rich mode of thought.

Multimodal presentations.   Culminating projects should allow for the use of many modes of thought, both by the students and by their audience. Students are very creative in thinking of ways to share their learning with others. Multimodal projects may include:

▼ a fair, in which stalls present the learned material in a variety of ways and in which live presentations play an important role;

▼ a multimedia presentation, possibly using computer technology to combine text, images, and sound through hypermedia so that there are many ways to access the material;

▼ a classroom or school museumlike exhibition, with words, objects, pictures, music, and audiovisual presentations;

▼ a tour, where information about different regions is presented in many modes to the "traveler"; and

▼ a "shopping mall," where students "sell" their products through a variety of different marketing approaches.

Notice that all of these multimodal presentations incorporate audience participation. This is congruent with some of the beliefs about learning that underlie the interdisciplinary theme approach:

▼ Learning occurs when the learner is engaged with what is to be learned and the media through which it is learned.

▼ Learning is an active process.

▼ Learning involves the investigation of meaningful questions.

▼ Learning can occur through a variety of modes of thought.

Members of the audience are perceived not as passive onlookers, but as active participants who will come away from the experience changed and enriched, and with new questions to explore.

THE ROLE OF THE TEACHER IN ASSESSMENT

Throughout this text, we have identified three teacher models—teacher-director, teacher-guide, and teacher-mentor—recognizing that you may use any of these models at different times to suit different situations and to meet different needs. In assessment, too, you can adopt one or more of these models as the situation demands.

Teacher-directors take major responsibility for planning, designing, and carrying out assessment throughout the theme study. As teacher-director, you may design rubrics, publish criteria, and assess student work. You identify the degree to which student efforts meet stated standards and provide assistance to those who have not met those standards. You design culminating activities, being careful to include a variety of products and performances that allow children to demonstrate their individual strengths and abilities. The end of the theme study is dictated both by outside demands and by your perception that it is time to close the theme study.

As teacher-guide, you encourage students to take responsibility for their own progress, within certain well-defined parameters. You make sure that learners understand the criteria for any part of the theme study and help them evaluate their own performance in relation to those criteria. For example, interviews with individuals or groups help you to enable children to assess their own progress, to reflect on what they have learned, and to see what they need to do next. You design culminating activities jointly with the learners, and these reflect children's interests and their pride in their achievements and learning. You determine the end of the theme study in consultation with the children when they feel that their work is reaching some stopping place or when outside influences indicate a need for closure.

As teacher-mentor, you work with the children to design their own criteria relative to the big idea, questions, and subquestions of the theme study. As co-inquirers, you and the learners continually review your work and check each other to ensure that you are all moving toward the same goal. "Where are we?" discussion sessions, for example, provide opportunities for looking backward and forward, in much the same way that regular project meetings help business and industry to stay on target and plan future work. Meanwhile, in journals, inquiry notebooks, day books, or computer records, children learn to record and evaluate their daily work. Culminating activities emerge naturally from the ongoing work. As teacher-mentor, you work closely with the children to decide when and how the theme study will end. Indeed, the learners may decide to bring closure and synthesis to one part of the theme study, while continuing with another line of inquiry within the same study.

Accountability and assessment raise serious concerns for teachers, students, parents, and communities. They are integral elements of learning and therefore deserve clear and sustained attention. In this chapter, we have looked at a variety of methods and approaches that should spark your thinking as you design and develop interdisciplinary theme studies with your students.

REFERENCES

Arnheim, R. (1969). *Visual thinking.* Berkeley: University of California Press.
Assessment as inquiry. (1997). *Primary voices 5*(1).

Bloom, B. S. (Ed.), *Taxonomy of educational objectives: The classification of educational goals: Book 1. Cognitive domain.* New York: Longman.

Dewey, J. (1938). *Logic: The theory of inquiry.* New York: Holt, Rinehart & Winston.

Eberle, R. (1987). *Scamper on.* East Aurora, NY: Dissemination of Knowledge.

Ennis, R. H. (1987). A taxonomy of critical thinking disposition and abilities. In J. B. Baron & R. S. Sternberg (Eds.), *Teaching thinking skills: Theory and practice* (pp. 9–26). New York: W. H. Freeman.

Gardner, H. (1983). *Frames of mind: The theory of multiple intelligences.* New York: Basic Books.

Guskey, T. R. (Ed.). (1996). *Communicating student learning.* Alexandria, VA: Association for Supervision and Curriculum Development.

Herman, J. L., Aschbacher, P. R., & Winters, L. (1992). *A practical guide to alternative assessment.* Alexandria, VA: Association for Supervision and Curriculum Development.

Hunkins, F. (1995). *Teaching thinking through effective questioning* (2nd ed.). Norwood, MA: Christopher-Gordon.

Krathwohl, D. R., Bloom, B. S., & Masia, B. B. (1964). *Taxonomy of educational objectives: The classification of educational goals: Handbook II: Affective domain.* New York: David McKay Co., Inc.

Margolis, H. (1987). *Patterns, thinking, and cognition: A theory of judgment.* Chicago: University of Chicago Press.

Marzano, R. J. (1992). *A different kind of classroom: Teaching with dimensions of learning.* Alexandria, VA: Association for Supervision and Curriculum Development.

Marzano, R. J., Pickering, D., & McTighe, J. (1993). *Assessing student outcomes: Using the Dimensions of Learning model.* Alexandria, VA: Association for Supervision and Curriculum Development.

National Council of Teachers of English & International Reading Association. (1996). *Standards for the English language arts.* Urbana, IL: National Council of Teachers of English; Newark, DE: International Reading Association.

National Council of Teachers of Mathematics. (1989). *Curriculum and evaluation standards for school mathematics.* Reston, VA: National Council of Teachers of Mathematics.

National Research Council. (1996). *National science education standards.* Washington, DC: National Academy Press.

Perkins, D. (1981). *The mind's best work.* Cambridge, MA: Harvard University Press.

Perrone, V. (Ed.). (1991). *Expanding student assessment.* Alexandria, VA: Association for Supervision and Curriculum Development.

Schwartz, B. (1996). Communicating student learning in the visual arts. In T. R. Guskey (Ed.), *Communicating student learning* (pp. 79–89). Arlington, VA: Association for Supervision and Curriculum Development.

Taba, H. (1962). *Curriculum development: Theory and practice.* New York: Harcourt Brace Jovanovich.

Tishman, S., Perkins, D., & Jay, E. (1995). *The thinking classroom: Learning and teaching in a culture of thinking.* Boston: Allyn & Bacon.

Traynor, D. (1994). Bald cypress along Cibolo wilderness trail. Unpublished inquiry project. The University of Texas at San Antonio.

Vines, R. A. (1994). *Trees, shrubs, and woody vines of the Southwest.* Austin, TX: The University of Texas Press.

Watt, K. H. (1996). Bridges freeze before roads. In T. R. Guskey (Ed.), *Communicating student learning* (pp. 6–12). Arlington, VA: Association for Supervision and Curriculum Development.

Wiggins, G. (1992). *Portfolios: Design ideas and criteria.* Geneseo, NY: Center on Learning, Assessment, and School Structure.

Wiggins, G. (1996). Honesty and fairness: Toward better grading and reporting. In T. R. Guskey (Ed.), *Communicating student learning* (pp. 79–89). Arlington, VA: Association for Supervision and Curriculum Development.

Conclusion

Throughout this book, we have encouraged you to build into your curriculum thematic interdisciplinary studies that support children's inquiry learning. Many factors in teaching and learning influence the roles you will choose for doing this, the ways you will engage your students with thematic content, and the particular fields of study that you will choose to integrate through those themes. We believe that every child deserves opportunities to formulate questions and explore them through various resources toward the discovery of large ideas. These opportunities are a legitimate and necessary part of schooling. When children develop the skills, knowledge of the methods, and habits of mind of interdisciplinary inquiry, they will become responsible for their own learning and realize that disciplinary boundaries are borders to be crossed and that barriers to learning are frequently those we impose on ourselves.

We sincerely hope that you find in this book a strong rationale, clear explanations, and good examples for ways to develop your personal style of interdisciplinary inquiry in your teaching practice for your students' learning and for your own professional development.

Bibliography

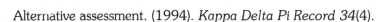

Alternative assessment. (1994). *Kappa Delta Pi Record 34*(4).

Arnheim, R. (1969). *Visual thinking.* Berkeley: University of California Press.

Assessment as inquiry. (1997). *Primary Voices 5*(1).

Babb, L. (1998). *Teacher's guide to the Van Raub Schoolhouse.* Unpublished manuscript.

Barber, J., Bergman, L., & Sneider, C. (1991). *To build a house: GEMS and the "thematic approach" to teaching science.* Berkeley, CA: Lawrence Hall of Science.
The LHS GEMS series includes nearly 40 teacher's guides for hands-on science and mathematics activities and handbooks on key educational topics. For more information, contact GEMS, Lawrence Hall of Science, University of California, Berkeley, CA 94720; (510) 642-7771.

Barber, T. (1993). *The human nature of birds.* New York: St. Martin's Press.

Bloom, B. S. (Ed.). (1956). *Taxonomy of educational objectives: The classification of educational goals: Book 1. Cognitive domain.* New York: Longman.

Bonser, F. G. (1926). Curriculum making in laboratory schools of experimental schools. *Twenty-sixth yearbook of the National Society for the Study of Education* (Pt. 1). Bloomington, IL: Public School Publishing.

Boslough, J. (1985). *Stephen Hawking's universe.* New York: Avon.

Brickman, W. W. (1962). Introduction. In J. Dewey & E. Dewey (Eds.), *Schools of tomorrow* (pp. ix–xxviii). New York: Dutton.

Bronowski, J. (1973). *The ascent of man.* Boston: Little, Brown.

Bruner, J. (1973). *Beyond the information given: Studies in the psychology of knowing.* New York: Norton.

Chatton, B. (1989). Using literature across the curriculum. In J. Hickman & B. E. Cullinan (Eds.), *Children's literature in the classroom: Weaving Charlotte's web* (pp. 61–70). Needham Heights, MA: Christopher-Gordon.

Cheney, M. (1981). *Tesla: Man out of time.* New York: Laurel Books.

Cremin, L. A. (1964). *The transformation of the school.* New York: Vintage. (Original work published 1961)

Dallas, D. (Producer and Director). (1993). *Richard Feynman: Take the world from another point of view* [Film]. Princeton: NJ: Films for the Humanities.

Dewey, J. (1900). *The school and society.* Chicago: University of Chicago Press.

Dewey, J. (1901). The place of manual training in the elementary course of study. *Manual Training Magazine, 2,* 193–194.

Dewey, J. (1933). *How we think.* Lexington, MA: D. C. Heath.

Dewey, J. (1938). *Logic: The theory of inquiry.* New York: Holt, Rinehart & Winston.

Dewey, J. (1956). *The child and the curriculum* and *The school and society.* Chicago: University of Chicago Press. (Original work published in 1900, 1902)

Dewey, J., & Dewey, E. (1962). *Schools of tomorrow.* New York: Dutton. (Original work published 1915)

Dillon, J. T. (1990). *The practice of questioning.* London and New York: Routledge.

Doris, E. (1991). *Doing what scientists do: Children learn to investigate their world.* Portsmouth, NH: Heinemann.

Eberle, R. (1987). *Scamper on.* East Aurora, NY: Dissemination of Knowledge.

Educational Testing Service. (1997). *Educational Testing Service 1997 Annual Report.* Princeton, NJ: Educational Testing Service.

Educator's Progress Service, Inc. (1996a). *Educator's guide to free health, physical education and recreation materials* (29th ed.). Randolph, WI: Educator's Progress Service, Inc.

Educator's Progress Service, Inc. (1996b). *Educator's guide to free home economics materials* (13th ed.). Randolph, WI: Educator's Progress Service, Inc.

Educator's Progress Service, Inc. (1996c). *Educator's guide to free science materials* (37th ed.). Randolph, WI: Educator's Progress Service, Inc.

Educator's Progress Service, Inc. (1996d). *Educator's guide to free social studies materials* (36th ed.). Randolph, WI: Educator's Progress Service, Inc.

Elementary Science Study. (1966). *The behavior of mealworms.* Nashua, NH: Delta Education.

Ennis, R. H. (1987). A taxonomy of critical thinking disposition and abilities. In J. B. Baron & R. S. Sternberg (Eds.), *Teaching thinking skills: Theory and practice* (pp. 9–26). New York: W. H. Freeman.

Feynman, R. P. (1988). *"What do you care what other people think?"* New York: Bantam Books.

Flam, J. D. (1973). *Matisse on art.* London: Phaidon Press.

Flexner, A. (1916). A modern school. *American Review of Reviews, 53,* 465–474.

Flexner, A. (1923). *A modern college and a modern school.* Garden City, NY: Doubleday.

Freedman, G., Hickman, D., & Morris, E. (Producers and Directors). (1991). *A brief history of time.* [Film]. Hollywood: Anglia Television/Gordon Freedman Productions and Paramount Pictures.

Gamberg, R., Kwak, W., Hutchings, M., & Altheim, J. (with Edwards, G.). (1988). *Learning and loving it: Theme studies in the classroom.* Portsmouth, NH: Heinemann.

Gardner, H. (1983). *Frames of mind: The theory of multiple intelligences.* New York: Basic Books.

Gardner, H. (1991). *The unschooled mind.* New York: Basic Books.

Gardner, H. (1993). *Creating minds: An anatomy of creativity seen through the lives of Freud, Einstein, Picasso, Stravinsky, Eliot, Graham, and Gandhi.* New York: Basic Books.

Gardner, H. (1997). The first seven . . . And the eighth. *Educational Leadership, 55* (1),8–13.

George, J. C. (1972). *Julie of the wolves.* Pictures by John Schoenherr. New York: Harper Trophey.

Golden, C. (1986). *American history grade 11: Course of study and related learning activities.* New York: New York City Board of Education, Division of Curriculum and Instruction.

Griffin, D. (1984). *Animal thinking.* Cambridge, MA: Harvard University Press.

Guilford, J. P. (1956). The structure of intellect. *Psychological Bulletin, 53,* 267–295.

Guskey, T. R. (Ed.). (1996). *Communicating student learning.* Alexandria, VA: Association for Supervision and Curriculum Development.

Hall, G., & Loucks, S. F. (1978). Teacher concerns as a basis for facilitating and personalizing staff development. *Teachers College Record, 80,* 36–53.

Harcourt Brace Jovanovich. (1988). *The United States: Its history and neighbors* (HBJ Social Studies: Landmark Ed.). Orlando, FL: Harcourt Brace Jovanovich.

Hardy, G. H. (1940). *A mathematician's apology.* Cambridge, England: Cambridge University Press.

Hawes, K. (1990). Understanding critical thinking. In V. A. Howard (Ed.), *Varieties of thinking* (pp. 47–61). New York: Routledge.

Heine, A. (1984). *Teaching the easy way (the multi-disciplinary approach).* Corpus Christi, TX: Corpus Christi Museum of Science and History.

Herman, J. L., Aschbacher, P. R., & Winters, L. (1992). *A practical guide to alternative assessment.* Alexandria, VA: Association for Supervision and Curriculum Development.

Hoffer, A. R., Johnson, M. L., Leinwald, S. J., Lodholz, R. D., Musser, G. L., & Thoburn, T. (1992). *Mathematics in action: Grade 5.* New York: Macmillan/McGraw-Hill School Publishing Co.

Hoskin, M. (1971). *The mind of the scientist.* New York: Taplinger.

Howard, V. A. (Ed.). (1990). *Varieties of thinking.* New York: Routledge.

Hughes, R. (1980). *The shock of the new.* New York: Knopf.

Hunkins, F. (1995). *Teaching thinking through effective questioning* (2nd ed.). Norwood, MA: Christopher-Gordon.

John-Steiner, V. (1985). *Notebooks of the mind: Explorations of thinking.* Albuquerque: University of New Mexico Press.

John-Steiner, V. (1997). *Notebooks of the mind: Explorations of thinking (Rev. ed.).* New York: Oxford University Press.

Johnson, D. W., & Johnson, R. T. (1990). *Cooperation and competition: Theory and research.* Edina, MN: Interactions.

Johnson, T. D., & Louis, D. R. (1987). *Literacy through literature.* Portsmouth, NH: Heinemann.

Junco, C., & Cook, G. (1998). Community Connections: The Madonna Center Project. *Primary Voices 6*(1), 24–31.

Kidder, T. (1981). *The soul of a new machine.* New York: Avon.

Kilpatrick, W. H. (1918). The project method. *Teachers College Record, 19,* 319–335.

Kilpatrick, W. H. (1931). A reconstructed theory of the educative process. *Teachers College Record, 32,* 530–558.

King, A. (1991). Effects of training in strategic questioning on children's problem-solving performance. *Journal of Experimental Education, 61*(2), 127–148.

King, A. (1994). Guiding knowledge construction in the classroom: Effects of teaching children how to question and how to explain. *American Educational Research Journal, 31*(2), 338–368.

Knull, K. R. (Producer & Director). (1988). *A world of ideas with Bill Moyers: August Wilson* [Video]. Alexandria, VA: PBS Video.

Kovalik, S. J., & Olsen, K. D. (1994). *Kid's eye view of science: A teacher's handbook for implementing an integrated thematic approach to teaching science, K–6.* Second edition. 17051 SE 272 Street, Suite 18, Kent, WA 98042.

Krathwohl, D. R., Bloom, B. S., & Masia, B. B. (1964). *Taxonomy of educational objectives: The classification of educational goals: Handbook II: Affective domain.* New York: David McKay Co., Inc.

Kuhn, T. S. (1970). *The structure of scientific revolutions* (2nd ed.). Chicago: University of Chicago Press.

Kyvig, D., & Marty, M. A. (1982). *Nearby history: Exploring the past around you.* Nashville, TN: American Association for State and Local History.

Learner-Centered Principles Work Group of the American Psychological Association's Board of Educational Affairs. (1997). *Learner-centered pyschological principles: A framework for school reform and redesign.* Washington, DC: American Psychological Association. <www.apa.org>

Lowenthal, D. (1985). *The past is a foreign country.* Cambridge, England: Cambridge University Press.

Lynch, J. (Producer & Director). (1998). *The proof* [Video]. NOVA: Adventures in Sciences. Boston: WGBH-TV.

Lynch, P. (1991). *Multimedia: Getting started.* Sunnyvale, CA: PUBLIX Information Products for Apple Computer.

Macauley, D. (1979). *Motel of the mysteries.* Boston: Houghton Mifflin.

Mallinson, G. G., Mallinson, J. B., Froschauer, L., Harris, J. A., Lewis, M. C., & Valentino, C. (1991). *Science horizons: Grade 5.* Morristown, NJ: Silver Burdett.

Mantel, H. (Producer & Director). (1974). *Einstein: The education of a genius* [Film]. Princeton, NJ: Films for the Humanities and Sciences.

Margolis, H. (1987). *Patterns, thinking, and cognition: A theory of judgment.* Chicago: University of Chicago Press.

Margolis, H. (1993). *Paradigms and barriers: How habits of mind govern scientific beliefs.* Chicago: University of Chicago Press.

Martinello, M. (1987). *The search for Emma's story: A model for humanities detective work.* Ft. Worth: Texas Christian University Press.

Martinello, M. (1992). *Cedar fever.* San Antonio, TX: Corona Publishing Co.

Marzano, R. J. (1992). *A different kind of classroom: Teaching with dimensions of learning.* Alexandria: VA: Association for Supervision and Curriculum Development.

Marzano, R. J., Pickering, D., & McTighe, J. (1993). *Assessing student outcomes: Using the Dimensions of Learning model.* Alexandria, VA: Association for Supervision and Curriculum Development.

Mayhew, K. C., & Edwards, A. C. (1936). *The Dewey School*. New York: Appleton-Century.

McKim, R. H. (1980). *Experiences in visual thinking* (2nd ed.). Monterey, CA: Brooks/Cole.

Milligan, B. (1990). *With the wind, Kevin Dolan*. San Antonio, TX: Corona Publishing Co.

Milligan, B. (1998). Growing a poet tree. In M. Martinello, G. Cook, & L. Woodson (Eds.), *Modes of inquiry: Voices of scholars across the fields of study* (pp. 19–23). Carrollton, TX: Alliance Press.

Mitchell, L. S. (1950). *Our children and our schools*. New York: Simon & Schuster.

Mora, P. (1986). *Borders*. Houston, TX: Arte Publico Press.

Moss, J. F (1984). *Focus units in literature: A handbook for elementary school teachers*. Urbana, IL: National Council of Teachers of English.

Narodick, S., & the Education Team. (1992). *Parent's guide to educational software for young children*. Redmond, WA: Edmark Corp.

National Council for the Social Studies. (1994). *Curriculum standards for the social studies*. Washington, DC: National Council for the Social Studies.

National Council of Teachers of English & International Reading Association. (1996). *Standards for the English language arts*. Urbana, IL: National Council of Teachers of English; Newark, DE: International Reading Association.

National Council of Teachers of Mathematics. (1989). *Curriculum and evaluation standards for school mathematics*. Reston, VA: National Council of Teachers of Mathematics.

National Research Council (1996). *National science education standards*. Washington, DC: National Academy Press.

Nelson, T. (1987). *Dream machine/computer lib*. Redmond, WA: Tempus Books.

NOVA Online/The proof/Solving Fermat: Andrew Wiles [Website] (1997). Boston: WGBH. <www.pbs.org>

Oberholtzer, E. (1937). *An integrated curriculum in practice*. New York: Teachers College Press.

Perkins, D. (1981). *The mind's best work*. Cambridge, MA: Harvard University Press.

Perkins, D., & Weber, R. (1992). Effable invention. In R. Weber & D. Perkins (Eds.), *Inventive minds: Creativity in technology* (pp. 317–336). Oxford, England: Oxford University Press.

Perlmutter, A. H. (Producer). (1991). *The creative spirit* [Television series, 4 parts]. Public Broadcasting System and IBM. New York: Ambrose Video.

Perrone, V. (Ed.). (1991). *Expanding student assessment*. Alexandria, VA: Association for Supervision and Curriculum Development.

Phenix, P. H. (1964). *Realms of meaning.* New York: McGraw-Hill.

Preble, D., & Preble, S. (1985). *Artforms.* New York: Harper & Row.

Roe, A. (1952). *The making of a scientist.* Westport, CT: Greenwood Press.

Ruef, K. (1992). *The private eye: Looking/thinking by analogy.* Seattle: The Private Eye Project.

Rutherford, F., & Ahlgren, A. (1990). *Science for all Americans.* New York: Oxford University Press.

Ryle, G. (1949). *The concept of mind.* London: Hutchinson.

Sanders, N. M. (1966). *Classroom questions: What kinds?* New York: Harper & Row.

Schwartz, B. (1996). Communicating student learning in the visual arts. In T. R. Guskey (Ed.), *Communicating student learning* (pp. 79–89). Arlington, VA: Association for Supervision and Curriculum Development.

Sebesta, S. L. (1989). Literature across the curriculum. In J. W. Stewig & S. L. Sebesta (Eds.), *Using literature in the elementary classroom* (pp. 110–128). Urbana, IL: National Council of Teachers of English.

Shafer, H. J. (1986). *Ancient Texans.* San Antonio, TX: Witte Museum of the San Antonio Museum Association and Texas Monthly Press.

Shamos, M. H. (Ed.). (1959). *Great experiments in physics.* New York: Dover.

Short, K. G., Schroeder, J., Laird, J., Kauffman, G., Ferguson, M. J., & Crawford, K. M. (1996). *Learning together through inquiry: From Columbus to integrated curriculum.* York, ME: Stenhouse.

Somers, A. B., & Worthington, J. E. (1979). *Response guides for teaching children's books.* Urbana, IL: National Council of Teachers of English.

Taba, H. (1962). *Curriculum development: Theory and practice.* New York: Harcourt Brace Jovanovich.

Tanner, D., & Tanner, L. N. (1980). *Curriculum development: Theory into practice* (2nd ed.). New York: Macmillan.

Tanner, L. N. (1997). *Dewey's Laboratory School: Lessons for today.* New York: Teachers College Press.

Texas Education Agency. (1991). *State Board of Education rules for curriculum: Essential elements.* Austin: Texas Education Agency.

Tishman, S., Perkins, D., & Jay, E. (1995). *The thinking classroom: Learning and teaching in a culture of thinking.* Boston: Allyn & Bacon.

Tippett, J. S., Coffin, R. J., & the staff of the elementary division of the Lincoln School of Teachers College, Columbia University. (1927). *Curriculum making in an elementary school.* Lexington, MA: Ginn.

Torrance, E. P. (1962). *Guiding creative talent.* Englewood Cliffs, NJ: Prentice-Hall.

Torrance, E. P. (1970). *Creative learning and teaching.* New York: Dodd Mead.

Traynor, D. (1998). *Bald cypress along Cibolo Wilderness Trail.* Unpublished inquiry project. The University of Texas at San Antonio.

Tufte, E. (1983). *The visual display of quantitative information.* Cheshire, CT: Graphics Press.

Tufte, E. (1990). *Envisioning information.* Cheshire, CT: Graphics Press.

Tufte, E. (1997). *Visual explanations.* Cheshire, CT: Graphics Press.

Van Kirk, S. (1980). *Many tender ties.* Norman: University of Oklahoma Press.

Vines, R. A. (1994). *Trees, shrubs, and woody vines of the Southwest.* Austin, TX: The University of Texas Press.

Voris, H. H., Sedzielarz, M., & Blackmon, C. P. (1986). *Teach the mind, touch the spirit: A guide to focussed field trips.* Chicago: Department of Education, Field Museum of Natural History.

Wallace, D., & Gruber, H. (1989). *Creative people at work.* New York: Oxford University Press.

Watson, J. D. (1968). *The double helix.* New York: Mentor Books.

Watt, K. H. (1996). Bridges freeze before roads. In T. R. Guskey (Ed.), *Communicating student learning* (pp. 6–12). Arlington, VA: Association for Supervision and Curriculum Development.

Weber, R. J., & Perkins, D. N. (eds.) (1992). *Inventive minds: Creativity in technology.* New York: Oxford University Press.

Webster's third international dictionary. (1981). Springfield, MA: Merriam-Webster.

Welty, E. (1983). *One writer's beginnings.* New York: Warner Books.

White, E. B. (1952). *Charlotte's web.* New York: Harper & Row.

Whitin, P., & Whitin, D. J. (1997). *Inquiry at the window: Pursuing the wonders of learners.* Portsmouth, NH: Heinemann.

Wiggins, G. (1992). *Portfolios: Design ideas and criteria.* Geneseo, NY: Center on Learning, Assessment, and School Structure.

Wiggins, G. (1996). Honesty and fairness: Toward better grading and reporting. In T. R. Guskey (Ed.), *Communicating student learning* (pp. 79–89). Arlington, VA: Association for Supervision and Curriculum Development.

Wilson, A. (Producer). (1995). *The piano lesson* [Video]. Hallmark Hall of Fame Productions, Inc. Los Angeles: Republic Entertainment, Inc.

Index